A Pictorial Treasury of
JEWISH HOLIDAYS
and CUSTOMS

A Pictorial Treasury of JEWISH HOLIDAYS and CUSTOMS

by

MORRIS EPSTEIN

KTAV PUBLISHING HOUSE, INC.
NEW YORK 2, NEW YORK

Book design by EZEKIEL SCHLOSS

Copyright 1959
Ktav Publishing House, Inc.

Library of Congress catalog card number 59-9972

TABLE OF CONTENTS

2	The Calendar
10	The Sabbath
24	The High Holy Days
36	Sukkot and Simhat Torah
48	Hanukkah
62	Tu Bi-Shevat
70	Purim
84	Passover
100	Lag Be-Omer
106	Shavuot
114	Tishah Be-Av
118	The Synagogue
138	The Cycle of Jewish Life
150	Bar Mitzvah
158	The Jewish Home
166	The World of Jewish Books
196	Index

PHOTOGRAPH CREDITS

American Friends of the Hebrew University   167

J. J. Breit   7, 20, 39, 118, 119, 142, 162, 170, 178, 183, 185

Colton Photograph   75

The Jewish Museum (Jewish Theological Seminary). Photos by Frank J. Darmstaedter.
4, 5, 11, 13, 14, 15, 16, 20, 21, 23, 25, 26, 27, 28, 29, 30, 32, 36, 41, 42, 44, 46, 47, 50, 52, 53, 54, 59, 61, 72, 79, 80, 81, 82, 84, 90, 93, 94, 95, 96, 99, 100, 101, 108, 113, 117, 124, 131, 132, 134, 135, 137, 138, 139, 140, 141, 142, 143, 149, 151, 153, 158, 160, 163, 164, 168, 169, 185

Defense Department, Department of the Army   43

Temple Emanu-El, New York, N. Y.   130

Forest Hills Jewish Center, Forest Hills, N. Y.   133

Hebrew Union College — Jewish Institute of Religion   127

The Jewish Museum, London   48

Jewish National Fund   68, 69

Jewish Theological Seminary   127

B. Manischewitz Company   90, 91

Matson Photo Service
33, 38, 51, 63, 64, 86, 87, 88, 89, 92, 105, 106, 107, 108, 110, 115, 171, 172, 173, 174, 175, 176, 177, 181

North Carolina Association of Jewish Men   126

Bernice B. Perry   126

Ezekiel Schloss Art Collection   77

Leo Stashin   116

Maurice Seymour   24, 31

Herbert S. Sonnenfeld
2, 10, 12, 17, 18, 19, 22, 34, 40, 45, 46, 50, 56, 57, 58, 70, 93, 95, 103, 112, 128, 137, 147, 150, 152, 154, 157, 161, 165, 166, 184, 194

Three Lions Inc.   19, 42, 132, 148, 169

Touro Synagogue   124

United Jewish Appeal   146

Roman Vishniac   122

M. Wolozin Inc.   156

Wide World Photos   125

Yeshiva University   127

Zionist Archives and Library
35, 38, 52, 55, 60, 61, 62, 65, 66, 67, 68, 78, 81, 83, 97, 98, 102, 104, 109, 111, 114, 120, 136, 188, 191, 192, 193

for
SHIFRA RIBEKA

A sundial heralds the approach of the Sabbath in the holy city of Jerusalem.

The Calendar

How accustomed we are to the conveniences of civilization! Is it too cold? Fix the thermostat. Do we have to get up early? Set the electric alarm. Want to know when to buy Purim gifts? Consult the Jewish calendar. It tells the date of every festival. Knowing how to read it yields a great deal of information, as you will soon see.

But what did people do *before* there was a printed calendar? How did they manage before a calendar in *any* form existed?

Thereby hangs a tale. How the Jewish calendar came into being is a fascinating account that begins with a story of people long ago.

In Early Days

In the earliest days of our history, in the days of the patriarchs Abraham, Isaac, and Jacob, the Jewish people were shepherds who wandered in search of green pastures for their flocks. They had no lamps. They often went to bed at sunset and got up at sunrise. Men, women, and children thought of the sun as a wonderful friend. They knew that without the sun it would always be dark and cold.

When our ancestors were wandering shepherds, they were concerned only with the seasons. "Now it is warm," the people said. "We can shear our sheep. We will have wool to make garments for the winter."

But then they learned to plant crops, and they found that they had to do more than just divide the year into seasons of winter and summer. Watching the sun rise and set did not help them.

Then someone said, "While you have been sleeping at night, I have been watching the moon and the stars. Sometimes the moon is full and round, sometimes it is only half its size, and sometimes I can't find it at all. It seems to disappear."

The shepherds of ancient Palestine were filled with wonder by the moon's changes. They did not know that the moon has no light of its own but is lighted like the earth itself only by the rays of the sun. Nor did they know that the changes in the size of the moon, its "waxing" and "waning," are caused by the moon's traveling around the earth.

Legend of the Moon

A legend even grew up about the moon. In the beginning (says the Talmud) the Lord created the sun and the moon equal in size. But the moon was not satisfied to share her glory with the sun. She complained. To punish her for being jealous, the Almighty shrank the moon down to her present size. But then He took pity on her and promised that some day the Israelites would celebrate the new moon and build their calendar on her movements.

Report to the Sanhedrin

Committees were appointed to watch the moon to see how often these changes happened. Special observers were placed at stations to wait for the appearance of the new moon. As soon as the slightest crescent showed in the sky, the observers rushed to Jerusalem. They presented themselves to the Sanhedrin, the High Court of the Jewish people. "We testify that we have seen the new moon," they swore. They stated the exact moment it had made its appearance.

It was a moment of high excitement.

Once the Sanhedrin had proclaimed the new month, runners were dispatched to light fires on the highest hills ringing the capital city. As soon as these signals were seen by the inhabitants of the next town, they in turn lit a fire on their highest hill. At last the signals reached the farthermost communities. The new month had officially begun.

But what about the settlements that lay

In ancient times, people used signs of the zodiac to distinguish seasons and months of the year. This mosaic was excavated from the floor of the 6th-century C.E. Bet Alpha synagogue in the valley of Jezreel, Israel.

Before the invention of printing, the preparation of a calendar was a laborious undertaking. This calendar or *luah* of 5036 (1276) was found in a Bible manuscript.

beyond the shimmering ocean? Jews of far-off countries like Persia and Italy and Egypt could not rely on messages which sometimes arrived very late. "We will observe the thirtieth day and the day after it as the new month," they decided. "In that way, we will be certain not to go astray."

That is why, according to tradition, our forefathers who lived too far from Judea to be reached by signals and messages added an extra day to the Passover, Shavuot, Sukkot, and Rosh Hashanah holidays. It meant a great deal to them to keep the customs of our people properly. In that way they were certain to do so.

The Sun and the Moon

Now a new problem arose to plague these pioneer calendar-makers. From the moon they had arrived at a month of 29½ days. Twelve moon-months added up to 354 days. But if they had followed the moon-calendar, they would at times have been celebrating Passover in the winter instead of the spring, and planting seasons would have been utterly confused.

Then the people watched the sun more closely than before. With remarkable wisdom, they discovered that a year calculated by the sun has 365 days. (We know the reason for this is that the earth, revolving once daily on its axis, takes 365 days to go completely around the sun.)

"We must devise a plan to keep the moon-month in step with the sun-year," the astronomers said.

Leap Year

There is a new moon every twenty-nine or thirty days. Twelve such months make up the normal Jewish year. This method of figuring, as we have seen, created differences between the solar, or sun year, of 365 days, and the Jewish, or lunar year of 354 days. To make up for this difference, the Jewish leap year has an additional month after Adar, called Adar Sheni (Second Adar). The second Adar month comes every third, sixth, eighth, eleventh, fourteenth, seventeenth, and nineteenth year.

A 13th-century calendar indicating the dating of the festivals was discovered interleaved in a Bible.

"Now we have it," the people said. "A calendar arranged in a cycle of nineteen years, and seven of the nineteen years are leap years."

Now you will understand what we mean when we describe the Jewish calendar as both a lunar (moon) and solar (sun) calendar. The months of the Jewish calendar are moon-months, but the year is a sun-year.

All this was accomplished and still there was no written calendar. Partly this was because there was a close-knit Jewish community and the known world occupied only a small part of the globe. Partly it was due to the fact that Jews were accustomed to hand down laws and traditions by word of mouth, from father to son and from generation to generation.

The passing of time brought important changes. Our people was driven out of the Jewish homeland. Jews were scattered to the four corners of the earth. There was no *central* Jewish community and no chief authority with regard to religious laws and customs. So it became necessary to have a written calendar, and a great Jewish scholar who lived about 1600 years ago prepared one.

A Written Calendar

In the year 359 C.E., Hillel the Second —so-called to set him apart from the famed Hillel who lived in the days of the Second Temple—set down the rules for making a calendar.

Taking quill in hand, he wrote down that the length of the Jewish month is the time it takes the moon to go around the earth. This month is 29 days, 12 hours, and 44 minutes. "We must be practical, however," said Hillel. "We will reckon the months by full days." So the law was laid down that some months should have 30 days and others 29. From that day forth, all Jews everywhere could determine the calendar for themselves and observe the festivals on the same day. Our calendar has remained the same since that time.

Now we know about the way our calendar began, but that does not explain how we number our years. Why is the Jewish year called 5718 instead of 1958, or 5719 rather than 1959? The answer to this question lies, as is very often the case, in the lap of Jewish tradition.

From the beginning of recorded time, calendar-makers have used events great and small as a starting-point for their date-guides. The Romans, for example, counted time from the founding of their capital city. Early Christians dated events from the birth of Jesus, which they called "the year 1." (Later calculations show that he was actually born about four years before that time.) Our everyday calendar follows that rule. It is called the Gregorian calendar, because it was revised by Pope Gregory XIII in 1582, and was adopted by England for herself and her American colonies in 1752. Jews, however, number the years from the time of the Creation of the World as accounted for in the Bible. And, in place of B.C. and A.D., which mean "Before Christ" and "Anno Domini" (the year of our Lord), we use B.C.E. and C.E., which mean "Before the Common Era" and "Common Era." The latter abbreviations are used in this book.

How Many 'New Years'?

One of the many interesting things about the Jewish year is that it has at least two "New Years." According to the Bible, the Creation took place in the beginning of the month of Tishri. That is the date of our *Rosh Hashanah*. It also marked the start of the rainy season in Palestine, an event of great importance to our shepherd-and-farmer ancestors.

Still, even though Tishri is considered *Rosh Hashanah,* or "The Head of the Year" and the first month of our calendar, the

Bible commands us to consider Nisan as the first of the months, since it was in the month of Nisan that our forefathers were freed from slavery in Egypt.

Names of the Months

You have just seen the months Adar, Nisan, and Tishri mentioned, and you probably know the names of at least some of the other months of our calendar. Where did the months get their names?

Originally, the Israelites used numerals to distinguish one month from another. The month in which the spring season began was the first month; the other months were called accordingly the second, third, and so on.

The Hebrew names of the months as we know them were adopted when our people lived in the Babylonian exile after the destruction of the First Temple in 586 B.C.E. The names were derived from the Babylonian calendar, which was itself based on an earlier Sumerian system.

Many authorities believe that the month-names refer to ancient Sumerian myths associated with various seasons of the year. For example, *Tamuz* is the month dedicated to the worship of a fruitfulness-spirit of that name. *Tishri*, on the other hand, simply means the "opening" month of the

A calendar based on the Bible was introduced by the Pilgrims in Massachusetts, 1666. The Pilgrims knew and revered the Bible; they used the Hebrew names of the months in this early American calendar.

7

Jewish calendars are today arranged in various ways, but they all provide certain basic information. Here are sample pages from a luah. *How much can you glean from the data on these pages?*

year. Other names, like Sivan, Nisan, Kislev, and Av, still baffle those who search for their origins.

Only a few of the names of the Hebrew months are mentioned in the Bible. They are: Tevet (*Esther 2:16*); Shevat (*Zechariah 1:7*); Adar (*Esther 3:7, 9:17, 19, 21*); Nisan (*Esther 3:7, Nehemiah 2:1*); Sivan (*Esther 8:9*); and Elul (*Nehemiah 6:15*).

We do know, however, that all the names of the Hebrew months—Nisan, Iyar, Sivan, Tamuz, Av, Elul, Tishri, Heshvan, Kislev, Tevet, Shevat, and Adar—were fully in use by the Jewish people by the fifth century, B.C.E.

Now Read the Calendar

We are now ready to greet our Jewish calendar as an old friend and to read it with ease and speed. At this point, it would be helpful if you were to take a Jewish calendar, or *luah,* as it is known in Hebrew, and place it before you. Glance at a few pages. Do you see that it is a guide to our religious observances as well as a date-reminder?

Observe that the day, in Jewish reckoning, begins at sunset. Saturday, which is the seventh day of the week, begins on Friday evening. That is because the Bible tells us, in the story of the Creation, that "there was evening and there was morning, one day." The very first day, the day of Creation, began not with daybreak but with sunset. All our holidays follow this order, and begin at sunset of the day before.

A detailed Jewish calendar tells us when the sun sets on the eve of a Sabbath or holiday; it informs Mother that she must light candles a scant half-hour before the sun

The earliest recorded Jewish calendar (and earliest Hebrew inscription) is this 10th-century B.C.E. clay tablet found near Gezer, Israel. Written by a farmer in ancient Hebrew script, the Gezer Calendar lists the agricultural seasons and the work associated with them.

dips below the horizon.

Look again at the calendar. It will tell you which portion of the Torah and Prophets will be read in the synagogue next Saturday.

When does the new Jewish month begin? Your calendar knows, and willingly points to the first day of the New Month, called *Rosh Hodesh,* and even to the exact second when the new moon is "born." In olden days special celebrations were held throughout Palestine to greet the new month. The custom of "blessing the new month" has come down to us. It is recited in the synagogue on the preceding Sabbath. In this prayer we ask that we may be granted a month of good health and happiness. On *Rosh Hodesh* day, prayers of thanksgiving are read at services. Many Jews also observe the custom of blessing the new moon —*Kiddush L'vanah.* In this ancient ceremony, Jews gather in groups outdoors. When the moon is visible to all, each says to his neighbor: "Blessed be the Lord, Who reneweth the months. Shalom Aleichem!" and everyone replies: "Peace be unto you ... may this month bring Mazal Tov ... good fortune to us and to all mankind!"

That is the story of the Jewish calendar. It is an old and trusted friend that has graced Jewish homes in every far-flung corner of the world. It reminds us of happy occasions such as festivals and of sad ones such as fast and memorial days. It is as old as written history and as timely as tomorrow's newspaper.

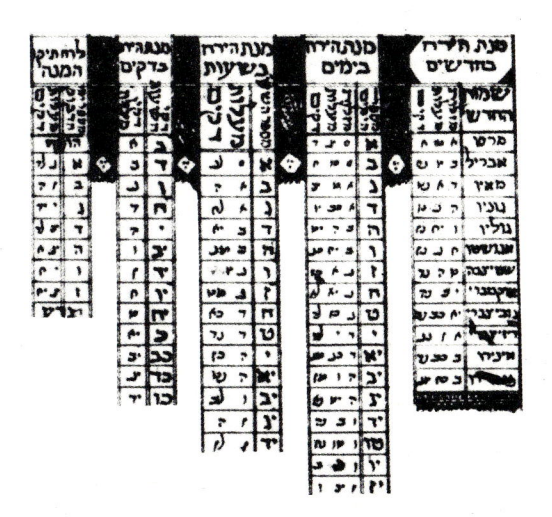

This Hebrew Almanac, prepared by the Jewish astronomer Abraham Zacuto, was used in translation by Christopher Columbus on his voyage to the New World. With it Columbus predicted an eclipse of the moon.

The Sabbath, Day of Rest, is ushered in with the lighting of the candles.

The Sabbath

Only one of all the Jewish holidays is observed every week throughout the year. It is the Sabbath, the day of peace and rest.

In the Ten Commandments, which are the cornerstone of the Jewish faith, the Sabbath alone of all the holidays is mentioned. Look at the Ten Commandments. The Fourth Commandment says, in part:

"Remember the Sabbath Day to keep it holy.

"Six days shalt thou labor, and do all thy work.

"But the seventh day is the Sabbath of the Lord thy God: in it thou shalt not do any work, thou, nor thy son nor thy daughter, thy manservant, nor thy maidservant, nor thy cattle, nor thy stranger that is within thy gates."

This Commandment gave something to the world that it had never had before: a weekly day of rest. Before that time people worked day in, day out, all through the year. No one even thought of a day of rest, just as no one could possibly have thought of tuning in a television program a generation ago. The farmer tilled the soil, the servant cleaned the house, the potter sat at his wheel, and the shepherd grazed his flocks from morning till night, without a day of rest.

Then Moses, who led the Jews out of slavery in Egypt, ascended Mount Sinai and, at God's command, brought down the Ten Commandments. Among them was the Fourth, establishing a day of rest for the Israelites, and later, for all mankind.

Blessings for candle-lighting for Sabbath and holidays, from an 18th-century Italian prayer book. Note the interesting Sabbath lamp and the Italian translation.

For the Christians, Sunday became the Day of Rest; the Mohammedans chose Friday. But everyone agrees that originally the *idea* of a Day of Rest was Jewish, and it has been accepted as a very important Jewish contribution to civilization.

The Oldest Holiday

The Sabbath is probably the oldest of Jewish holidays. Just when the first Sab-

Father blesses the children. For a boy he says: "May God make you like Ephraim and Manasseh." For a girl: "May God make you like Sarah, Rebekah, Rachel, and Leah."

bath was celebrated we really do not know. But, according to one legend, long before the world was created, God created the Angels and the soul of Adam. And on the first Sabbath after their creation, they assembled in Heaven and sang:

"It is Sabbath unto the Lord! May the glory of the Lord last forever!"

Sabbath in Heaven

There is another legend which describes an Angel of the Sabbath who sits upon a special Throne of Glory, and on the Sabbath day thousands of angels dance before this Sabbath Throne of Glory and sing in praise of the day of peace and rest, which, they say, is a foretaste of the World-to-Come, when all the people of the earth will live in everlasting peace, and every day will be as happy as the Sabbath.

Preparing for the Queen

Since the Jewish day is measured from sunset to sunset, the Sabbath arrives on Friday evening. The house is neat as a pin. Mother has been busy all afternoon, cleaning, cooking, and perhaps even baking. For the Sabbath is considered the "Queen" of all our holidays, and one is happy to work very hard to welcome the Sabbath Queen.

Now the table is set. A silver *Kiddush* cup and candlesticks have a place of honor.

Two *Hallot*—the twisted loaves of Sabbath bread—are placed at the head of the table and are covered with a white cloth.

A hallah-cloth covers the two loaves. This delicately-embroidered cloth was made in 19th-century Germany.

Why the Twist-Bread (Hallah)?

The two hallot are known as *lehem mishneh* (double bread). They remind us that the Israelites, while in the wilderness on their way to the Promised Land, gathered on Friday a double portion of *manna* to last them for two days, because on the Sabbath they were not permitted to gather *manna*, the food that descended to them from the skies. The coverlet on the hallot recalls the dew which covered the *manna* every morning.

In many homes, the old custom of dropping coins into a charity box is still followed. This is the moment for it. And now Mother steps up to the table. She covers her head and lights the candles. Shielding her eyes with the palms of her hands, she recites the age-old prayer: *Blessed art Thou, O Lord, our God, King of the Universe, Who hast made us holy by Thy Commandments, and commanded us to kindle the Sabbath lights.*

Father, in turn, blesses the children. Placing his hands over the bowed head of each child, he recites the prayer for a boy: *May God make you like Ephraim and Manasseh;* and for a girl: *May God make you like Sarah, Rebekah, Rachel, and Leah.*

No one saw her enter, but she is here. Silently, invisibly, the Sabbath Queen has come into the home. A sense of peace and quiet fills every corner of every room. It is a special feeling, hard to describe, but as real as the snowy tablecloth and the best china and the sparkling silverware and the delicious aroma of food simmering on the range.

Welcoming the Sabbath

The Friday evening service in the synagogue is short. The prayers include a song with the words: "Come, my friend, let us welcome Sabbath the Bride!" Kiddush over wine is recited in the synagogue just as it once was in medieval days when strangers often spent the entire Sabbath in the house of prayer.

The ceremony of *Kabbalat Shabbat*, the greeting of the Sabbath on Friday evening, was first introduced at the end of the sixteenth century. It was begun among the Kabbalists, the religious mystics of Safed,

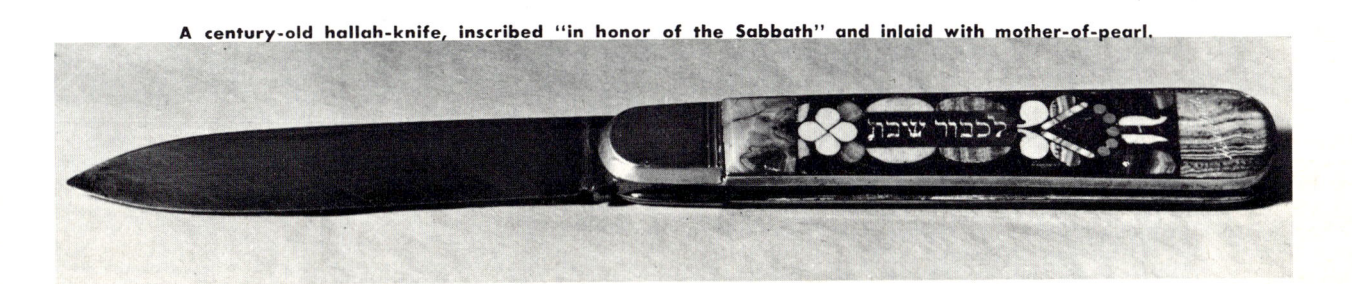

A century-old hallah-knife, inscribed "in honor of the Sabbath" and inlaid with mother-of-pearl.

These 18th-century candlesticks, made in Germany, have scenes from the Bible on their bases. On the right one you can see Moses tending sheep.

Palestine, of whom the greatest was Rabbi Isaac Luria.

They had read in the Talmud that sages of the third century would dress in Sabbath clothes on Friday evening and say "Come, let us go out and meet the Sabbath Queen!" The Kabbalists revived this custom. On late Friday afternoons, they marched in a procession outside the town to greet the queen and bride Sabbath. They sang psalms and ended with "Come, bride; come, bride!" One of these Kabbalists composed a poem *"Lekha Dodi"* ("come, my friend, to meet the bride.") This poem by Solomon Alkabets is the one mentioned above which is still chanted in our Friday evening services.

After the synagogue services, Father comes home. Cries of "Shabbat Shalom!" ring through the house. And you can tell that *this* household is one that has disappointed the Bad Angel once more.

The Happy Angel

It is an old, old story, that tells of two angels that fly with every man as he leaves the synagogue on Friday evening and wends his way homeward. One angel is a Good Angel, dressed in white, with a kind face and a sweet smile. The other is a Bad Angel, with tousled hair and a scowl on his brow. When they reach the house, the angels rush ahead and peek inside. If the house is not cleaned, if the candles are not lit, the table not set—in short, if the people who live there are not ready to meet the Sabbath Queen—the Bad Angel claps his hands in glee. "Ha!" he cries. "May all the Sabbaths of this family be like this one! So be it! So be it!" And the Good Angel, much as he dislikes to, must say "Amen."

But if there is a special Sabbath glow and a spirit of warmth and expectation fills every nook and cranny of the house, the Bad Angel's scowl deepens and he slinks

A very rare Sabbath lamp, made by a Persian craftsman in the 13th or 14th century.

away, while the Good Angel laughs and flutters his wings, saying: "Ah! May all your Sabbaths be like this one, dear friends!" And the Bad Angel, grumpy though he is, is forced to say, "Amen!"

In Olden Times

Even in ancient times the Sabbath was a day of celebration as well as of rest. Work was halted and the Temple was crowded. When our people were exiled to Babylonia after the destruction of the First Temple, the Sabbath took on a deeper meaning, for there we had no Temple, and prayers took the place of sacrifices. The synagogue now began to play a vital role both as a house of prayer and a house of study. Here the Jew could hear the Torah read, and follow a portion of the Prophets, and listen to an explanation through a sermon.

Slowly, Sabbath customs and interpretations of laws for the Sabbath developed and grew, and the Talmud, that great treasury of Jewish law and lore, devotes the closely-printed pages of two volumes solely to the Sabbath. These pages are witnesses to the hours of discussion and debate spent by our Rabbis and Sages on the subject of the Sabbath.

The Precious Gift

One story in the Talmud tells that when Moses went up to Mount Sinai, God said to him:

"I have a precious gift in my treasury, and I wish to present it to Israel."

"Is it the Ten Commandments?" asked Moses.

"I shall give them the Ten Commandments too," said God.

"Is it the Sacred Books of the Law?" asked Moses.

"I shall give them the Holy of Holies in the Temple of Jerusalem," said God. "But this gift is even more precious."

"What can it be?" asked Moses.

"It is the Sabbath," said God.

This double pitcher for ritual hand-washing was made by a Jewish artisan in North Africa about 200 years ago.

The Spice of Life

There are many other legends about the Sabbath. According to one, so different is the Sabbath from the weekdays that with the appearance of the evening star on Friday, the air becomes filled with a delightful fragrance no perfume can equal. But this fragrance is enjoyed only by those who observe the Sabbath and keep it holy.

This aroma even enters the food of faithful Jews and flavors it more deliciously than any known spice on earth.

It is said that once a Roman governor visited a great rabbi on the Sabbath. After the governor had eaten the food offered him, he exclaimed:

"How good this food tastes!"

"It is the spice that gives its flavor," said the host.

"Then I must order a large quantity of this spice. What is its name?"

"It is named 'the Sabbath,'" the rabbi replied.

"I have never heard of a spice named 'the Sabbath,'" said the governor. "Where

15

does it grow?"

"It does not grow," said the rabbi, "because it is not an herb. It is the Day of Rest, which we call 'the Sabbath.'"

"How is the Sabbath different from any other day?" asked the governor scornfully.

"How are you different from any other Roman?" asked the rabbi.

"The emperor was pleased to honor me and he appointed me Governor."

"God was pleased with the seventh day and He appointed it the Sabbath," the rabbi replied.

Stuffed Fish

It is in the Talmud that we are told to make every Sabbath meal into a feast. And many stories are told how the faithful, who try very hard to prepare for the Sabbath, are rewarded.

A pewter Sabbath plate made in Germany over a century ago shows the lighting of the Sabbath candles.

For example, one tale relates how there was a prince who wanted fish for dinner. But when the royal cook came to the fish market, there was only one fish left for sale, and a poor Jewish tailor was bidding for it. No matter how much the royal cook offered for the fish, the tailor offered more.

When the prince was told about it, he grew very angry and ordered the tailor to be arrested and brought before him.

"Tomorrow is the Sabbath," explained the tailor, trembling with fear. "God has commanded us to make the Sabbath meals into feasts. It was not my intention to anger you, but to serve my God well."

The prince realized that the man had intended no wrong, and ordered that the fish be given to the tailor for the Sabbath. When the tailor returned home and opened the fish, he found in it a pearl of such great value that he and his family lived happily ever after.

And that, says the story, is how the Lord rewards the faithful.

To Honor the Sabbath

The Sabbath has been honored by our people throughout history. The Sages of our Talmud say that the Prophet Ezra, upon returning from the Exile in Babylonia in 459 B.C.E., made many laws for the good of our nation. One of these laws ordered Jewish women to rise early on Friday morning and bake bread to supply poor people with hallahs for the Sabbath.

In those days too, it was declared that every person, no matter how great or how rich, must honor the Sabbath personally. Even the most famous Jewish scholars of Talmudic times made certain to do something, some special bit of work, to usher in the Sabbath with reverence. Rab Hisda, for example, cut radishes for the Sabbath. Rabbah and Rab Joseph used to chop wood for the Sabbath cooking. Rab Zera, though he had many servants, would be sure to light the fire himself for the Sabbath cooking. Rab Nahman used to put the house in order, bringing in all the utensils needed for the Sabbath and putting away the things used only during weekdays.

In Jerusalem, a priest, standing on a high tower of the Temple, blew the *shofar* as a

Sabbath afternoon is a time for study and rest. Here, yeshiva students in Israel review their weekly lessons.

signal to put away all work and begin the Sabbath. This custom has been revived in modern form in Israel today. In many towns of Eastern Europe, the *shammash* or sexton announced in the marketplace that it was time to close up and prepare for services in the synagogue. Hurry, good people, hurry! he said. And everyone did.

Sabbath and Song

The whole of the Sabbath Day is spent in happiness and relaxation. Sabbath meals are feasts, and they are accompanied by the singing of *Z'mirot*, which are special songs composed by rabbis and poets in different periods of our history in honor of the Day of Rest. These songs express the joy which is to be found in the Sabbath. One of the most famous of our Z'mirot is called *Koh Ribbon Olam*, composed in the sixteenth century by Rabbi Israel Najara, who wrote more than three hundred songs. This song, chanted on Friday evening all over the world, describes the wonders of God's creation and ends with a prayer that God may rebuild Jerusalem, the city of beauty. Here are two of the stanzas, translated into English.

> *Lord, O master of all the world*
> *You are the King of Kings.*
> *Your majesty is e'er unfurled*
> *We see Your wondrous deeds.*
> *Return to Your most holy shrine*
> *There all souls rejoice*
> *In chanting hymns of lasting praise*
> *To You we raise our voice.*

After the meal, *Birkhat Ha-mazon*, or Grace, is said and then the family chats, entertains Sabbath guests, reads, or perhaps goes to the synagogue to enjoy a late Friday service or a forum.

The morning of the Sabbath is taken up by services in the synagogue, which include the Torah reading and junior congregation for boys and girls. Then, another sunny Sabbath meal, more *Z'mirot*, and the blessing after the food.

An old Jewish custom is the Sabbath afternoon farher or test, administered by teacher, father, or grandfather.

The afternoon is spent in several ways. It is a good time to take a walk. It is a wonderful time to visit your grandparents and to dip into Grandma's never-empty cookie jar. And in the summer there is the pleasant duty of reading a chapter of *Pirke Avot*, the "Ethics of the Fathers," which contains words of wisdom to guide us in our daily conduct.

Order of Prayer

There are three daily services in the synagogue: morning (Shaharit), late afternoon (Minhah), and evening (Maariv). On Sabbaths, new moons, and festivals, there is a fourth, known as the additional (Musaf) service, which follows the reading from the Torah after Shaharit. On Yom Kippur, the Ne'ilah (closing service), is added at the end of Minhah. The Kiddush (Sabbath and festival consecration service), the Havdalah (separating the holy day from the weekdays) and the Birkhat Ha-mazon (grace after meals) are outstanding examples of prayers for the home.

Among the most important daily synagogue prayers are the Shema (*Deut.* 6:4) which proclaims the unity and sovereignty of God; the Shmoneh Esre (or Amidah), consisting of eighteen basic benedictions which comprise the main portion of every service; the Ashre (*Psalm* 145) and the Alenu.

Torah Readings

On Sabbaths, a Sidra, or Torah portion is read. (Torah readings are also held at new moon, holiday, and fast-day afternoon services.) Congregants are honored by be-

The Torah is read twice at Sabbath services—in the morning and in the afternoon at the Minhah service.

Sabbath is observed by Jews the world over. Here you see Moroccan Jews in the courtyard of their synagogue during Sabbath morning services.

ing called up to the reading. This act of going up is called an Aliyah.

The section from the Prophets recited at the conclusion of the reading from the Torah is called the Haftarah, or "conclusion." Each portion of the Torah has a specific Haftarah of its own; there is some connection between the Torah reading and the Haftarah. Some Sabbath days are named after the Haftarah reading, such as Shabbat Hazon ("Sabbath of Vision"), when the first chapter of Isaiah (beginning with the words "The vision") is read. From the Talmud we learn that the practice of Haftarah readings on the Sabbath goes back to the first century C.E. Today, boys who are celebrating their Bar Mitzvah, and young men about to be married, are honored by being called up for the reading of the Haftarah.

Sabbath in Israel

Sabbath takes on a special meaning in Israel. A spirit of peace and holiness descends upon the whole land. Offices, factories, stores, schools, theatres, are closed.

Flower shops do their best business on Friday afternoons. Almost everyone brings home bouquets of flowers for Shabbat.

In Mea Shearim ("One Hundred Gates"), an old, very Orthodox section of Jerusalem, men and boys dressed in long cloaks, or Kaftans, many with fur hats ("streimlach") hurry to the synagogue. There are many tiny synagogues in this quarter of Jerusalem. Each is frequented by a group of worshippers who have been praying together for many years. From these synagogues comes the chant of fervent praying. If we could look inside, we would see the worshippers swaying as they prayed, welcoming the Sabbath with all their hearts and all their souls.

Oneg Shabbat

On Saturday afternoon it has become the custom in Israel to gather for Sabbath discussion, song, and refreshments. This beautiful tradition is only a generation old. It was originated by the outstanding Hebrew poet of modern times, Hayyim Nahman Bialik, and is called Oneg Shabbat ("Sabbath Joy"). The custom has since taken root in America and in many synagogues

The Holy Scroll containing the Five Books of Moses is the most sacred possession of the Jewish people.

This Sabbath and festival lamp, made in Germany about 1710, was designed to be suspended from ceiling or wall.

the Oneg Shabbat is a regular Sabbath feature, ending in the *Se'udah Shelishis* (the "third meal" of Shabbat), evening prayer, and *Havdalah*.

Farewell to the Sabbath

In the late afternoon, the daylight begins to wane. The Sabbath is slipping away. Of course, we will not let the Queen leave without a suitable farewell. There is an afternoon service *(Minhah)*, a third Sabbath meal (the *Se'udah Shelishis*), and the closing Sabbath service. Then we have a *Havdalah* ceremony. Havdalah means "separation" and it marks the close of a Sabbath (or other festival) and the beginning of the weekdays that follow.

When three stars appear in the sky, it is time for Havdalah. First, Mother bids the Sabbath farewell by chanting a beautiful prayer beginning with, "God of Abraham, Isaac, and Jacob." In this prayer, she offers thanks to the Almighty for His gift, the holy Sabbath, and prays for the health and happiness of her own family and for all of Israel.

The head of the family brings out a small box of fragrant spices *(besamim)*. A ceremonial Havdalah candle, used especially for this occasion, is lit. The family watches quietly. Father says a blessing over wine, spices, and light. He pronounces the blessing over the light to remind us that light was the first thing God created. The spices have replaced the burning of incense which was customary at festive events. The spice box may be made of gold, silver, or fine wood, in plain or special form. Often it resembles a tower, and is called by the Hebrew word for tower—*migdal*.

The family inhales the aroma of the spices and silently prays for a week that will be as sweet as the delicate smell of the spices. Each one comes close enough to the lighted candle to hold his fingers near enough to throw great shadows on the ceiling.

We bid farewell to the Sabbath at the Havdalah ceremony, using the spicebox, the braided candle, and the cup of wine.

A silver spicebox in the form of a fish—symbol of fertility and abundance—made in the 18th century.

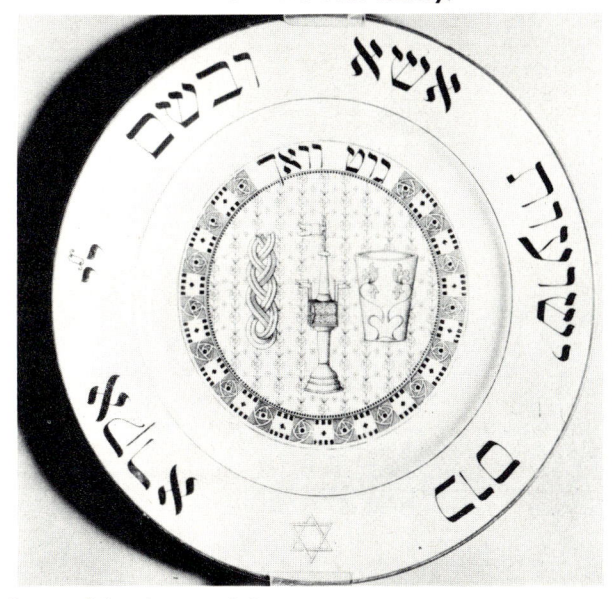

A porcelain plate used for the Havdalah ceremony, made in 19th-century Germany.

The head of the family says solemnly: *"Blessed art Thou, O Lord our God, King of the Universe, Who made a distinction between light and darkness, between the holy and the ordinary, between the Sabbath and the weekday."*

He sips of the wine and dips the candle-tip into the wine that remains. The flame sputters out.

The Sabbath is over.

We are a little saddened when we part with the Sabbath Queen. She has been such a pleasant visitor. One thought makes us happy, however. In six days she will return to us.

And our home will be filled with Sabbath warmth and gaiety once again.

This intricately decorated Havdalah candlestick (Germany, 1710) has a drawer for spices.

21

Oriental Jews study the Talmud on a Sabbath afternoon in Safed, Israel.

Special Sabbaths

Several Sabbaths preceding and following certain festivals or fasts have a special character. While they may be mentioned elsewhere in this book, this would be a good place to group them all together with a brief description of each.

a) *Shabbat ha-Gadol.* The Saturday before Passover is known as Shabbat ha-Gadol, the Great Sabbath. We feel that the holiday is just around the corner. A Passover spirit fills the synagogue when we recite a portion of the Haggadah. Just before the afternoon services, the rabbi gives his holiday sermon, in which he usually explains the complicated laws of *hametz*. He may also present rabbinical interpretations of the exodus from Egypt, the Song of Songs, or of anything else associated with Passover.

b) *Shabbat Hazon and Shabbat Nahamu.* The Saturday before Tisha Be-Av is called Shabbat Hazon and the following Saturday is called Shabbat Nahamu. These names refer to the portion of the prophets read in the synagogue on each of these Sabbaths. On the first Sabbath, the reader chants from the first chapter of Isaiah, which begins with the Hebrew word *Hazon* (vision, or prophecy). The chapter foretells the gloomy events which were to face Israel after the destruction of the Temple.

Tied up with the feeling of mourning was the hope for happier days to come. Therefore, on the Sabbath after Tishah Be-Av, we mark Shabbat Nahamu, the Sabbath of

Comfort. On that day, the fortieth chapter of Isaiah is chanted in the synagogue, the chapter beginning with *Nahamu, Nahamu, Ami* (Comfort ye, comfort ye, My people).

c) *Sabbath Before Rosh Hodesh.* To welcome in each new month we have a special ritual. There is a special prayer in the synagogue on the Sabbath before the New Moon and there is a ceremony blessing the New Moon which is recited outdoors when the New Moon appears. The Sabbath before the New Moon is called the "Sabbath of blessing." After the reading from the Torah, the exact time of the forthcoming arrival of the New Moon is announced and a special prayer for health and happiness is recited by the congregation.

d) *Shabbat Shuvah.* The Sabbath between Rosh Hashanah and Yom Kippur is called Shabbat Shuvah ("return"). It receives its name from the first word of the portion of the Prophets which is read on that day. Since we are in the midst of the Ten Days of Penitence at this time, Shabbat Shuvah takes on an especially holy air. In the afternoon, the rabbi delivers a long sermon in which he encourages the congregation to repent and atone and to determine to live noble lives in the days to come.

e) *Shabbat Zakhor.* The Sabbath before Purim is called Shabbat Zakhor ("remember"), because an extra passage from the Bible is read, which says, "Remember what Amalek did to thee as ye came forth out of Egypt." The Haftarah, the portion of the Prophets that is recited, is from the Book of Samuel and tells of Saul's war against Agag, king of the Amalekites. (Haman is often described as an Agagite, a direct descendant of Amalek, enemy of our ancestors.)

f) *Shabbat Shirah.* The Sabbath on which we read Sidrah Be-shalah (about two months before Passover) is called Shabbat Shirah ("song"). This is because the Sidrah contains the Song of Moses, the description of how the Almighty helped our ancestors cross the Red Sea to freedom.

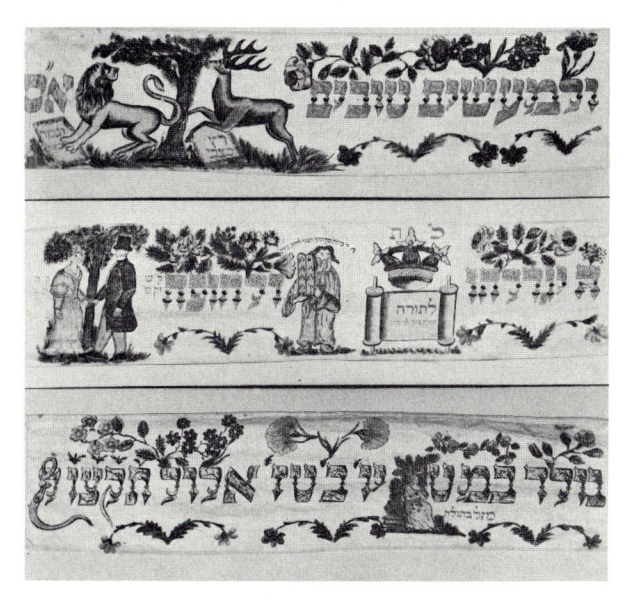

Sections of an embroidered mappah; Germany, 19th century. A "mappah" is the sash which is tied around the middle of the Torah before it is replaced in the Ark.

The call of the shofar resounds in synagogues the world over on Rosh Hashanah.

The High Holy Days

Summer has slipped away and autumn is in the air. Like candles flaring brightly before they go out, the leaves on the big maple out front have taken on brilliant hues of red and orange and yellow. "Take a last look," they seem to say. "Remember us when we are gone!"

And the Jewish calendar on the wall is almost down to its last page, for the Jewish year is slowly drawing to a close. Suppose we turn to that last page. The month is *Elul*, last in the Jewish year. It ends with the twenty-ninth day of the Hebrew month. This is the day before the Jewish New Year.

The New Year begins with a period of ten days, called the Ten Days of Repentance. This period is also known as the Solemn Days, the High Holy Days, and the Fearful Days. The first two of these days are called *Rosh Hashanah*.

The Month of Elul

The whole month preceding Rosh Hashanah has always held a special meaning for Jews. In the little towns of Eastern Europe, the whole community would await the coming Holy Days with awe and excitement.

At daybreak, the old *shammash*, or sexton, of the synagogue would march through the silent streets, a large wooden hammer in his hand.

"Knock, Knock!" went the hammer on the doors or shutters of the little houses. The shammash was calling the people to *Selihot*, the special prayers said in the month of Elul.

Children had special duties. They went into the field to gather little pears. These were nicknamed "Elul pears." When all the baskets were full, the pears were stored in the attic, to be eaten all winter long on Friday nights after the Sabbath meal.

There would be visitors in the month of Elul—booksellers with prayerbooks, messengers with white beards who collected contributions for Jewish institutions in Palestine, a traveling cantor with a choir of boys who practiced their chants for the Holy Days in the lodging-house.

When the High Holy Days came, every

A museum piece, this Rosh Hashanah plate, used for hallah, apples, and honey, was made in Delft, Holland, about 1700.

one was ready to greet the New Year.

The Seventh Month

"Rosh Hashanah" means "the beginning of the year"—but it really is not that. For it comes on the first and second days of Tishri, the seventh month of the Jewish calendar.

In the distant past, our ancestors had several dates in the calendar marking the beginning of important seasons of the year. The first month was Nisan, in the spring. The fifteenth day of the month of Shevat was considered the New Year of the Trees. But the first of Tishri was the beginning of the economic year. This was also the time when the old harvest year ended and the new one began.

In the autumn, too, the first rains came in Palestine, and the soil was plowed for the winter grain. So, in time, the first of Tishri became the beginning of the year, and business dealings, sabbatical years (every seventh year), and jubilee years (every fiftieth year) were all counted from the first of Tishri.

In the Bible

The Bible calls Rosh Hashanah "The Day of the Sounding of the Ram's Horn." In the Bible we read, *"In the seventh month, in the first day of the month, shall be a solemn rest unto you, a memorial proclaimed with the blast of horns, a holy gathering..."*

As they do about all festivals and folkways, legends have clustered about Rosh Hashanah. Many important moments in the history of our people came to be associated with the New Year. It was said that this was the day on which Adam was created out of clay; it was also the birthday of Abraham and Isaac and Jacob; it was the day on which Joseph was released from prison in Egypt, and it was the day Moses appeared before Pharaoh, demanding that

Zodiac symbols were used in many olden calendars. This mosaic design is from the floor of the 6th-century C.E. Bet Alpha synagogue in Palestine.

the king let our people go out of Egypt.

The Mood of Rosh Hashanah

The whole spirit of Rosh Hashanah and of the entire Ten Days of Repentance is one of seriousness and solemnity. The sounding of the shofar is to stir those who have drowsed in their duties and who have forgotten that man is but a very tiny being in the eyes of God, Who keeps a constant watch over His world.

It is a Jewish belief that has been handed down from generation to generation that there is a Book of Life in heaven in which every act, word, and thought of each human being is written down during the twelve months of the year.

On Rosh Hashanah, this Book of Life is opened and the good and evil deeds of each of us is carefully examined. This record is the basis upon which the fate of every person is decided. Into the Book of Life is written everyone's fate for the coming year.

On the Scales

Interesting about Rosh Hashanah is the fact that the Zodiac sign for Tishri is *Scales*.

The ancients, watching the skies, noticed different formations of stars each month. Their imagination gave these twelve groupings, or constellations, various shapes, and they called them by names: ram, bull, twins, crab, and so on. Later, these groups of stars became known as the "signs of the Zodiac," which comes from the Greek word for "animal." At one time or another, many peoples used the Zodiac to tell men's fortunes. (Today, of course, we no longer believe that the future can be predicted by studying the stars, but we still say *"mazal tov,"* which originally meant "may you have a lucky constellation of stars.")

The Zodiac sign for the month in which Rosh Hashanah occurs is *a pair of scales*. This is a symbol reminding us that one's deeds are weighed and judged in the Heavenly Book of Life on the New Year.

L'Shanah Tovah Greetings

When Rosh Hashanah approaches, we like to wish our relatives and friends a happy, healthy, and joyous New Year. Since we cannot visit them all, we follow the custom of sending greeting cards especially printed for the occasion. Many people even send New Year's telegrams, or insert messages in newspapers and magazines that reach Jewish homes. Whichever method we use, the greeting card always says, "L'Shanah Tovah Tikatevu!" which means, "May you be inscribed for a good year!"

Selihot

On the Saturday night before Rosh Hashanah, after the clock has struck twelve and the world has become very quiet, Jews the world over go to the synagogue to say *Selihot*. Services begin after midnight, and we are in a very grave mood as we enter the house of worship. For this is a time to recite special prayers of repentance and Selihot are prayers asking for forgiveness. Some of the prayers are beautiful poems composed by Jewish scholars and poets. They recall the hardships of exile, perse-

Selihot—prayers of repentance—as found in a 19th-century European prayer book.

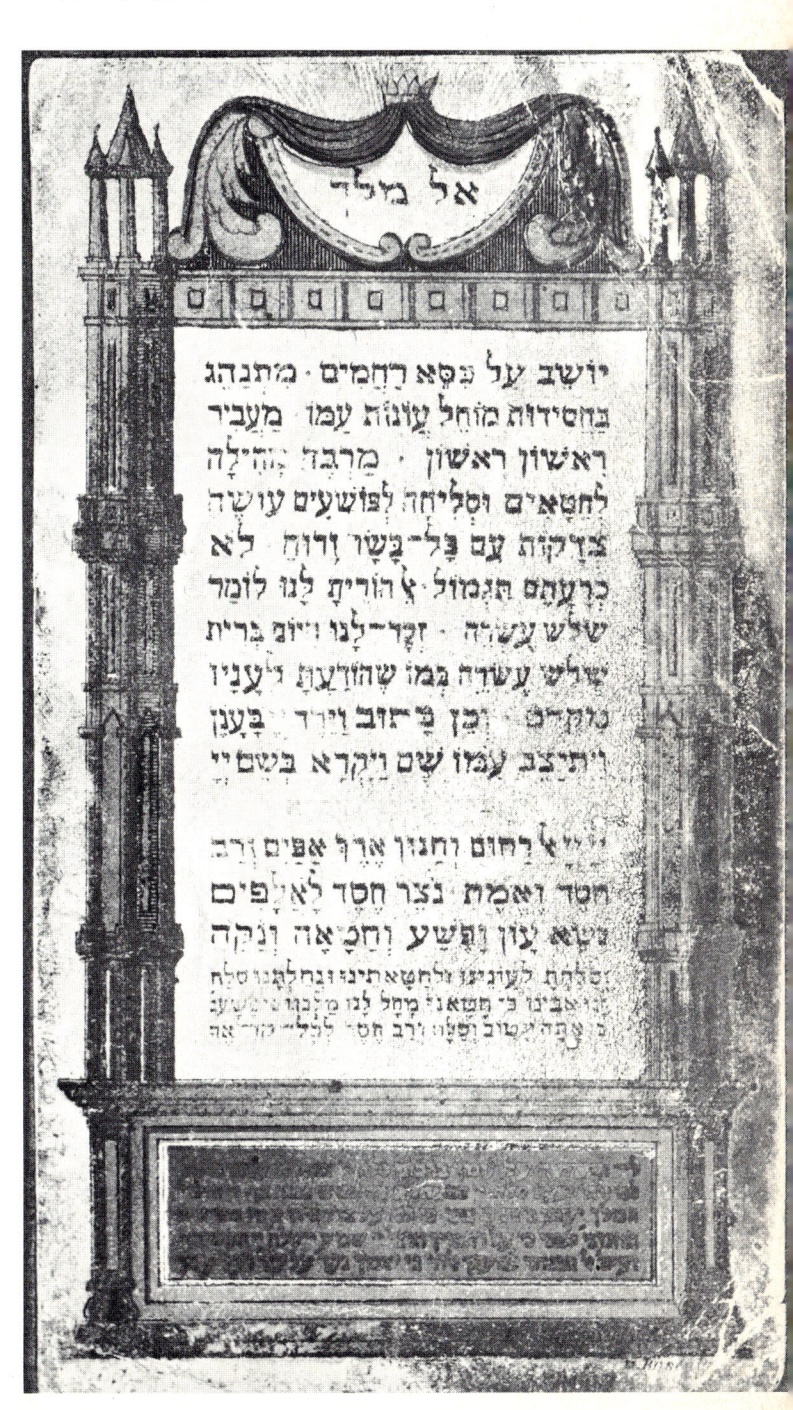

cution, and martyrdom which our people have endured. Selihot are also said during the rest of the Ten Days of Repentance. When we recite Selihot, we ask the Lord to forgive our sins and to send His help when mankind needs it most.

The Shofar

The shofar is blown every day in the month of Elul, except on the Sabbath. It provides the most impressive moment of the morning service of Rosh Hashanah. (If the first day of Rosh Hashanah is on Saturday, the shofar is not blown till the second day.) Not a whisper is heard as the shofar is raised for the hallowed sounds.

This decorated shofar was prepared for memorial blowing on the New Year in Germany in 1782.

How the Shofar is Made

How is the shofar made? Usually it is made of a ram's horn, although it may also be made of the horn of any other clean animal except a cow or an ox. The horn is boiled in water until it gets soft. The inside is then hollowed out and the horn flattened somewhat. But it is not flattened too much for then air could not be blown through it. The mouthpiece is then carefully shaped and the horn is put aside to harden. When the hardening process is complete, we have a shofar. Sometimes, the shofar has only a slight curve; sometimes, particularly in lands of the Middle East, the shofar is long and very curved.

The Meaning of the Shofar's Call

In biblical times, the shofar was used to herald great moments. It proclaimed the ascent of a king upon the throne, it announced the Jubilee every fiftieth year, the Sabbath and festivals. In wartime, it signalled the army.

Indeed, the shofar has been so long associated with Jewish tradition that it has become a holy symbol. It recalls the offering of Isaac by Abraham, for that was when God, recognizing our people's devotion to Him, ordered Abraham to substitute a ram for his son as a sacrifice on the altar.

It reminds us of the giving of the Ten Commandments to the accompaniment of shofar blasts on Mount Sinai. Maimonides, the great Jewish philosopher of the twelfth century, found a special message in the call of the shofar. He said that the shofar proclaimed:

> Awake, ye sleepers, and consider your deeds; remember your Creator and repent. Be not of those who hunt after shadows and who waste their years seeking empty things. Look well into your souls; leave your evil ways and thoughts, and return to God, so that He may have mercy on you.

Before the shofar is blown, we recite Psalm 37, which says that the shofar will one day announce God's dominion over all peoples. Then the horn is sounded. There are three variations in the call: *Tekiah*, *Shevarim*, and *Teruah*. Tekiah is a long blast starting on a low note and rising nearly an octave; Shevarim consists of three shorter notes; Teruah is made up of nine quick, sharp calls ending with a high note. Every man, woman, and child listens intently to the call of the Shofar. It is a symbol of our people's unity and has been that for thousands of years.

The Prayer Called Unetaneh Tokef

One of the most important of the hymns and prayers read on Rosh Hashanah is one that is also recited on Yom Kippur. It is called *Unetaneh Tokef* and was composed by Rabbi Amnon of Mayence. According to the story that was handed down from one generation to another, Rabbi Amnon was pressed time and again by the local bishop to leave his faith and be converted to Christianity. He always refused. Once, instead of refusing immediately, he requested a period of three days in which to consider his decision. When he was left alone, he felt so guilty for having delayed his reply that, when he was called to the bishop, he asked that his tongue be cut out. Instead, the bishop had the rabbi's hands and feet amputated. In this condition, the rabbi was carried to the synagogue for the High Holy Day services. As the *kedushah*, or sanctification service, was about to begin by cantor and congregation, Rabbi Amnon asked permission to offer a prayer he had composed. As soon as the last word had left his lips, the rabbi's life was mercifully ended.

Unetaneh Tokef expresses the idea of

A silver plate, made by a Persian craftsman in the 19th century, portrays the shofar ceremony in the synagogue.

holiness and awe which fills the Rosh Hashanah service. It says, in part:

> We will celebrate the mighty holiness of this day, a day of awe and terror... You open the Book of Records... a great trumpet is sounded, and a still, small voice is heard... The angels proclaim: This is the day of judgment, and all who enter the world You cause to pass before You as a flock of sheep. On the New Year it is written, and on the Day of Atonement it is sealed, how many are to pass away and how many are to be born; who shall live and who shall die; who shall perish by fire and who by water; who by hunger and who by thirst; who shall become poor and who rich... But Penitence, Prayer, and Charity avert the evil decree!

At Home

After services, the family gathers for a festive meal. After the blessing over wine, father says the *Ha-Motzi* over the hallah and passes pieces of it around. Often the hallot are baked in the shape of a ladder, a bird, or a crown. The ladder symbolizes our wish that our Rosh Hashanah prayers may go upward and be heard by the Almighty. The bird is a symbol of mercy, for God has mercy even upon birds. The crown stands for the kingship of God.

The members of the family dip a small piece of hallah into honey and say to each other, as if it were a toast: "May it be Thy will, O Lord, to grant us a sweet and happy year!"

Tashlich

On the afternoon of the first day of the New Year (or on the second day if the first is a Sabbath) many Jews gather near a flowing body of water to "cast all sins into the depths of the sea." *Tashlich* means "you will cast." Often crumbs of bread, symbol of sins and of broken promises, are thrown into the moving water.

There are many lessons that Rosh Hashanah can teach us. Perhaps all of them may be summed up in the saying of one of our rabbis of old. He said, "A man should live in such a way that he can truthfully say 'I have not yet wasted a single day of my life.'" To every Jew, Rosh Hashanah renews that challenge at the beginning of each year.

Fast of Gedaliah

The day after Rosh Hashanah is called Tzom Gedaliah, the Fast of Gedaliah. Gedaliah was a governor appointed to rule the Jews of Judea by Nebuchadnezzar some 2,500 years ago. On this day, Gedaliah was assassinated, and wicked Nebuchadnezzar instituted a reign of terror against the Jewish inhabitants of Palestine. Tzom Gedaliah has since then been considered one of the minor fast days in the Jewish calendar.

Tzedakah—righteousness—is a virtue especially associated with Yom Kippur. This silver tzedakah box was made in Germany in 1880.

The Day Before Yom Kippur

After the New Year, the Days of Repentance continue. The Sabbath between Rosh Hashanah and Yom Kippur is a special Sabbath, called Shabbat Shuvah, or the Sabbath of Penitence. The rabbi usually delivers a sermon dealing with this subject of repentance on this Sabbath.

The ninth day is the day before Yom Kippur, and an air of hush and expectancy is everywhere. No one has a moment to spare. There are so many things to be done. There is an afternoon service and we hurry not to be late.

In some synagogues we see a long table covered with charity plates. Tzedakah, or charity, according to tradition, may save one from punishment. Each plate has an identification card on it, calling attention to the charitable organization it represents. We pass the plates slowly, distributing our contributions. We know that when we do this we take part in the time-honored custom of doing righteous deeds.

Yom Kippur is the holiest day in the Jewish calendar. On this "Sabbath of Sabbaths," the entire day is spent in prayer and worship.

Why We Fast

In the late afternoon, we eat the feast that precedes the fast of Yom Kippur. The fast-meal must be eaten before sunset. After that, everyone except children under thirteen and sick persons will fast until after sunset on the following day.

We do not fast in order to punish our bodies, but to enable us to concentrate on the meaning of Yom Kippur. By not touching food, we think only of the loftiness of this day—the holiest in the Jewish calendar.

A very pious rabbi once said, "If I had my way, I would do away with all fasts except two: the one on the Ninth Day of Av, for who *could* eat on that day? And the other, the holy and awesome day of Yom Kippur—for who *needs* to eat on that day?"

Kol Nidre

Before leaving home for the Kol Nidre service, Father blesses the children. This old custom dates back to our Patriarchs, Abraham, Isaac, and Jacob. Father holds his hands over the heads of the children and says: "May God make you as Ephraim and Manasseh. May it be the will of our Father in Heaven to plant in your heart love of Him. May you wish to study the Torah and its commandments. May your lips speak the truth and your hands do good deeds. May you be inscribed for a long and happy life."

At dusk, men, women, and children gather in the synagogue. The Torahs are taken out of the Holy Ark. The congregation rises. The cantor begins the famous Kol Nidre prayer in the chant that is known round the world. It is thrilling to think that in every Jewish community on the face of the earth, the Kol Nidre service is taking place. Three times the cantor chants the prayer.

Kol means "all" and *Nidre* means "vows." The words of the Kol Nidre prayer state that all vows and oaths not carried out are hereby cancelled and made void. To understand the meaning of this prayer, we must know something of Jewish history. In the

Yizkor—memorial prayers—are recited on Yom Kippur. This Burial Society cup was made in Hungary in 1692. (The Hevra Kadisha—burial society—of a synagogue supervises customs of burial.)

A section of an 18th-century Italian Holy Ark curtain bears a Yom Kippur message of repentance.

days of the Inquisition in fifteenth-century Spain and Portugal, Jews were often forced to give up their faith. Though they became Christians outwardly, these Jews, whom we call Marranos, secretly continued to observe Jewish customs. In the Kol Nidre prayer they begged God to forgive them for their vows which they knew they could not keep because they practiced their religion in secret. Kol Nidre released them from the vows they had been pressed to make. Kol Nidre refers only to vows made by man to God. Other promises which we make in the course of everyday life cannot be done away with by reciting a prayer.

Actually, the Kol Nidre prayer goes back much further than the Inquisition. In fact it is first mentioned in the ninth century. But it came to have a greater and deeper meaning in the evil days when Jews were forced to give up their faith.

The Book of Jonah is read on Yom Kippur afternoon. Shown here is the traditional resting place of the Prophet Jonah, not far from Nineveh. He was sent to Nineveh to persuade its citizens to repent.

The music of Kol Nidre is as impressive as are the words. The sad and haunting melody, which first appeared among the Jews of southern Germany in the mid-sixteenth century, has left an indelible mark upon our synagogue services.

Yom Kippur Day

Services begin early on Yom Kippur day and last until evening. Several times during the day the congregation makes a confession to every possible kind of sin and wrongdoing, just in case any of the sins has been committed unknowingly. This prayer of confession is called *Al Het*. In it we ask for forgiveness for such sins as dishonesty, disrespect for parents, cruelty, and the like. The confessions are made by the congregation as a whole, and forgiveness is asked for the congregation as a whole.

In this book, we learn how Jonah fled to a distant country because he wanted to escape the presence of God. But his efforts were in vain, for he learned that God is everywhere. This reading teaches us that no matter where we live, in whatever age or country, God is with us and His love embraces all people on His earth.

Repentance

The day wears on and still the services continue. More and more we see the central message of Yom Kippur: *Repent* for wrongs you have done.

The Tear of Repentance

A story that explains the importance of confession and atonement on Yom Kippur tells of an angel whom God punished for wrongdoing by sending him to earth to bring back the most precious thing he could find there.

The angel returned with a drop of blood from a soldier dying for his country. This was precious, but not *most* precious!

Back to earth flew the angel. This time he came back with the last breath of a heroic woman who had sacrificed her life for others.

This was more precious, but still the angel was sent back to find something *most* precious. Despairingly, he flew this way and that. Suddenly something caught his eye and he swooped down just as a criminal was about to kill an innocent man.

At the very last moment the criminal felt sorry for his victim. He repented and did not do the terrible deed. As he watched the man struggling in his grasp, the attacker blinked and a tear rolled down his cheek. The angel scooped up the tear and brought it back to Heaven.

The *tear of repentance* was the most precious thing on earth and the angel was forgiven and was accepted once more in Heaven.

At a solemn moment in the service, the cantor kneels before the Holy Ark.

Memorial Prayer

Part of the Yom Kippur service is the *Yizkor,* or memorial prayer for the dead. Yizkor is recited for the departed on several important holidays—Yom Kippur, Shemini Atzeret, the last day of Passover, and the second day of Shavuot. The soul being mourned is mentioned by name and the mourner pledges to give Tzedakah as a memorial tribute.

Reading Jonah

In the afternoon, the Portion of the Prophets which is read is the Book of Jonah.

Ne'ilah

Weary as we are, we summon our strength for the last service of the day of Yom Kippur. It is called Ne'ilah, or closing. The cantor and the congregation chant:

> Open the gate for us,
> For the day is nearly past;
> The sun is low, the day grows late—
> Open Thy gates at last!

At the very end of the evening service, the shofar is blown for the first and only time on Yom Kippur. The note is a long and steady one—as long as the breath holds out.

The Day of Atonement is over. People hurry home to break the fast that has lasted since sunset of the day before.

The High Holy Days are at an end. After a brief Havdalah service, we relax and enjoy a light meal. We are happy and hopeful that our prayers have been answered, that we are indeed on the threshold of a good New Year.

The Western Wall in the Old City of Jerusalem is all that remains of the Second Temple.

A Torah Ark carved of wood; Italy, 1450.

Sukkot and Simhat Torah

Five days after Yom Kippur, the holiest day of the Jewish Year, comes one of the happiest of all festivals. It is called Sukkot, which means "booths" or "tabernacles." One of the nicest things about Sukkot is that it lasts for nine days and contains a variety of celebrations. (Reform Jews observe only one of the first two days, and combine the last two days.)

In the Bible, Sukkot is called: *Hag Ha-Sukkot,* the Festival of *Booths* (or Tabernacles), and *Hag Ha-Asif,* the Festival of *Ingathering.*

The Origin of Sukkot

In the history of every people there are great moments which it likes to recall in order to be reminded of the past and to learn from the past a lesson for the future.

In our own history there is one event that we can never forget. Nor do we wish to. Every Shabbat, when we recite the blessing over the wine, we repeat the words *zekher l'yitziat Mitzra-yim,* "in remembrance of the departure from Egypt." And in several of our holidays, we commemorate events connected with our emancipation from slavery.

Sukkot is one of these holidays.

Years of Wandering

After our ancestors left Egypt, the Bible tells us, they wandered for forty years in the desert before they reached the Promised Land. During all these years they lived in makeshift shelters made of dry palms and such branches as they could find. The Bible tells us to dwell in booths seven days each year in remembrance of the years of wandering and hardship.

Gathering the Crops

After our forefathers had settled in Canaan, they discovered that the autumn, when Sukkot was celebrated, was also the time when they gathered in the crops. So Sukkot became a double celebration. We were grateful that we were no longer wan-

A father in Casablanca, North Africa, stands proudly before the Sukkah he has made and decorated.

derers in the desert; and we offered thanks to God for the gathering-in of the crops. Thus Sukkot became the Jewish Thanksgiving.

Sukkot is the third of the "*Shalosh Regalim*," the three pilgrimage feasts on which Jews from all parts of Palestine used to make pilgrimages to the Holy Temple in Jerusalem.

Happy Harvest

Sukkot is also known as *Hag Ha-Asif*, the Harvest Festival. The fruit harvest was finished in ancient Palestine at this time. The grapes were ready to be made into wine, the olives pressed into oil. Today in Israel, this old meaning of the holiday has taken on a fresh importance, and Israelis celebrate Sukkot with great thanksgiving.

Sukkot and Thanksgiving

Did you know that there is a close connection between our American holiday of Thanksgiving and the Jewish festival of

In olden times, olives were a basic crop of the Israelite farmer. Today, many Arabs still extract oil in primitive fashion by rolling a rock over the olives.

On Sukkot we give thanks for God's plenty. Here grapes are sorted near the wine-cellars of Zikhron Yaakov, Israel.

Sukkot? There is a direct link indeed; it makes an interesting footnote to American history and reveals how much influence has been wielded by our Book of Books.

The First Thanksgiving

In the fall of 1621 the settlers in Plymouth colony gathered to give thanks to God for a bountiful harvest after their first hard year in the New World. That was America's first Thanksgiving. In 1789, after Congress had adopted the Constitution, President George Washington proclaimed November 26 as a day of Thanksgiving for the new nation. From then on, some states observed it one day, some on another. Later, Mrs. Sarah Josephs Hale, a teacher and author (we remember her best for her poem "Mary Had a Little

Lamb"), thought it proper for all Americans to celebrate Thanksgiving as a national holiday on the same day. For thirty-five years she wrote letters to governors and Presidents about her plan. At last, in 1863, President Lincoln proclaimed the fourth Thursday in November as a national Thanksgiving Day.

Pilgrims and the Bible

Where did the early Pilgrims get the idea for a Thanksgiving Day? They were religious men and women. The book they loved most dearly was the Bible. Many of their laws and customs were based on the Bible, and they gave their children Biblical names like Ezekiel, Moses, Solomon, and Hannah.

The Pilgrims even called America "the new Canaan." Cotton Mather, who was a Puritan historian, spoke of the Pilgrims as "our happy Israel in America," and of William Bradford, the second governor of Plymouth, as "Moses." Mather called the early magistrates *ba'ale nefesh,* which is a Hebrew term meaning "men of spirit." The ministers were referred to as *hasidim harishonim,* "first pious men," while John Winthrop, who was governor of the Massachusetts colony, was called *Nehemias Americanus,* the "American Nehemiah," after the Nehemiah who was the Jewish governor of Palestine when our people returned from exile in Babylonia.

The Bible's Command

The pilgrims also knew of the festival of Sukkot, and the Biblical command: *"When you have gathered in the fruits of the land, you shall keep the feast of the Lord"* (*Leviticus 23:39*).

So we can be certain that the Pilgrims drew their inspiration for Thanksgiving from the Bible. Thus, the spirit of the Bible, as well as Jewish history and custom, were

American Pilgrims drew their inspiration for a Thanksgiving Day from the festival of Sukkot in the Bible. They loved the Bible, even based their calendars on it. In this early American calendar of 1666, Pilgrims used the Hebrew names of the months.

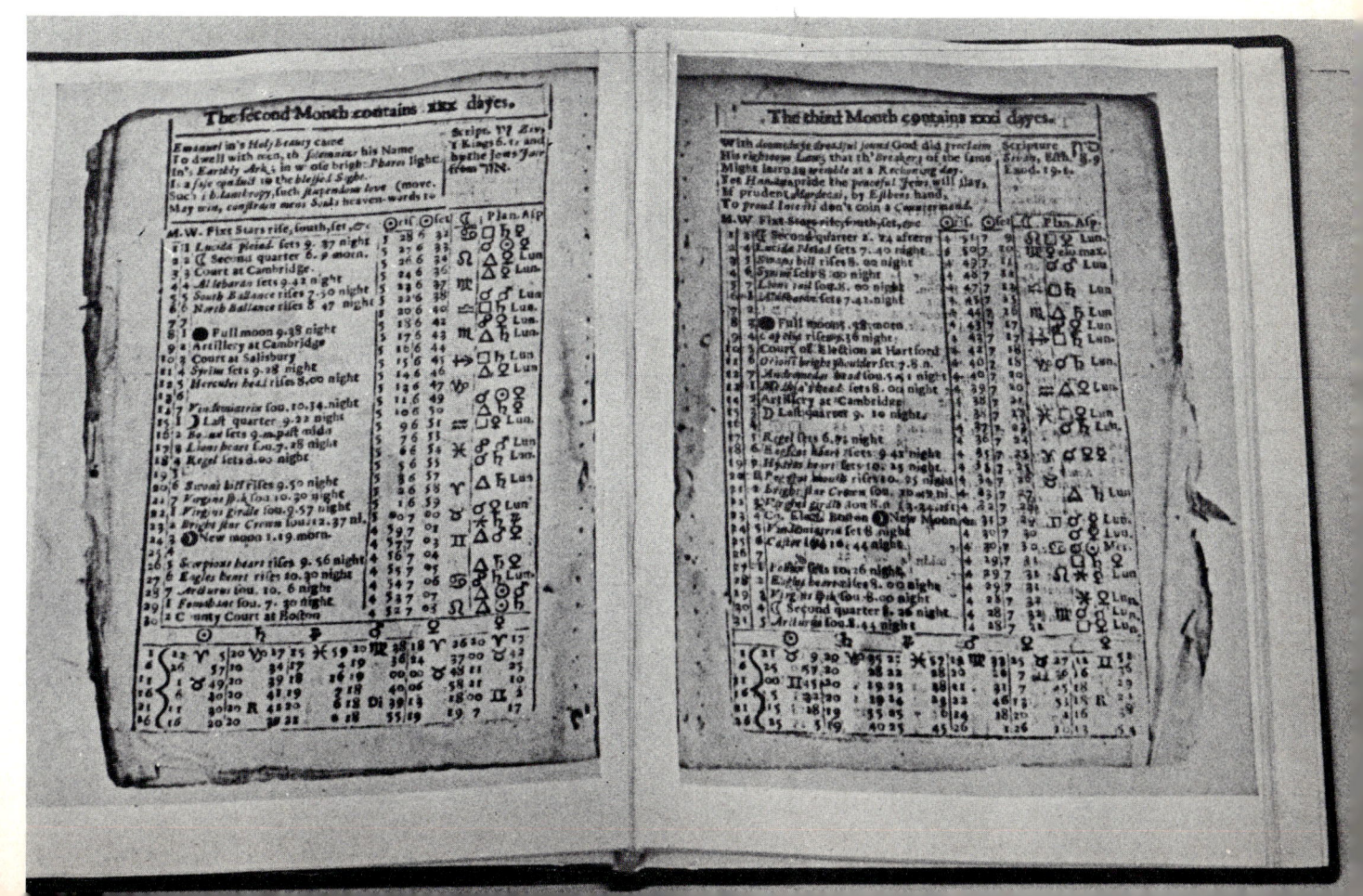

Every morning during the first seven days of Sukkot (except on the Sabbath) we take the etrog, lulav, myrtle, and willow, and recite a blessing. Here the blessing is said under the fragrant branches adorning a Sukkah.

all expressed in the first Thanksgiving celebrated by the Pilgrims in the autumn of 1621. In this way our great heritage helped form the character and backbone of the American way of life.

Building the Sukkah

To show that Sukkot was close at hand, it became a custom to drive in the first nail or stake for the erection of the Sukkah at the end of the Day of Atonement.

In the days that follow, the whole family participates in building the Sukkah. It is placed in the yard or on the roof; in gardens where people have gardens, or on a porch which has an open roof. The Sukkah is not covered from above with boards, but with separate twigs, so that the stars may shine through. Mother and the children decorate the Sukkah with apples, pomegranates, clusters of grapes, Indian corn, and all kinds of flowers.

In the Sukkah all meals during the festival are eaten. The Sukkah is treated with respect and dignity. Mother does not wash the dishes there, nor is any other housework done within its walls. The table is set in the Sukkah so that it shines with warmth and beauty. Freshly baked hallot are placed on a white tablecloth. Candlesticks and candles are brought into the Sukkah, and Mother lights them while pronouncing a prayer over them and reciting a special prayer for the occasion.

Citron and Palm

In the Sukkah, too, except when they are being used in synagogue services, are the *etrog* and the *lulav*. The etrog is a citron, yellow and fragrant; it nestles in a paper container or a wooden box or a silver dish filled with cotton wool to protect its delicate contents. The lulav is a sheaf of long palm fronds, fastened with myrtle and willow twigs. But to say that is hardly to say anything at all; it is like describing an ocean by calling it a huge body of water.

The 'Four Kinds'

The Bible commands us to take four things—the etrog, the lulav, myrtle branches, and willows of the brook—and rejoice before God for seven days when celebrating the harvest festival. In this way our forefathers showed their appreciation for God's goodness.

Every morning during the first seven days of Sukkot (except on the Sabbath), we take these "four kinds" and recite a blessing. The prayer is recited while stand-

A pewter plate (Germany, 19th century) depicts a Sukkot scene taking place in a synagogue.

Etrog (citron) container, made a century ago in Germany. The etrog lies in the box when it is not in use.

ing and holding the lulav in the right hand and the etrog in the left with the part that was attached to the stalk pointing upward. As soon as the blessing is ended, the etrog is turned upside down and, with the etrog held close to the lulav, so that they are as one unit, they are waved together slightly so that the lulav rustles.

What the 'Arba Minim' Mean

Why do we use these "Arba Minim," these "four kinds"? Our rabbis of old thought of several reasons. One explanation is that the etrog is like the heart, without which man cannot live. The lulav is the spine, the myrtle is the eye, and the willow leaves are lips. Together they declare that a human being ought to serve God with all his soul and body.

Another explanation is that the "four kinds" symbolize the Jewish people. Would you like to know how?

The etrog, you will notice, tastes good and has a delightful aroma. The fruit of the date-palm, from which the lulav comes, has taste but no fragrance. The myrtle has fragrance but no taste. The willow has neither taste nor fragrance.

Have you ever seen a Torah case like this one? The case opens down the center, and there is no velvet mantle for the Holy Scroll. This is the Oriental fashion; the photo was taken in Cochin, near the southern tip of India.

So it is, say our sages, with our own people. Some possess both knowledge of the Torah and good deeds; some possess knowledge of the Torah but no good deeds. Some possess good deeds but no knowledge of the Torah; some (like the lowly willow) possess neither knowledge of the Torah nor good deeds. And what does God do with these? He will not destroy them, nor does He wish in any way to harm them. So He says:

"Let them all be tied together with one bond of brotherhood, and let one find forgiveness for the other."

On each of the first seven days of the Sukkot festival, the Ark in the synagogue is opened after the *musaf* or additional service, and a procession takes place. First in line is the cantor, followed by the rabbi, after whom come all those who hold an etrog and lulav. They march around the *bimah,* or down the aisles, while the cantor chants the Hoshanah prayer.

In the Days of the Temple

Sukkot has been celebrated in the very same way for thousands of years. In the days when our Temple stood in Jerusalem, however, there was an additional and very colorful ceremony. This was known as *simhat bet ha-sho-ayvah,* the "feast of water-drawing."

At the morning service on each day of Sukkot, an offering of water was made together with the pouring of wine. The water was drawn from the famous Pool of Siloam —the remains of which have been found in our own time—and it was drawn in a golden pitcher.

In solemn procession, while all the spectators stood awed and silent, the pitcher was borne to the water-gate of the Temple. Then everyone halted while the shofar was blown.

On the night of the first day of Sukkot, the outer court of the Temple was brilliantly lit with four golden lamps. Each contained one hundred and twenty measures of oil. The lamps were placed on high columns, whose tops could only be reached by tall ladders. Crowds filled the court. Special galleries were built for women. Their shining eyes reflected the torches held

This 150-year-old festival kiddush cup was engraved by its designer with a Sukkot scene.

Sukkot is everywhere. All over the world Jewish GIs celebrate holiday at services arranged by the National Jewish Welfare Board. Here, American soldiers stationed at Nuremberg, Germany, participate in Sukkot prayers.

aloft by the men below, who were dancing and singing psalms of praise to God. The Levites, pressed together on fifteen steps of the Gate of Nicanor, chanted the fifteen "songs of degrees" (*Shir Ha-Ma'alot*) of the Book of Psalms, accompanied by flutes and other instruments.

All night long the festivities lasted, and the gaiety and the light penetrated every corner of Jerusalem. It must truly have been a rare feast for the eyes.

Hol Ha-Mo'ed

The four days following the first two days of Sukkot are called Hol Ha-Mo'ed, or semi-holidays. The Hallel prayers are recited at the morning service, and the procession with etrog and lulav takes place. When one of the days of Hol Ha-Mo'ed falls on the Sabbath, the book of *Kohelet,* or Ecclesiastes, is read before the reading of the Portion of the Torah.

Hoshanah Rabba

These two words mean the "great help." They mark the seventh day of Sukkot. It is the day when the palm fronds and the willow and myrtle will be given to the children. They will make rings and bracelets, bows and tassels out of the palm fronds.

But more important to the children than the charms is the midnight of Hoshanah Rabba. For exactly at midnight, it is said, are much longer. Seven times around the synagogue we march, carrying our lulav and etrog. Each person holds a little bunch of willows called hoshanot, and at the close of the service, these willows are beaten on the benches until all or most of the leaves have fallen off. Thus do we "rid ourselves of all our sins." This, too, is an old, old custom, harking back to Temple days when our forefathers circled the altar bearing willow branches.

Shemini Atzeret and Simhat Torah

On the eighth day of Sukkot, the etrog and lulav are laid aside, for this is an entirely new festival, called Shemini Atzeret (the Eight Day of Solemn Assembly).

Several special features mark the morning service. Memorial prayers (*Yizkor*) are said for the dead. A prayer called *Geshem* (rain) is recited. In it, we ask God to provide rain in this season. In the Holy Land, the summer is the dry season, when

Silver Torah breastplate, with figures of Moses and Aaron, made in Poland in the 18th century. At the bottom you can see hands raised in priestly blessing.

A Torah decked with the appropriate ceremonial objects: crown, mantle, breastplate, and pointer.

the skies open. And anyone who makes a wish exactly at that moment when the skies open will have the wish come true. During the seven days of Sukkot, after the morning prayer, special prayers called *hoshanot* are recited. On Hoshanah Rabba, the hoshanot

44

On Simhat Torah, the Holy Scrolls are carried around the synagogue in a gay procession. Children, holding Simhat Torah flags aloft, follow the adults as they circle the synagogue.

there is no rain at all. It rains only during the winter. And in Israel the crops of the spring depend on the rains of October.

As a mark of devotion to our ancient homeland, all of us pray for the rain that is so necessary and that will be stored away to be used during the dry season.

And then, at last, comes one of the gayest days in the Jewish year—Simhat Torah, the Rejoicing in the Law.

It is not a holiday in memory of a great hero.

It is not a holiday commemorating emancipation from slavery or the gaining of independence.

It is not a nature holiday.

It is a holiday dedicated to a book—the greatest book of all—the Torah.

On this day we end the reading of the Five Books of Moses in the synagogue and begin all over again with the wonderful story of Creation. The last chapter in Deuteronomy is chanted, and the first chapter in Genesis is read. Thus the cycle of Torah reading continues and the circle of the Torah is eternal, without beginning or end.

In the synagogue, Simhat Torah is celebrated with great merriment. Everybody comes—young and old, tall and small. Children carry flags, topped with apples. A special prayer which begins with the words *Atah Horayta* is recited, spoken sentence by sentence, by the grown-ups in the synagogue.

Procession of the Torahs

On this festive occasion, all the Torah

45

place. Seven times the procession makes its rounds. Before homegoing time, refreshments—candy, cake, fruit—are distributed to all the children.

The Morning Service

In the morning service, every male over thirteen years of age is called to the Torah to recite the blessing over the reading of the last Sidrah or Portion of the Book of Deuteronomy. The last person to be called up is the *Hatan Torah* (the bridegroom of the Torah), because he has the great honor of reciting the blessing over the conclusion of the Five Books of Moses. Then another person is called for the reading of the first chapter in Genesis; he is called the *Hatan Berayshis* (the bridegroom of Genesis).

Just before these two are called, a very unusual ceremony occurs. All boys under

The honor of carrying the Torah is bestowed upon an American soldier home from an overseas tour of duty.

scrolls are taken out of the Ark and carried lovingly around the synagogue in a procession known as *hakafot*. Children follow the grown-ups, gaily carrying their flags on high. When the synagogue has been circled, singing and dancing with the Torahs takes

An early paper flag for Simhat Tórah shows King David kneeling. The text: "David rejoiced on Simhat Torah."

The Ten Commandments taken from the Torah Ark of the former synagogue of Danzig.

the age of thirteen come up to the Torah. A large tallit is spread like a canopy over their heads. All together, in one voice, they recite the blessing over the Torah. This is called *Kol Hanearim* (all the children) and it marks the one time during the Jewish year when even small boys are given the honor of being called to the Torah.

Thus, in happiness and festivity, Simhat Torah slowly draws to a close, ending the High Holy Day season. The sukkah will be dismantled, to be used again after a twelve-month has taken its course. The calendar on the wall tells us that there will be no other holiday for another two months.

And that is all to the good, for after a period of quiet, we will be able to enjoy the festivals to come all the more.

Torah Ark curtain made in Germany and dated 1768.

Silver Hanukah menorah; Germany, 1769
For eight days each year we light our menorah in commemoration of the Festival of Lights and the triumph of freedom.

Hanukkah

Sukkot and Simhat Torah are now far behind us. Autumn leaves have been raked away; trees are bare and branches empty.

Just when it seems that holidays are so few and far between, the calendar announces that another festival is on its way. And as if to make up for lost time, this holiday will be *eight* days long. Its name is Hanukkah.

Stories of heroism and bravery never die. They are told and retold from generation to generation, and from father to son. Then, when they have become part of a people's culture, they are written down by a talented scribe. Thus they enter the world of literature to be judged and appreciated by everyone who can read.

When it comes to tales of dauntless courage and spirit in the face of overwhelming odds, Hanukkah is one of the world's greatest sagas.

Setting the Scene

To see the picture clearly, to know just what Hanukkah means to every Jew and indeed to every free man, no matter what his race, religion, or creed, it is important to set the scene for this stirring episode of history. And to do that, you have to turn the time machine back well over two thousand years.

In the year 336 B.C.E., Alexander the Great, mighty king of Macedonia, assembled a huge army and crossed from his native Greece into Asia. He shattered the troops of Darius, king of Persia, and thus became ruler of the entire Persian empire, which included Syria, Palestine, and Egypt.

'In the Name of the King'

The rabbis tell many interesting stories about Alexander. One of them explains why "Alexander" is a name common among Jews to this very day.

When Alexander the Great marched in triumph through Jerusalem, he asked the High Priest that a statue in his image be erected in the Temple to commemorate his visit to the Holy City.

"O Alexander," said the High Priest, "it is forbidden by Jewish law to place statues or images of any kind in the Temple of God."

Alexander was displeased. At that moment, the High Priest had a brilliant inspiration.

"I shall build a living memorial to remind the Jewish people of Alexander's kindness

Alexander the Great, king of Macedonia (336-323 B.C.E.), figures prominently in Jewish legend.

Ancient Hebrew coins from the Hasmonean period to the Bar Kochba war. Bottom row: "Holy Jerusalem" inscribed on a silver shekel with three pomegranates (68 C.E.).

to them," he said. "Every male child born during the year of the king's visit to Jerusalem shall bear the king's name—Alexander."

And the king was pleased. Thus it was decreed, and thus it came to pass that the name of Alexander the Great has remained alive among our people to our own day.

War Over Palestine

In time, Alexander the Great died. His great empire was broken into four kingdoms. There was war between two of these kingdoms, Syria and Egypt, for almost a hundred years. Little Palestine was forced to serve as a land bridge between these two kingdoms and it was torn by the invading armies.

Finally the war ended, leaving Syria in possession of Palestine. Once more, peace came to the little Jewish state.

But it was a peace that depended on the whims of the Syrian kings. And it was the whim of such a king that destroyed the peace once and for all and provided us with the wonderful festival of Hanukkah.

A Madman for King

In 175 B.C.E. Antiochus Epiphanes ("the glorious") became king of Syria. Known for his occasional fits of insanity, he was nicknamed "Epimanes," the "madman," by his close friends. The Jews became his subjects.

From the very beginning of his reign, he hated the Jewish people. His chief reason was that they remained faithful to their own God and their own religion and refused to accept the idol-worship of the Greeks.

Antiochus believed that he was God and he decided to destroy the Jewish religion. He issued orders forbidding the observance of Jewish ritual laws.

Bronze coin from the reign of Antigonus Mattathias (40-37 B.C.E.). This is the first known appearance of the candlestick as a Jewish symbol.

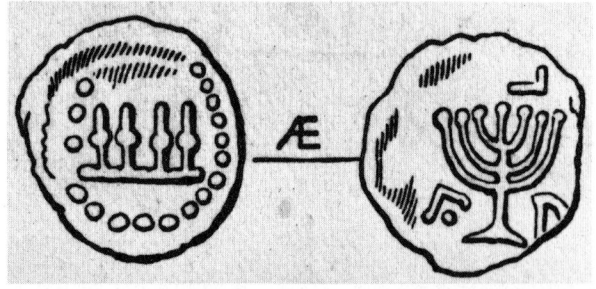

This is Modi'in, where, according to tradition, the heroic Maccabees are buried.

Most shameful of all was the fact that Menelaus, then the High Priest, stood at Antiochus' side and guided and helped him in all his evil deeds. It was he who advised Antiochus on ways and means to uproot the Jewish religion. He was a vile traitor to our people.

Despite Antiochus' villainies, the Jews remained steadfast in the faith of their fathers. So the mad king went further. Everywhere Greek altars and statues were erected. Antiochus sent an army to Jerusalem to dedicate the Holy Temple to Olympia and Zeus.

A pig was offered on the altar of the Temple. Its blood was sprinkled in the Holy of Holies; its meat was cooked and the broth poured upon the Scrolls of the Law.

Antiochus appeared unexpectedly everywhere. "I am God!" he would roar. "The Jews shall eat forbidden foods! They shall not keep the Sabbath! And they will bow down before the altars of our Greek gods!"

What were our people to do? Terrified, some of them unwillingly performed the required sacrifices. But many refused to budge a fraction of an inch in obedience to the tyrant's commands.

A Woman's Heroism

It was in these days that a woman named Hannah displayed fortitude so remarkable and heroism so matchless that her name still arouses a thrill of reverence and admiration, although two thousand years have passed since she lived.

One day Hannah was ordered to appear before the king together with her seven

The story of Judith and the tryant Holofernes (see page 57) as told in a 14th-century manuscript poem.

A carved menorah in a rock-cut tomb at Bet Shearim, a central burial place for Jews in the 2nd to 4th centuries.

sons. All the king's officers were gathered and there was a large group of spectators besides. Turning to Hannah's eldest son, the king said:

"At my side, you see an image of Zeus. I order you to bow to this image!"

The youth paled but stood his ground, firm and strong.

"Has not our Heavenly Father commanded us to bow to no man and to no idol?" he asked in a brave voice. "I will not bow to this image of stone!"

The king clenched his hand and his knuckles were white.

"You will bow," he said in a low voice, "or you will die."

Although his face was ashen and his eyes moist, the lad held his head high as he was led away to his death.

The second son was summoned. Fortified by his faith in God, his tongue remained silent and before many minutes had passed, he walked the same path as his brother.

So it went with one son after another, until six of Hannah's children had been taken from her, never to lay eyes upon their dear mother again.

The Youngest Son

Finally it was the turn of the youngest to be brought before the king. But even this son, young though he was, refused to bow to the king and to the idols.

When the king saw this he was very angry, both with the lad and with himself. "Can I not persuade even a small child to obey my commands?" he thought.

Craftily, he turned to the young one.

"Listen to me, boy. I will speak unto your heart. You need not bow to these images. Lo, I will let my ring fall to the floor. You will then pick it up for me and the people will be deceived. For they will think that you have bowed to the idols."

There was a pause. Then, "Well, what do you say?"

The lad did not hesitate at all.

"O mighty king," he cried, "I will not seek safety at the expense of my honor. Do what you wish to me. As for my people—they will never be defeated!"

Seething with rage, the king ordered the boy executed. When Hannah saw the last

A very rare menorah of about the 9th century. The triangular trough for the shammash candle shows that this is a Hanukkah menorah.

52

The spoils of the Second Temple carried in the triumphal procession of Titus, who conquered Jerusalem in 70 C.E. Shown here is an 18th-century Italian copy in bronze based on the Arch of Titus in Rome.

of her sons led to slaughter, her heart could not longer bear the strain and she expired there in the hall of the king.

And it was said later by the great rabbis of Israel that Hannah's soul flew instantly to Heaven, where she was permitted to share everlasting happiness with her beloved children.

Such happenings seemed only to make Antiochus grow wilder and more vicious by the day. "Destruction" was his emblem, and he lay awake at night thinking of new ways to torture the freedom-loving, God-worshiping Jewish people. "What is their most sacred possession?" he asked himself. Ah, the Temple, of course. So he sent his battle-hardened soldiers into the Holy Temple at Jerusalem. They left the Temple a shambles. Antiochus himself entered the Temple's Holy of Holies, which no man might enter save the High Priest, and he only on Yom Kippur, the holiest day of the Jewish year.

Grunting pigs slithered and slipped across the polished floors of the sacred chambers.

Holy ceremonial objects were robbed by coarse, unfeeling hands. They took the golden altar, the candelabra, and the precious objects.

Jewish women and children were torn from the Temple's sanctuary, to which they had fled in terror, and were sold on the auction block to the highest bidder. Slavery! The dread word seeped poisonously into every street and alleyway of old Jerusalem.

It seemed that the sun would never shine on Israel again. And then, as so often happens, a ray of light appeared when the heavens appeared darkest.

In a Village Named Modi'in

The ray of light shone first in the little village of Modi'in, where a man named Mat-

A bronze oil lamp of the 2nd century, C.E., found in Syria.

tathias, of the Hasmonean family, saw an officer of Antiochus approach a Jewish altar in the market place. The officer laughed a hearty laugh, drew his knife and, with a swift thrust, slew a young pig and offered it as a sacrifice to his pagan gods on the Jewish altar.

Mattathias could not bear the sight nor the smell of this evil deed. He knew at once that only one course of action was open for him.

He rose and advanced upon the officer. The crowd watched, disbelief stamped on every face, as Mattathias plunged his dagger deep into the breast of the officer of the king.

Thus, without fanfare or heroics, was struck the first blow for freedom.

Now Mattathias summoned his five stalwart sons—Judah Maccabee and Jonathan, Johanan, Eleazar, and Simon.

"Whoever is for God, follow me!" cried Mattathias. Together with a hardy band of patriots, the Hasmoneans fled to the hills.

Guerilla Fighters

Enraged, Antiochus sent four new armies against the Hasmoneans, now transformed into hunted fugitives. Mattathias and his men became guerilla fighters, taking advantage of the night's darkness and of their familiarity with the uncharted terrain.

In hills encircling Jerusalem was heard the cry: "Death to the invader!" Men without training, carrying pitchforks and swords, moved only when it was dark. When a cloud blanketed the moon, they struck. One after another, they laid low the armies of Antiochus, whose soldiers were the best-fed, best-led troops in the East.

The Secret Weapon

Meanwhile, Antiochus fumed. How would he ever conquer these rebels who refused to be governed by his iron fist? He tried a new approach, a dread weapon. One day, a cry of terror was heard in the Jewish garrison: "Elephants!"

Lumbering elephants, thick-skinned and huge, bore down upon the defenders, leaving havoc and destruction in their path.

But the Maccabees proved resourceful in their desperation. Assembling their finest archers, who were sharpshooters all, they strung their bows and let fly. Caught by surprise, Syrian officers toppled off the miniature forts on the elephants' backs. Eleazar bravely made his way to the lead elephant, sank his spear into its vulnerable belly. Down came the giant beast, crushing its petrified riders.

Antiochus' secret weapon was vanquished!

The Last Stronghold

The final test came at a town named

Masada, near the Dead Sea, was an ancient Jewish fortress on a lofty, isolated rock. It was the last Jewish stronghold against the Roman invaders and fell in the year 72 C.E.

Emmaus, which stood on the road to Jerusalem. Judah Maccabee had heard the report of his observers. The town quartered a large force of Syrians whose tents bristled with spears. They blocked the road to Jerusalem. Judah Maccabee marshaled his men. There was no sleep that night in the Jewish ranks. If this move failed, all was lost.

At dawn, the signal shrilled: "Attack!"

The armies clashed in the first rays of the morning sun. Soon it was all over. The Syrians sank back to lick their bleeding wounds. Their commander bowed to mark the victory of Judah Maccabee.

And it came to pass that in 165 B.C.E. the Jews returned to Jerusalem. With unbounded eagerness and anticipation, they turned their faces to the City of Zion, where once King Solomon had reigned: Jerusalem, the center of Jewish hopes and ideas from time immemorial!

Return of the Hunted

When they reached the holy city, their joy turned to bitterness. For they beheld a view that made strong men sick. The Syrians had done their work thoroughly. Dirt and desolation met the eye everywhere. The Maccabees entered the Temple Area and saw the Scrolls of the Torah torn to bits and scattered about. Statues of Greek gods and goddesses had been placed in the Temple. Swine had been sacrificed on the Holy Altar.

The people braced themselves and set about their tasks. They cleaned the Temple and scrubbed it. On the twenty-fifth day of Kislev in 165 B.C.E. the Temple was rededicated. With a little flask of oil—the *only* holy oil they could find amid the destruction—they re-lit the great Menorah.

Exceeding all expectations, the oil miraculously lasted for eight long days. And

The ceremony of Hanukkah candle-lighting is practiced by joyous boys and girls in a Jewish school.

since that time, we have celebrated Hanukkah, which means "dedication," for eight days each year, in commemoration of the Festival of Lights and the Triumph of Freedom.

* * *

Hanukkah Lights

Hanukkah is a gay festival. It is marked by the lighting of candles in the home, beginning with one candle on the first night and adding one on each following night of the holiday.

Many of us buy Hanukkah candles made in Israel. Candles come forty-four to the box—enough for all the eight nights of Hanukkah. For we light one candle each night that acts as the *shammash* (which means "one who serves") with which we light the other candles.

The oldest historical sources that deal with the festival of Hanukkah are ancient works known as the Books of the Maccabees. They tell us how Judah and his brothers came to the desolate Temple, how they cleansed it and re-dedicated it on the twenty-fifth day of the month of Kislev. Slowly, the custom of lighting Hanukkah lights in every Jewish home was developed until Hanukkah became the widespread festival that it is today.

For All to See

So that everyone may know that Hanukkah is here, we place the candles near a window which faces the street. The lighting ceremony is accompanied by blessings and followed by song. The most popular Hanukkah song is *Ma-oz Tzur,* or Rock of Ages.

There are no special Hanukkah services in the synagogue. At the regular evening service, however, the candles are lit just as they are at home. Services during Hanukkah also contain a number of additional prayers. One is *"Hallel,"* which consists of selections from the Book of Psalms. Another is the *Al Ha-Nissim* ("for the miracles") which is repeated during the *Shmoneh Esreh* (the Eighteen Blessings) and in *Birkhat Ha-Mazon,* the Grace after meals.

Hanukkah Foods

A favorite Hanukkah food is *latkes,* or potato pancakes. Originally, the pancakes were made of cheese. From the custom of eating cheese delicacies grew the custom of eating pancakes of all kinds. During the Middle Ages, Jews explained this custom by connecting it with the story of Judith which they linked with the story of Hanukkah. Judith, according to legend, was a daughter of the Hasmoneans. She fed cheese to the leader of the enemies of the Jews. He was made thirsty by the cheese and began to drink much wine. When he grew quite drunk, she cut off his head. For this reason, it was said, Jews ate cheese delicacies on Hanukkah.

The Hanukkah Dreidel

A favorite custom is the giving of gifts. What would you like for Hanukkah? A bicycle, doll, electric train, books? Make a wish (out loud). Perhaps it will come true.

Hanukkah is a time for "Hanukkah gelt." When the Maccabees returned to Jerusalem, they re-lit the Menorah and struck coins to show they were a free people.

A Hanukkah menorah, symbol of the Festival of Lights, stands proudly silhouetted against the sky in Israel.

Ancient coins of Israel still exist, but we have our own version for Hanukkah: "Hanukkah gelt."

You can expect "Hanukkah gelt" in this holiday and you may try to increase your share by playing a game of *dreidel.* For this game you need a dreidel or four-sided top whose four Hebrew letters stand for *Nes Gadol Hayah Sham*—"a great miracle happened there."

According to an old legend, the Hanukkah top was invented during the time of the Maccabees. Antiochus forbade the study of Torah. Nevertheless, people gathered in small groups and studied the Torah secretly and by heart. If soldiers approached, the group scattered. Another means they used to escape detection was the dreidel game. The dreidel lay on the

Hanukkah is not complete without a jolly dreidel-spinning game. Nun, gimel, hay, and shin, are the Hebrew letters on the Hanukkah top. They stand for Nes Gadol Hayah Sham, "a great miracle happened there."

table. At the lookout's warning, the students spun the top. When the enemy arrived, all he could see was Jews playing an innocent game. Thus the dreidel saved many a life.

Since that time, the popular little dreidel has been part of Hanukkah fun everywhere. In Eastern Europe, the tops were made of lead. Pouring the lead into molds was begun weeks earlier. They were cast in wooden forms. Made of wood, tin, lead, plastic, or what-have-you, the dreidel always bears the letters *Nun, Gimel, Hay, Shin*. These are initials for *Nes Gadol Hayah Sham:* a great miracle happened there. Spin it, and the dreidel tells you how you've done. *Nun,* and you take nothing from the pot. *Gimel,* and you take all. *Hay* means you get half. *Shin* tells you to put in.

The Hanukkah Menorah

When Judah Maccabee triumphantly regained Jerusalem, the lamps of the Temple Menorah were re-lit and the rededication of the Temple was celebrated for eight days with feasting and with song.

Long before anyone thought of Hanukkah, even while the Children of Israel were in the wilderness, the sacred Tabernacle had a beautiful seven-branched Menorah. When the Israelites entered the Promised Land, they set up the Tabernacle at Shiloh, and graced the Inner Sanctuary with the Menorah. The Sanctuary of Shiloh was destroyed by the Philistines, and no one knows what happened to the Menorah, though some believe that it later stood in the Temple of Solomon.

But there it was not the only lamp, for no fewer than ten candlesticks shed their brilliant light in Solomon's Temple. After its destruction in 586 B.C.E., the candlesticks, with other precious Temple vessels, were brought to Babylon. From there, they were restored by the great Persian conqueror Cyrus, who allowed our people to return to Palestine and rebuild the Temple.

However, from that moment on, we hear no more about the *other* candlesticks. Henceforth only the large, magnificent, golden Menorah, which was perhaps the same one made by Moses in the wilderness, drew the attention of friend and foe alike. Antiochus had the Menorah removed and broken, but the Maccabees repaired it and lit it again with the oil which miraculously burned for eight days.

Since then the Menorah has been used by our people in every place where we have lived. In Africa—in great Alexandria, down the Nile at the Cataracts, and in busy Carthage; in Asia—in Yemen, Babylon, Persia, Palmyra, and on the border of the desert in the Decapolis and Pentapolis, in the Greek colonies in Syria and Asia Minor; in Europe—in Athens and Rome, in the Islands of the Mediterranean, in all these places the Menorah became a symbol of our people.

The Menorah grew to be a symbol of light and truth. We place it near a window so that all may see it and remember what it stands for. By the light of the Menorah, Jewish children were told the tale of Judah Maccabee, the hero who died for freedom.

The Hanukkah Menorah also became recognized as a symbol of our people's love for liberty. It shone in the synagogue, it

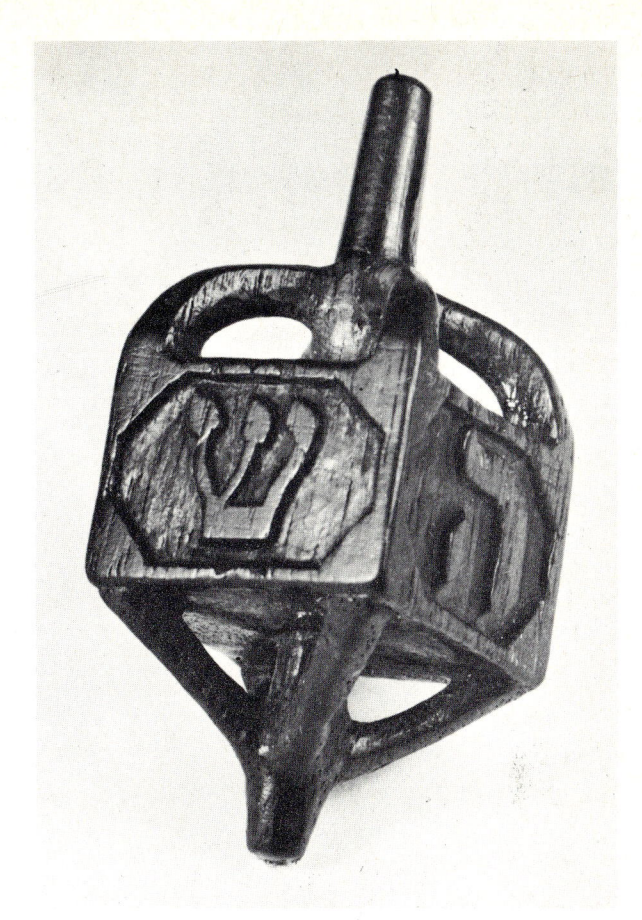

Dreidels are made in many shapes. This one, of wood, is an Eastern European 19th-century dreidel.

A very unusual menorah for seven and six lights, made in Morocco or Libya, 18th century.

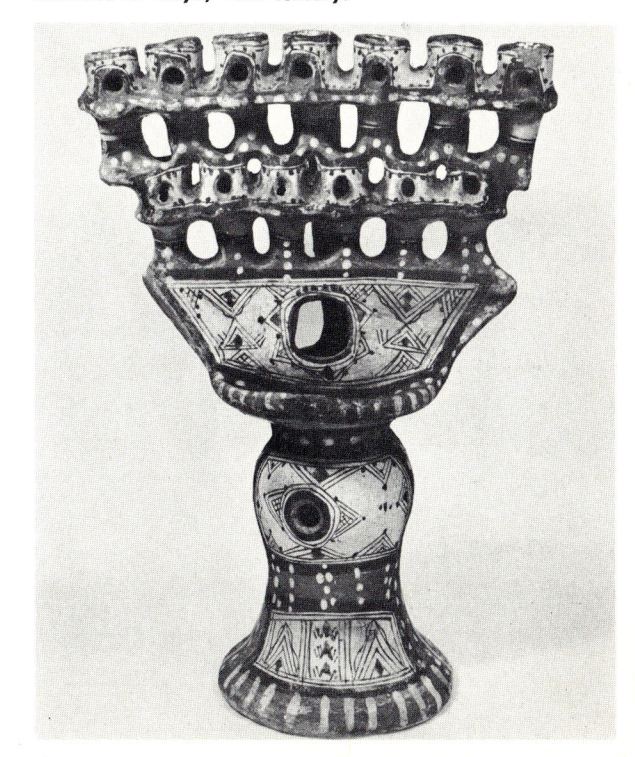

The Great Synagogue in Tel Aviv displays a Hanukkah menorah during the eight-day celebration.

glowed in the home, it guided the Jew through his life and often even accompanied him when he died, as an emblem on his tombstone.

When our ancestors made the first Hanukkah Menorahs, they knew that it was forbidden to imitate the seven-branched candlestick of the Temple. Besides, they wished to commemorate the little jar of oil that had lasted for eight days when the Temple was rededicated. For that reason, a special Hanukkah lamp was designed for the festival of light, with an individual shaft for the shammash (servant) by which all the wicks were lit.

Many artists have produced wonderful Menorahs, though none could equal the magnificence of the Temple candelabrum, which was taken by Titus, after the destruction of the Second Temple, to Rome where it was carried in his triumphal procession. On the famous Arch of Titus, which can still be seen in Rome, the Menorah is still prominently portrayed.

Thus the Menorah, and especially the Hanukkah Menorah, awakens in every generation memories of a heroic past and rekindles a hope and faith in the future.

Menorah in Israel

Even though the ancient Temple Menorah may have disappeared forever, its symbol has been revived in Israel, where it has become the emblem of the State. In Israel, incidentally, we may find the largest Hanukkah Menorahs, for they shine atop the

A Maccabiah youth team leader holds high a torch symbolic of the ancient Maccabees.

water towers of the settlements and decorate public buildings in every city.

Torch Relay

Israel also boasts another meaningful Hanukkah custom—the torch relay. In Modin, where the first blow was struck for liberty against the invaders thousands of years ago, a torch is lit and raced in relay fashion to the Great Synagogue in Tel Aviv.

All men owe much to the ancient Maccabees. Had their spirit been snuffed out, not only would Judaism have disappeared, but its two daughter religions, Christianity and Mohammedanism, would never have been born.

Hanukkah, then, tells us to be ever watchful against those who would harm us. It tells us to grow closer to our faith and our people and to drink deep from our ancient heritage.

Above all, it tells us that we are heirs to a great tradition. Hanukkah teaches us that we do *our* part only if we keep this noble tradition alive and transmit it to each succeeding generation.

A terra cotta oil lamp (Palestine, 3rd century, C.E.) showing the columns of the Temple.

In Israel, growing things begin to blossom on Tu Bi-Shevat, the New Year of the Trees.

Tu Bi-Shevat

Towards winter's close, we celebrate the New Year of the Trees. If this seems a strange kind of birthday to you, think of the millions of Chinese who annually observe the Birthday of the Flowers!

Flowers and trees and all growing things mean so much to every human being. Our ancestors knew this. They realized that trees are among our best friends. Trees help feed and clothe us. They give us wood for our houses, paper for books, fruit to eat, and shade from the hot sun. Trees keep the soil rich and fertile and they give beauty to the world.

'Tu' Equals Fifteen

Our ancestors were aware of this and they set aside the fifteenth day of the month of Shevat (Hamishah Asar Bi-Shevat; or "Tu Bi-Shevat," for "Tu" represents the two Hebrew letters which numerically equal fifteen) as Jewish Arbor Day.

In Israel, the rainy season lasts till sometime in February; then the first buds on the trees appear and lo—it's Tu Bi-Shevat!

It was in the Talmud that the New Year of the Trees received its name. But long before that the Torah showed the way. The Bible, for example, says that fruit trees may not be cut down even in time of war (*Deuteronomy* 20). The Torah itself is called a "tree of life" (*Proverbs* 3:18). And King David, in the *Book of Psalms*, says that a righteous man is "like a tree planted by the streams of water" (Psalms 1:3).

There are many references to trees in the Bible. They show our love for trees and how they were used in matters of religious importance. Here are a few references:

Cedar: And Solomon built the Temple, and finished it ... and he built the walls with boards of cedar ... all was cedar; there was no stone seen.
1 Kings 6:14, 16, 18

Willow: By the rivers of Babylon we sat down and wept, when we remembered Zion. We hanged our harps upon the willows ...
Psalms 137:1, 2

This is the stately cedar. Its wood was used by King Solomon in building the Temple.

Palm: Take on the first day (of Sukkot) the branches of palm trees ... and dwell in booths seven days.
Leviticus 23:40, 41

Citron: On Sukkot ... take the fruit of the beautiful trees ... this is the fragrant citron, or etrog.
Leviticus 23:40

Cypress: And King David and all the house of Israel played before the Lord on all kinds of instruments made of cypress or fir wood, on harps and on drums.
II Samuel 6:5

Gopher: And God said to Noah: Make an ark of gopher-wood ... and come into the ark with your sons, your wife and your sons' wives ... and of every living thing bring two of each sort into the ark ...
Genesis 6:14, 18, 19

Fig: Adam and Eve sewed fig-leaves together and made themselves aprons.
Genesis 3:7

Olive: The Lord spoke unto Moses, saying: Command the children of Israel to bring pure olive oil, beaten for the Menorah, to cause a light to burn always in the tabernacle of your congregation.
Exodus 27:20, 21

Carob: In the days of Bar Kochba: a great teacher named Simeon Bar Yohai refused to obey the Roman decree against the study of Torah. He continued to teach his pupils, though his life was in danger. At last he had to flee. He hid in a cave in the mountains of Galilee. For thirteen years he lived in this hideaway. According to a legend, the carob tree grew up at the mouth of the cave so that the scholar might have food.

First fruits blossom on a fig tree. The Talmud says: "When one sees a fig tree one should make a blessing, thanking God for creating it."

* * *

Judgment Day

On the New Year of the Trees, it was said by the rabbis of old, trees are judged in Heaven, just as we are on *our* Rosh Hashanah. On this judgment day, it is decided that some trees will grow strong and flourish and others will weaken and die. So, from olden times on, people prayed that the new year would be good to all *trees*.

Strength and Fragrance

Many customs grew up around Tu Bi-Shevat. In ancient Palestine, it was customary to plant a tree when a child was born: a cedar for a boy, and a cypress for a girl. The cedar stood for height and strength, the cypress for tenderness and fragrance. When the children grew up and were married, branches from their own trees were cut and used to support the bridal canopy, for good luck. Between birth and marriage they cared for their own trees. Through this custom everyone learned to love trees.

In the Heder

When our people were forced to leave the Holy Land, they did not forget Tu Bi-Shevat. In the cities and townlets of Russia and Poland, Tu Bi-Shevat came in the winter. In the *heder,* or Jewish school, after Hebrew lessons, the children opened the little bags they had brought from home—bags filled with tropical fruit that reminded them of Zion—dates, figs, raisins, and bokser, the dry fruit of the carob tree.

Faraway Customs

Other customs, odd and unusual to us, sprang up. In Kurdestan, raisins and other sweet fruits used to be placed in a ring around trees on Tu Bi-Shevat. Then the people prayed for an abundant fruit season and for the birth of many children.

In sixteenth-century Palestine, some communities drank four cups of wine on Tu Bi-Shevat. The first cup was white wine, to symbolize winter. The second was light red, for spring. The third: deep red, for summer. The fourth: red mixed with white, to symbolize fall.

A third unusual custom was that observed in Safed, Israel, long ago, where on Tu Bi-Shevat inhabitants would do their best to sample at least fifteen (for "hamishah asar" which equals 15) different kinds of fruit!

And, finally, a touching custom was that followed by Sephardic Jews of the sixteenth

One of the most important missions of the Jewish National Fund is forest conservation, for trees give shade, fruit, and lumber, and help hold sandy soil in place thus preventing land erosion.

An orange orchard in Israel's Plain of Sharon. Citrus fruit exports aid Israel's economy.

century. They had a *Ma-ot Perot* fund: money was collected to provide fruit for the poor on Tu Bi-Shevat.

In Israel Today

In modern Israel, Tu Bi-Shevat marks the end of the rainy season and is celebrated in all its ancient glory. In 1949, on the first Tu Bi-Shevat of the Jewish State, thousands of people gathered to plant life-giving trees in a forest which will one day contain six million trees—the number of Jews killed by Hitler's wrath. It is to be known as the "Forest of the Martyrs."

Tu Bi-Shevat also reminds us of the way Israel has bloomed under the tender care of the halutzim—the pioneers—in recent years. Jewish settlers have worked wonders of reclamation in the cool northern regions of Galilee, in hot waterless plains of the Negev, and in the tropical coastal areas.

Imaginative Jewish farmers introduced the grapefruit and varieties of oranges into Israel. They developed crop rotation so that the soil would not become weary and barren from growing the same plants over and over.

A quarter of a century ago, there were very few vegetables in Israel. The soil was too dry. Jewish pioneers sank wells to tap underground sources. Today there are thousands of acres of truck farms. Only twenty years ago, potatoes were a big farm problem in Israel: no one knew how to store them. Then it was discovered that if enough ventilation was provided, the potatoes would keep from sprouting little shoots before the market was ready for them.

'Land of Promise'

Today, when you visit Israel, you will find a great variety of growing things. In the north, where it is cooler, grow apples and pears. Galilean villages produce peaches and apricots. The tropical Jordan

Crates of oranges are ferried to a steamer in an Israel port waiting to depart for foreign markets.

By hacking down giant clumps of cactus, large areas of Israel's soil are reclaimed for useful planting.

valley has banana, persimmon, avocado, and papaya groves.

The maritime plain along the shore of the Mediterranean boasts the large citrus belt—oranges, grapefruits, and lemons.

Lots of other crops, including tobacco, grapes, melons, almonds, pistachio nuts, and pomegranates, to name but a few, show that Israel has truly earned its description as "a land of promise."

We Help the JNF

One way we in the United States observe Tu Bi-Shevat is by contributing to the Jewish National Fund, which plants young trees in Israel. These trees help reclaim for cultivation the earth which has been worn out by centuries of erosion and shifting sand dunes. In more than half a century of existence, the JNF has planted millions of trees and built hundreds of agricultural settlements.

In these five decades, the JNF has dedicated itself to the following tasks:

1. To use voluntary contributions to acquire land in Israel.
2. To lease this land to farmers and home builders.
3. To drain swamps, plant and conserve forests, develop water resources and irrigation.
4. To lease land for housing new immigrants.

Much of the credit for making Israel bloom as it did in days of old belongs to the JNF. When, for example, the famous Valley of Jezreel was bought by the JNF, it was a wasteland, a mass of swamps. Today the Emek is a beautiful valley, studded with orchards, grain fields, vegetable gardens and little farms. All this was achieved by the halutzim with the help given by Jews everywhere through the *Keren Kayemet Le-Yisrael*, the Jewish National Fund.

Eating Fruits of Israel

We also show our love for Tu Bi-Shevat and the ideals for which it stands by eating fruits from Israel on this day. And there's even something else which many children enjoy doing. That is growing plants and little trees indoors.

Still in use in some areas of the Middle East are olive-crushers and presses like this one.

Have You a 'Green Thumb'?

All you need for this is earth, water, flower pots or jars, and seeds. In your own kitchen you can grow fine plants from grapefruit seeds, date pits, avocado seeds, peas and lima beans, just to name a few. In most cases, all you need do is plant a few seeds in earth, water them and put them in a fairly warm place. In about three weeks, when your seeds sprout, place them in the sun and water them a little every day. With a little patience you can have a lovely indoor garden.

* * *

Tu Bi-Shevat Flower Legend

Not only customs, but legends as well have clustered about Tu Bi-Shevat and its flowers, plants, and trees. One legend describes the history of the shy and graceful Cyclamen, also called *Nezer Shlomo*, the "Crown of Solomon." It is said that when Solomon became king, he chose the lovely Cyclamen as a model for his crown. Centuries later, when Jerusalem was conquered by the enemy, the royal crown was stolen from the king's treasury. The Cyclamen bowed its head in sorrow, saying: "Only when a son of David again ascends the throne and the crown is returned to Jerusalem shall I once more stand erect." To this day, the Cyclamen droops its head.

Tu Bi-Shevat marks the start of Israel's spring season. The fields from the Negev in the south to the Galil in the north are covered wih wild flowers.

Tu Bi-Shevat is devoted to planting saplings, for trees play an important part in the growth of the Jewish State.

'Rip Van Winkle'

Another beautiful legend that has arisen is that of Honi and the carob tree.

Said Rabbi Johanan: All his life Honi, the righteous one, was troubled about this verse *(Psalms, 126:1):* "When the Lord brought back those that returned to Zion, we were like unto them that dream." Seventy years elapsed between the destruction of Jerusalem and the return to Zion. Is it possible for anyone to sleep for so long a period without interruption? One day, while walking on the road he noticed a man planting a carob tree. Said Honi to the man: "You know that it takes seventy years before a carob tree bears fruit; are you sure that you will live seventy years and eat therefrom?"

"I found this world provided with carob

trees," the man replied. "As my ancestors planted them for me, so I plant them for my children."

Thereupon Honi sat down to eat and was overcome by sleep. As he slept, a grotto was formed around him, which screened him from the human eye. There he slept for seventy years. When he awoke, he saw a man gathering carobs from the carob tree and eating them. "Do you know who planted this carob tree?" Honi asked. "My grandfather," the man replied. "I too must have slept seventy years!" Honi exclaimed.

* * *

That, then is the story of Tu Bi-Shevat, which is celebrated by Jews the world over. It is a festival that symbolizes our love for the Holy Land and which shows our people's feeling for trees and plants as living, fruitful things. Tu Bi-Shevat can also remind us that when God created the world, he planted the Garden of Eden and placed Adam in it.

The fruit of the carob tree ("bokser"), dry and hard, is a traditional Tu Bi-Shevat specialty.

Purim means Megillah-reading, hamantashen, masks and merry-making.

Purim

Purim is a holiday of gift-giving and great fun. No other holiday makes us feel so gay and cheerful; on no other holiday are there so many goodies eaten. Because Purim celebrates the downfall of a tyrant who wished to wipe out our people and because the *Megillah*—the Scroll of Esther which is read on Purim—tells us to keep the 14th of Adar as a day of joy and happiness, the Feast of Lots has always been a time for merry-making.

In days gone by, bands of musicians roamed the streets on Purim, going from home to home, to play and then to receive Purim gifts. In every Jewish school and center, Purim plays and carnivals are the order of the day. In fact, just as the robin is a messenger of spring, so a rehearsal with wigs and make-up and poppy-seed cakes is a sign that Purim's around the corner.

The story of Purim is so full of human interest, of excitement and hair-breadth escapes, that we have never grown weary of telling it. Like the picture of the boy holding a box of cereal portrayed upon the wrapper of a *real* box of cereal, the Purim tale is a story set within a framework-story. And this is how it goes:

Once Upon a Time . . . .

Long ago there was a king named Ahasuerus, ruler of the Medes and the Persians. So mighty was he that his domain extended from Ethiopia to India, and he ruled over one hundred and twenty-seven provinces.

Now it happened once that King Ahasuerus ordered a feast in Shushan, his capital, and he invited all the princes and governors of his provinces. For seven days, he showed off his riches and ate and drank with his guests.

When the feasting was at its height and the king was quite drunk, he began to boast. Anything that he had, he said, was the best in the world. His horses were the best, his jewels the finest, his gardens the most luxurious.

"And your queen?" asked the princes.

The Boast That Failed

Queen Vashti, replied Ahasuerus, was the most beautiful woman in the whole world. To prove it, he would order her to appear at once, dressed only in her royal crown!

The queen was deeply insulted and re-

The supposed tomb of Mordecai and Esther in Hamadan, Iran (Persia).

fused to appear. Her husband, who saw the princes giggling behind their wine goblets, was infuriated. He ordered Vashti driven from the palace and he banished her from his kingdom.

Now King Ahasuerus found himself very lonely and he issued a proclamation, stating that all the fairest maidens of the land were to gather before him. The one whom he found most pleasing would be made queen in place of Vashti.

Beauty On Parade

Hundreds upon hundreds of contestants arrived and paraded before the king. Now there was in the royal palace at Shushan a certain Jew named Mordecai, who had been carried away from Jerusalem with the captives by Nebuchadnezzar, the king of Babylonia. He had adopted Esther, his uncle's daughter, for she had neither father nor mother. The maiden was very beautiful, and, after her father and mother died, Mordecai took Hadassah, that is, Esther, as his own daughter.

When the king's command was made known, among the many maidens brought to the royal palace at Shushan, Esther also was taken and placed in charge of Hegai, who took care of the women.

'Long Live the Queen!'

Esther had not revealed who her people were or her family, for Mordecai had told her not to tell. When Esther's turn came to go in to the king, Ahasuerus loved her more than all the other women. He placed the royal crown on her head and made her queen instead of Vashti.

In those days, while Mordecai was sitting in the king's gate, two of the king's servants, who guarded the entrance of the palace, plotted to kill King Ahasuerus. Mordecai learned of the plot and told it to Queen Esther; and she told the king in Mordecai's name. When the truth was

A Scroll of Esther case, set with semi-precious stones, made in late 18th-century Russia.

known, the men who plotted against the king were both hanged on a tree. And the incident was written down in the daily rec-

72

ord of events that was kept before the king.

The Man Who Didn't Bow

Now, King Ahasuerus promoted Haman, the Agagite, and gave him a place above all the princes who were with him. All the king's servants who were in the king's gate bowed down before Haman, for so the king had commanded. But Mordecai did not bow down before Haman. Haman was very angry. He decided to plot to destroy all the Jews in the kingdom of Ahasuerus.

Haman told King Ahasuerus:

"There is a certain people in the provinces of your kingdom; and their laws differ from those of every other people; and they do not keep the king's laws. Let an order be given to destroy them, and I will pay ten thousand talents of silver into the royal treasury."

The king took up his ring and gave it to Haman, and said:

"The money is yours and the people also, to do with them as you wish."

Messages then were sent to all the king's provinces, to destroy all the Jews on the thirteenth day of the twelfth month, which is Adar.

Trouble in Shushan

When Mordecai learned all that had been done, he tore his clothes and put ashes on his head as a sign of mourning, and went out into the city and raised a loud and bitter cry of sorrow. He went as far as the king's gate.

When Esther's maids and servants told her about it, she was greatly troubled. She sent Hatach, one of the king's servants, to learn what this meant.

Hatach went to Mordecai, who told him all that had happened and told him to urge Esther to go to the king and plead with him for her people.

When Hatach came and told Esther

This scene of Ahasuerus and his merry-making was made in the 17th century. From a Megillah in the Bersohn Museum, Warsaw.

what Mordecai had said, she commanded Hatach to go and say to Mordecai:

"Death is the punishment for any man or woman who goes to the king into the inner court without being called, except for the one to whom the king may hold out the golden scepter, which means that he may live. Now for thirty days I have not been called to go in to the king."

Mordecai's Message

When Mordecai was told what Esther had said, he sent back this answer to Esther:

"Do not think that you alone of all the Jews will escape because you belong to the king's household. If you keep silent at this time, help will come to the Jews from some-

A relief taken from the doorway of a palace courtyard at Persepolis, Iran, shows Persian ruler Darius the Great (seated) receiving petitioners.

In a 17th-century Purim-shpiel *sketch, downcast Haman leads triumphant Mordecai. Note the costumes: they belong to the period when the play was presented, not to the ancient Persia in which the story is set.*

where else. Who knows: perhaps you have been raised to the throne for an emergency like this!"

Then Esther sent this message to Mordecai.

"Go, gather all the Jews in Shushan and fast for me. Do not eat or drink anything for three days and nights. I and my maids will fast also, and I will go in to the king, although it is against the law. And if I perish, I perish."

Mordecai went away and did as Esther directed.

Audience With the King

On the third day, Esther put on her royal robes and stood in the inner court of the royal palace opposite the king's house. The king held out to her the golden scepter that was in his hand. Esther went up and touched the tip of the scepter. Then the king said to her:

"Whatever you wish, Queen Esther, and whatever you ask, it shall be granted, even to the half of my kingdom."

Esther replied:

"Let the king and Haman come today to the feast that I have prepared for him."

The king said:

"Bring Haman quickly, that Esther's wish may be granted."

So the king and Haman went to the feast that Esther had prepared, and she then invited them to come to another feast on the following day.

Haman went out that day joyful and happy; but when he saw Mordecai in the king's gate and noticed that he neither stood up nor moved for him, he was furiously angry with Mordecai. Haman went home and told his friends and Zeresh, his wife: "Queen Esther brought no one with the king to the feast which she had prepared but me, and tomorrow also I am invited by her along with the king. Yet all this does not satisfy me, as long as I see Mordecai, the Jew, sitting at the king's gate."

A Wicked Plot

Then Zeresh, his wife, and all his friends said to him:

"Let a gallows seventy-five feet high be built and in the morning speak to the king and let Mordecai be hanged on it. Then go merrily with the king to the feast."

This advice pleased Haman, and he had the gallows built.

In the Dead of the Night

That night the king was unable to sleep. He gave orders to bring him the books that told of great deeds; and they were read before the king. And in them was written how Mordecai had told about the two servants of the king who had tried to kill King Ahasuerus. Then the king said:

"How has Mordecai been honored and rewarded for this?"

The king's courtiers replied:

"Nothing has been done for him."

The king demanded:

"Who is in the court?'

Now Haman had just entered the outer court of the king's house to speak to the king about hanging Mordecai on the gallows he had prepared for him. So the king's courtiers said to him:

"Haman is standing there in the court."

The king commanded:

"Let him enter."

Haman entered, and the king asked him:

"What shall be done to the man whom the king delights to honor?"

A Little Mix-Up!

Haman thought to himself, "Whom besides me does the king delight to honor?"

So Haman said to the king:

"Let a royal garment be brought, which the king has worn, and the horse on which the king has ridden and on whose head a royal crown has been placed. Then let the garment and the horse be placed in charge of one of the king's noble princes and let him clothe the man whom the king delights to honor and make him ride on the horse through the city square and proclaim before him: 'This is what is done to the man whom the king delights to honor.'"

Then the king said to Haman:

"Make haste and take the garment and the horse, as you have said, and do thus to Mordecai, the Jew, who sits in the king's gate."

Haman obeyed the king.

Mordecai returned to the king's gate, but Haman hurried to his house, mourning, with his head covered.

Then the king's servants came and escorted Haman to the feast that Esther had prepared. The king and Haman went to drink with Queen Esther. And the king said to Esther:

"Whatever you ask, Queen Esther, it shall be granted you, even to the half of my kingdom."

Esther Speaks Out

Queen Esther answered:

"If I have won favor, O king, and if it seems best to the king, let my life and my people be given me at my request; for I and my people have been sold to be destroyed, to be killed, and to perish!"

King Ahasuerus said to Queen Esther:

"Who is he and where is he who dares to do this?"

Esther answered:

"A foe, an enemy, this wicked Haman."

Haman shrank in terror before the king, and the queen; and Harbonah, one of those who waited on the king, said:

"There, standing in the courtyard of Haman's house, is the gallows, seventy-five feet high, which Haman built for Mordecai."

The king said:

"Hang him on the gallows."

A pewter Purim plate showing the ten sons of Haman. Persia, about 17th century.

Purim players in a copper engraving of 1657. Their weapons are brooms and mops!

The Plot Boomerangs

So they hanged Haman on the gallows that he had prepared for Mordecai. And the wrath of the king was quieted.

King Ahasuerus then made Mordecai one of the king's advisers. The king also drew off his signet ring, which he had taken from Haman, and gave it to Mordecai.

Then Esther begged the king to prevent the evil that Haman had planned against the Jews. King Ahasuerus said to Queen Esther and to Mordecai:

"Write in behalf of the Jews in the king's name, and seal it with the king's ring; for what is written in the king's name and sealed with the king's ring no one may disobey."

Good News!

Thus Mordecai did. And he sent by messengers, who rode the king's swift horses, mules, and camels, the king's command that the Jews who were in every city should gather together and protect their lives. Mordecai told them to keep the fourteenth day of the month of Adar, and the fifteenth day also, each year, the days on which the Jews were saved from their enemies, and the month which was turned for them from one of sorrow to gladness, and from mourning into a holiday; that they should make them days of feasting and gladness, and of sending presents to each other and gifts to the poor.

The command was also given out in the royal palace at Shushan; and Mordecai went out from the presence of the king in royal garments of violet and white and with a great crown of gold and with a robe of fine linen and purple. The people of Shushan shouted and were glad. To the Jews there came light and gladness, joy and honor. And in every city and country, where the king's command came, there was gladness and joy among the Jews, and a holiday.

On the fourteenth day of the month of Adar, the Jews rested and made it a day of feasting and rejoicing. Therefore the Jews keep the fourteenth day of the month Adar as the day of rejoicing and feasting and a holiday, and as a day on which they send gifts to one another. But the Jews in Shushan rested on the fifteenth day of the same month and made it a day of feasting and rejoicing.

Purim Means *Lots*

The Jews made it a custom for them, and for their children, and for all who should join them, so that it might not be changed, that they should observe these two days as feasts each year. For Haman had plotted to destroy the Jews completely, and he cast *pur,* that is, *lots,* to destroy them. For this reason these days are called Purim.

That is the story of Esther and of Purim as it is told in our Megillah.

How the Purim Play Began

Because happiness and fun are the keywords of Purim, play-acting or mummery has been a traditional part of this holiday for centuries. The Purim play, a standard feature in Jewish schools today, has a long and honorable ancestry. Purim plays were first presented in Italy and Germany, and spread to Russia, Poland, Lithuania, Galicia, Rumania, and other countries in Eastern Europe.

Purim-time became the Jewish theatrical season, and in some European communities, Purim "show-time" lasted for two whole weeks.

Strolling Purim-players, accompanied by an "orchestra," presented their shpiel wherever an audience gathered. An original etching by Ezekiel Schloss.

The story of Joseph and his brothers was often presented as a Purim-shpiel. This scene was drawn by a 19th-century Russian Jewish artist, who decided to dress his Bible characters in Hassidic costume.

The Megillah's tale of Esther and Mordecai was not the only one portrayed. Also popular was the story of Joseph in Egypt and David and Goliath. In Germany a play about Joseph and his brothers was so successful that it was performed before large audiences in Frankfort and Metz. This play had a theatrical manager and the actors were Jewish students from Prague and Hamburg.

Usually the *shpieler,* or actors, made up their lines as they went along, throwing in as many jokes as possible. Clowns and Fools and other fanciful characters somehow mixed their way into the performances, until often the only link between a *Purim-shpiel* and the Feast of Lots was the date on the calendar. In one play, there was a clown named Pickle-Herring, who played practical jokes on spectators in the audience.

Sometimes the playscripts were printed and sold. The title of such a play, published in Germany in 1708, reads: "A beautiful new Ahasuerus play, composed with all possible art! ... Whoever will buy it will not regret his purchase, because God has commanded us to be merry on Purim."

Most of the time, the plays were presented with song and dance by the wandering Purim-shpieler, accompanied by musicians. They visited house after house, performed their show, and received con-

Purim parties in school must have a king and a beautiful queen, costumes and tempting refreshments. It's all in the age-old tradition of jolly Purim when anything goes!

tributions after they sang a jingle like this one: *Today is Purim, tomorrow no more; Give me a penny, I'll be gone from your door!* Sometimes, when the Purim plays were given out-of-doors, the crowds were so large that they had to be held back by soldiers.

These Purim plays gave way to indoor plays, carnivals, and masquerades. In Israel, the Adloyada Carnival, with colorful pageants, parades, and festivity, has been revived. In the United States, Purim celebrations are on the calendar of every Jewish school, center, and organization, the length and breadth of the land.

The Megillah and Art

Beginning with the Middle Ages, the Scroll of Esther was often ornamented with beautiful illustrations. Cases of graceful and unusual design, delicately carved in silver and gold, were made to house the Megillah.

The earliest dated Purim scroll is one of 1637; it may be seen in the Jewish Museum of London. Handsomely designed Megillot also appeared in other countries, including Holland, Italy, Germany, Poland, and Russia.

Illustrations in Purim scrolls include

scenes from the story, such as Haman on the gallows, and Mordecai being led on the king's horse. Many scrolls were intended for the use of youngsters and are illustrated in a fairy-tale style. The borders of Megillot were usually decorated with flowers, birds and animals, and graceful designs.

Purim Words

The following words belong to the Purim "vocabulary" that has developed with the holiday as it has been celebrated for thousands of years in every land where there has been a Jewish community. These words will enrich the meaning of Purim for you.

Gragger: Noisemaking at the mention of Haman's name in the reading of the Scroll of Esther is an old, old custom. The *gragger* has been in use since the thirteenth century in France and Germany. It combines two primitive instruments: the "bullroarer" and the "scraper." The "bull-roarer" consisted of a long stick at the top of which

An ingenious wooden gragger, made in Poland in 1935, depicts Haman and his 20th-century counterpart, Hitler.

A beautifully illuminated Esther scroll, parchment, 17th-century France.

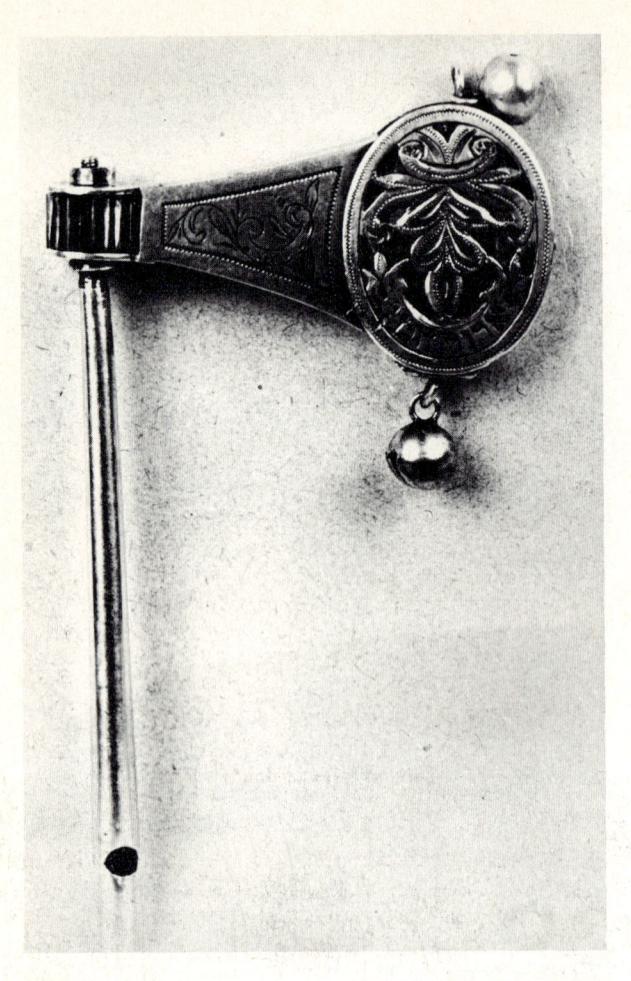

An 18th-century silver gragger, made in Poland, complete with bells to add to the confusion when Haman's name is read.

was attached a string and at the end of the string a thin board. When this was twirled, it made a strange noise. The "scraper" was a notched shell or bone which was scraped with a stiff object. The *gragger* combines both these objects. In some countries, Haman's name was written on the soles of the shoes, which were rubbed on the floor during the Megillah reading.

Mishloah Manot: Often called Shalach Monos, this means the "sending of gifts." The custom is mentioned in the *Book of Esther*—"make them days of feasting and joy, of sending portions to one another." That's where we get the oh-so-wonderful custom of giving and receiving presents on Purim!

Zakhor: It means "remember," and Shabbat Zakhor is the Sabbath before Purim. An extra portion of the Torah is read. This portion tells of what evil Amalek did to our ancestors. The *Haftarah,* or portion of the Prophets, read on Shabbat Zakhor, describes King Saul's meeting with Agag, ruler of the Amalekites. The point is that Haman is portrayed as an Agagite, a direct descendant of Amalek.

Fast of Esther: The day before Purim (the 13th of Adar) is the Fast of Esther. We remember on this day the fast decreed by Esther and the gathering of the Jews for public fasting and prayer on the day before the date set by Haman for the massacre of the Jewish people.

Hamantashen: These are the Purim pastries without which no Purim celebration would be complete. They are three-cornered little cakes filled with poppy-seeds or plum-jam. Some say that the name comes from *mohntashen,* or "poppy seed pouches"; others claim that the cakes resemble Haman's hat! An interesting sidelight is that in Hebrew a hamantash is called *ozen Haman,* or "Haman's Ear"!

Adloyada: There's a talmudic saying that one should drink merrily on Purim,

A Purim "gift-exchange" plate for sending Shalah Manot. Made in France, 18th century.

80

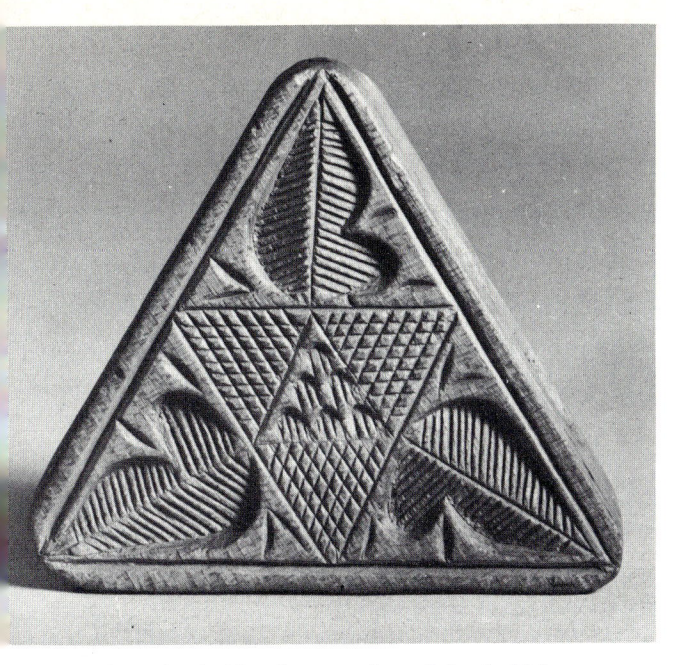

A form for baking hamantashen; Poland, 19th century.

until one is so tipsy that one knows not (*ad d'lo yada*) the difference between "blessed be Mordecai" (*barukh Mordecai*) and "cursed be Haman" (*arur Haman*). This expression has given the name to the annual Adloyada Purim Carnival in Tel Aviv, a gala affair, complete with floats, streamers, costumes and balloons.

Purim Katan: This means "small Purim." During Jewish Leap Year, Purim occurs in Second Adar (or the month of Adar Sheni). When that happens, the fourteenth day of the First Adar is called Purim Katan.

Shushan Purim: The day after Purim is called *Shushan Purim,* or Purim of Shushan, capital of Ahasuerus' empire. According to the *Book of Esther,* the Jews of Shushan celebrated the victory over Haman a day

At an Israel Adloyada carnival, a float announces that "Joy reigns in the city of Shushan."

81

Machatzit Hashekel: Before the Scroll is read, every adult contributes to charity, in remembrance of the biblical tax of one half-shekel which was used to keep up the Holy Sanctuary.

Special Purims: One of our ancient sources of wisdom, the Midrash, says—"any man, and especially the inhabitants of a city to whom a miracle has happened, may make that day Purim." There have been at least thirty such Purims when Jewish communities have set aside a special day to commemorate deliverance from great evil. One example is: *The Purim of the Baker Woman,* 1820: the city of Chios in Greece was attacked by Greek rebels, and a baker woman accidentally shot off a cannon. This warned the Turkish forces and the city was saved.

Another Purim took place two centuries earlier in Germany. It became known as *Vincenz Purim* (or Purim Fettmilch) after Vincenz Fettmilch, a baker who called himself a "new Haman" and blamed the Jews for Germany's hard times. He spurred an attack first on the ghetto of Worms and then on the ghetto of Frankfort. Luckily, the governor looked upon these pogroms as acts of civil disobedience. He quickly quelled the riots and the "new Haman" was hanged. The governor ordered damages

A silver-gilded Megillah case made to hold the Scroll of Esther in Eastern Europe over a century ago.

later than did the other Jews because they were engaged in battle an additional day.

Megillah: The Book (or Megillah, or Scroll) *of Esther* is found in the third part of the Holy Scriptures (in the Ketuvim, or Writings). It is the last of the five Megillot, or Scrolls. The Megillah is read in the synagogue after the evening service on the Eve of Purim, and again on the morning of Purim.

A pewter Purim plate with engraved decorations made in Holland about 1700. Inscription on rim: ". . . sending portions to one another and gifts to the poor" (Esther 9:22).

paid to the Jews. The Jews of Frankfort established a special Purim in 1614.

Still another special Purim was the *Purim of Tiberias*. A Jewish community had settled in Tiberias. Shortly thereafter Suleiman Pasha, the Governor of Damascus, attacked the city. During the eighty-three days of siege, the Jews helped bravely in the defense. They knew that capture would spell disaster for them. At last the attackers withdrew; before they could prepare a second assault, their Pasha died. The Jews of Tiberias gratefully established a special Purim to commemorate their escape from danger.

Would you like to know the names of some other special Purims? Here are a few: Purim of Shiraz, Curtain Purim, Purim of Bandits, Purim of the Poisoned Sword, and Purim of the Bomb. They have all been described in books and perhaps one day you will want to read about them.

* * *

The ways in which *you* can add to Purim fun are many indeed. You can make Purim costumes, prepare Purim gifts, set the table for the Purim "seudah," or feast, sing Purim songs, play Purim games. When you remember that Purim recalls the downfall of a tyrant and the joyous victory of our freedom-loving ancestors, you will realize *why* Purim has been always a day of gladness and will continue to be so forevermore.

Jonah can't seem to escape from the whale in this float drawn in a Tel Aviv Adloyada procession.

Porcelain Seder plate to hold the symbolic foods, made in England, 19th century.

Passover

"How does this night differ from all other nights? On all other nights we eat bread and matzah; why on this night do we eat only matzah?"

"We were slaves to Pharaoh in Egypt; and Moses was sent down to free our people from bondage..."

The question is the same every year, and so is the answer. For both are part of a ceremony that has remained unchanged for centuries upon centuries. This ceremony is called the Seder, and it marks the beginning of Passover.

What Passover Is

Passover is many things. It is a Festival of Freedom, when we recall how the Almighty released our forefathers from slavery in Egypt and helped a free people come into existence.

Passover is an Agricultural Festival, reminding us of the Land of Israel in the time of the First and Second Temples. In those days, our ancestors were farmers tilling the soil for a livelihood. Passover marked the beginning of the grain harvest.

Passover is also a Pilgrim Festival. Three times during the year, the Israelites, according to the laws of the Torah, went in joyous procession to Jerusalem, there to celebrate the festivals of Passover, Shavuot, and Sukkot.

Passover is all of these things, but it is especially a holiday for children. Our ancestors were instructed: "You shall tell it to your son." The Seder Service, the reading of the Haggadah, the Four Questions, the "stealing of the afikomen"—all these are meant for boys and girls, to teach them the importance of this great holiday in the history of the Jewish people.

Turn Back the Clock...

To learn the story of Pesah we must wend our way across the sands of time, to a distant age and to a strange land. There, in ancient Egypt, lived Joseph, the favorite and gifted son of Jacob. Joseph had been sold by his brothers to Midianite merchants, who in turn had brought him to Egypt. One day he was thrown into prison on false charges. Soon afterwards, the ruler of

Stele of King Mernephthah of Egypt on which the name Israel is first mentioned.

A camel caravan, plodding across the desert sands, recalls the trek of the ancient Israelites.

Egypt had a strange dream in which seven lean cows devoured seven fat ones. Not a single wise man or wizard in all the land could tell the meaning of the dream. Then Joseph, who had interpreted dreams for the royal cupbearer and baker, was called before the Pharaoh.

"I have dreamed a dream and none can interpret it," said the Pharaoh.

Joseph answered, "God is the interpreter of dreams. Perhaps through me He shall grant the Pharaoh peace of mind."

Joseph listened and then told the Pharaoh that his dreams meant that seven years of famine would follow seven years of plenty in the land of Egypt.

Joseph Becomes Governor

The king rewarded Joseph by making him governor over all the land. The new governor built huge granaries to be filled during the years of plenty. When the years of famine came, the full granaries saved Egypt from starvation.

While he was governor, Joseph had the good fortune to see his brothers again. They had come to Egypt to buy grain during the famine. Joseph recognized them at once and forgave them for what they had done.

"Take with you as much grain as you need," he said. "And—promise me this: you shall bring our father here, so that he may spend his last years in this great land of plenty."

So the family was re-united and Jacob lived out his days together with his favorite son.

A New Pharaoh

Many years passed. Pharaoh and Joseph and his father and brothers died. Generations came and went. A new Pharaoh rose, who did not know of Joseph and his good deeds. The new Pharaoh feared that the Israelites might grow so numerous that they would overrun the land. To avoid this, he determined to enslave them and oppress them, so that their numbers would diminish.

According to tradition, Joseph was buried at this spot in the shadow of Mt. Gerizim in the hills of Ephraim.

For many years, the Children of Israel toiled under the taskmasters of Egypt. And then it happened that this Pharaoh, too, dreamed a dream. He saw an old man with scales in his hand: on one side was a small, tender lamb; on the other, all the great men of Egypt. And the little lamb outweighed all the Egyptians.

The next morning, one of Pharaoh's wise men interpreted his dream. He warned the king that the lamb represented the Israelites and that a child would be born to one of them who would overthrow the Kingdom of Egypt and set all the Israelites free. This child would excel all men in wisdom and his name would be remembered forever.

'Death to the Israelites!'

In panic and desperation, Pharaoh commanded that every baby boy born to the Israelites be cast into the Nile. Thousands of children were drowned by this decree and there was great mourning and weeping among the Israelites.

There lived among the Israelites a man named Amram, of the tribe of Levi. Jocheved, his wife, had given birth to a boy. Wishing to save the child from the hands of the cruel Egyptians, his mother hid him well. Now Pharaoh had sent out spies to search for all the new-born babes. Jocheved made a cradle of bullrushes, the long weeds at the river's edge, and daubed pitch over the cradle to make it waterproof. She put the child into the cradle and set it afloat. Miriam, the child's sister, watched by the river bank, her heart throbbing with anxiety.

Rescued from the Nile

Then it happened that Thermuthis, daughter of Pharaoh, came to the river to bathe. She heard a child crying and rescued the little boy. Miriam timidly approached the princess and offered to call

Tourists today can still see this huge statue of the Pharaoh Rameses II at Memphis, Egypt, where once the Hebrews were held in bondage.

one of the Hebrew women to nurse the child. Receiving the princess' permission, Miriam soon returned with her mother. Thus little Moses was reared by his own mother. Afterwards, the princess took the child Moses to the palace.

Although Moses grew up in the palace of the Pharaoh, he never forgot that he was an Israelite. When he saw his people slaving in the hot sun, he determined that he would help end their misery. Once, after he had grown to manhood, Moses saw an Egyptian taskmaster beating an Israelite. Moses struck down the officer and buried him in the sand. When Pharaoh discovered this, he became angry and sentenced Moses to death.

Adventure in Midian

Moses fled to Midian. There he sat down to rest near a well where shepherds gathered. Among them were the seven daugh-

Site of the ancient city of Memphis in Egypt.

ters of Jethro, priest of Midian. Moses helped the girls water their flock, and Zipporah, the eldest daughter, invited Moses to her father's home.

Moses married Zipporah, and for many years he tended the flocks of Jethro. One day he came near the mountain called Sinai. While grazing the sheep, he saw a fire spring up in a thornbush. Amazingly, the bush was not consumed. Moses wanted to approach but the voice of God called out to him from the fire and ordered him to stand still. Then God commanded Moses to go to Egypt and set the children of Israel free.

Before the King

With his brother Aaron, Moses appeared before the king and asked him in the name of God to free the Israelites. Pharaoh laughed and said that he had never heard of the God of the Hebrews. Moses threw down his rod, and it became a snake. Pharaoh laughed; his magicians could perform the same feat. And even though Moses' rod swallowed all the other rods, Pharaoh remained unconvinced.

Moses told Pharaoh that if he would not set the Israelites free, God would turn all the waters of Egypt into blood. The plague took place but the king's heart remained unsoftened. Then came the plagues of frogs, of darkness, and of wild animals. Each time Pharaoh offered to let the Israelites free if only the plague would cease, and each time he refused to fulfill his promise.

The Last Plague

Then came the final plague that broke the will of Pharaoh, the plague that brought death to every first-born in every Egyptian home. In the dead of night, Pharaoh, whose own son lay dead, called for Moses and begged him to take his people out of the land. Moses gathered the Hebrews and left Egypt in great haste. They baked unleavened bread because they had no time to allow the dough to rise. Thus were prepared

Palm trees shelter Egyptian shepherds; in the distance a pyramid rises against the cloudless sky.

the matzot which were to become such an important symbol in our celebration of Pesah.

The Israelites marched for three days. Meanwhile, Pharaoh summoned his army and began to pursue them. On the sixth day he found the Israelites resting near the Red Sea. The fleeing Israelites were terrified. The sea was in front of them and the mighty Egyptian army behind them. How were they to escape?

Moses prayed to God for aid, and the Lord parted the waters and left dry land upon which the Israelites could go across. Pharaoh followed them into the sea. Then another miracle occurred: the waters became as they had been before, and swallowed the entire army of Pharaoh. Only Pharaoh himself was saved so that he might live to see and hear the glories of God.

The Long Trek

The Israelites wandered for forty years until they reached Canaan, the Promised Land beyond the River Jordan. In Canaan, with the Ten Commandments which God had given them through Moses on Mount

Legend says that Aaron is buried in this tomb at the summit of Mt. Hor. (See the Bible—Numbers 20:22-9.)

This is the Red Sea and these are the waters which the Bible tells us were crossed by the Israelites in the Exodus.

Sinai, they began a new life. They built homes and planted vineyards and celebrated their harvest festivals.

Since those days, we have celebrated Pèsah beginning with the eve of the fifteenth day of Nisan. During the eight days we eat unleavened bread to remind us of the bread our fathers baked in haste when they left the land of Pharaoh. (Reform Jews do not observe the eighth day.)

Preparing for Passover

Preparations for the holiday begin in every home many days before Passover. Everything in the house is scrubbed and polished. Carpets are cleaned, floors are scrubbed, fresh curtains are hung. Just before Passover, all-year-round kitchen utensils are put away, to be replaced by those specially reserved for Passover.

Then comes the matzah—enough to last through Passover. Matzot are the only kind of bread permitted in a Jewish home on Passover. The Bible does not tell us exactly how matzot are prepared, but the Talmud gives us details as to the ingredients used (—wheat flour and water—), the proper thickness of the cakes, and other information.

From earliest times, matzot were perfo-

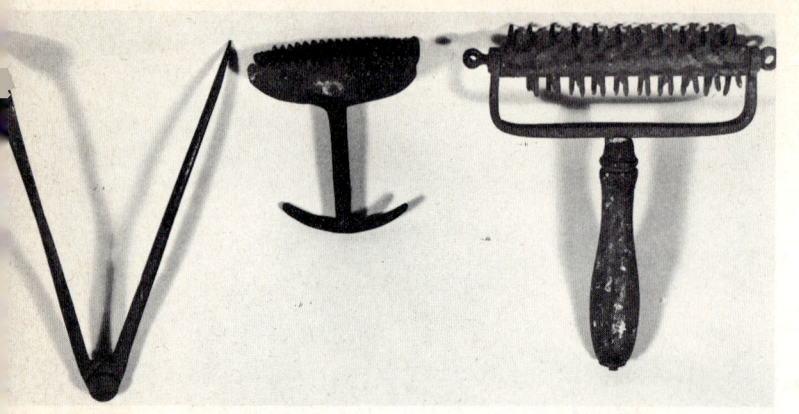

Old European tools for matzah-making. Right: a compass to measure the round matzot. Left and center: wheels to make the tiny perforations in the matzot before baking.

rated after being rolled into shape, and before baking. This was to keep the matzot from rising and swelling in baking.

Matzah Designs

In the days of the Talmud, the perforation of the matzot was quite artistic. In the house of Rabbi Gamaliel, the little holes in the matzot shaped figures: animals, flowers, and such. The perforating was done with a tool that looked like a comb. One rabbi suggested stamping the matzot with ready-made figured plates. But other scholars felt that every one had a right to design his own perforated figures.

In later years, the perforating tool was a wheel; it had sharp teeth and a handle. The "perforator" would run his wheel through the matzot at right angles and about one inch apart.

In olden times, matzot were made in the home as well as by professional bakers. During the Middle Ages, there were community ovens. The matzot were usually made in a round shape, but sometimes they were triangular.

Ma-ot Hittim

A fund known as *Ma-ot Hittim* ("money for wheat") was set up in every community. This was to provide Passover provisions for the poor and the needy. In our day, we can participate in the mitzvah of Tzedakah by contributing to the *Ma-ot Hittim* fund.

A Special Matzah

A special kind of matzah is that called *Matzah Shemurah* ("guarded matzah") which many Orthodox Jews use, particularly on the two Seder nights. Shemurah matzah is made of wheat that is watched during harvesting, milling, and baking. The wheat is carefully protected against leavening, either by rain swelling the grains or dampening the flour, or by too much kneading and slow baking.

About 1875, matzah-baking machinery was invented in England. Soon after, it was introduced in America. Although some matzot are still made by hand, most Passover matzot today are made by machine. Actually, matzot are used all year round. On Passover, however, only matzot which are prepared for the holiday may be eaten. The only day one may *not* eat matzot is the day before Passover, so they may be eaten with greater enjoyment during the Seder.

Selling the Hametz

Since we may have no *hametz* or leavened bread in our homes on Passover, we perform a ceremony known as *mekhirat hametz* several days before the holiday. A bill of sale is written out and all our hametz is "sold" to a non-Jew for the duration of Passover. This transaction is usually handled by the rabbi for each of his congregants, but every member must personally

Matzot today are watched as they roll along conveyor belts. They must move swiftly and never touch *hametz*.

The ritual of the Seder table, the special foods and ceremonial objects, all help retell the story of the great liberation from slavery, when the Almighty led our ancestors out of Egypt.

ask the rabbi to be his agent for him. The bill of sale is prepared with the understanding that it will be returned immediately after the holiday.

The Search for Hametz

The last cleansing ceremony, *B'dikat Hametz*, takes place on the night before the first Seder night arrives. To symbolize the change from the old to the new, from the leavened to the unleavened bread, Mother has taken bits of bread and put them on window sills and shelves. Now Father takes a goose-quill and a wooden spoon, and with his children close at his heels to watch him, he goes looking for hametz. Naturally, he finds the bits of bread easily enough, for this is a symbolic search. He brushes the bread onto his wooden spoon, wraps spoon and bread in a piece of cloth, and puts it away till morning. Then he burns it, together with any bread left at breakfast. After ten in the morning of the day before Passover (*erev Pesah*) no hametz may be eaten. Neither are matzot eaten that day so that the real Pesah matzot will taste fresh and new when they are eaten at the Seder.

Everything has been taken care of. The holiday is about to be ushered in. For eight

Present-day Samaritans in Israel, who claim descent from the tribes of Ephraim and Manasseh, have their own customs. Here they bake matzot for Passover.

days, beginning at sundown of the fourteenth day of the month of Nisan, the family celebrates the Festival of Pesah. The first and the last two days are observed as full holidays; the intervening four days (Hol Ha-Moed) are half-holidays.

Here at Last

The evening of the first Seder comes at last. Dressed in bright, new clothes, in a home fragrant with the sweet odors of matzot and wine and holiday food, the family begins its celebration of the Festival of Freedom. The Seder celebration is held on the first and second nights of the holiday.

The Seder

On the first Seder night the table is decked in gleaming white, the candles cast a warm, flickering glow, and the proud wine cups stand ready to play their part in the annual drama of the Pesah Seder. The Seder table helps us to celebrate Passover properly. "Seder" means *order* or *arrangement*; and the arrangement of foods at the Seder reminds us of the many-sided meaning of Passover, the great festival that marked the birth of a free people thousands of years ago and that still has an important message for every one of us.

What do we find on our Seder table? As we look about, we see—

Candles. As on every Sabbath and festival, candles grace the table. The blessing over the candles gives warmth to their light as they cast a holiday glow over the Seder and those who have come to celebrate Passover.

The Haggadah. "You shall tell it to your son," says the Torah. The Haggadah (from the Hebrew *haggeyd*, to tell) recounts the Passover story, and adds thanksgiving prayers and children's songs. It makes Pesah a holiday the whole family looks forward to.

Four Cups of Wine. Everyone at the Seder table drinks them, in the order mentioned in the Haggadah. There are *four* because of God's four expressions of promise to free the Israelites from slavery.

Cup of Elijah. Because Jewish tradition says that the prophet Elijah will one day bring peace to the world, we set a goblet for him on the table, open the door (the Haggadah tells us when) and "welcome" him in.

Roasted Egg. The egg symbolizes the festival offering sacrificed by Pilgrims in the Temple. The egg is used in the Seder because it is a Jewish symbol of mourning, in this case for the destruction of our ancient Temple, where the sacrifices were brought.

Maror. The bitter herbs (usually horseradish) remind us of the bitterness of slavery. It was bitter in Egypt in those days; it is no less bitter for our people there today and elsewhere where there is tyranny.

Karpas. Greens (lettuce, parsley, or celery) symbolize the poor nourishment the Israelites had while in Egyptian slavery. We dip the *karpas* into salt water to re-

Silver Passover plate; Austria, 1907. The three compartments are for the three matzot. Decorations: Moses, Aaron, and Miriam and three groups of men, carrying the small dishes for the symbolic foods of the Seder.

member the salty tears they wept under Egypt's cruel yoke.

Matzah. After the ten plagues, the Israelites, pressed by the Egyptians to leave, snatched up their unbaked dough, though it was unleavened (which means it hadn't yet risen, like bread). There are three special matzot at the Seder. Half of the middle of these matzot will be used as the afikomen, or dessert. For children who snatch the afikomen unseen there will be a present for returning it upon request.

Shankbone. This roasted bone is a symbol of the Pesah lamb sacrified at the Temple of our ancestors.

Haroset. Although this mixture of apples, almonds, cinnamon, and wine symbolizes the mortar (or cement) made by our forefathers under the lash of Egyptian taskmasters, it tastes delicious. Why? Because its sweetness, it is said, is a symbol of God's kindness, which made even slavery bearable.

On the Seder Plate itself we find:

1. Three whole matzot covered.
2. Zeroa—a roasted meatbone, symbol of the paschal lamb.
3. A roasted egg.
4. Maror—bitter herbs, usually horseradish.
5. Haroset—a mixture of nuts, apples and wine.
6. Karpas—celery, parsley or potatoes, to be dipped in salt water.

At the Seder we eat matzah to remind us of the days of slavery and the freedom we enjoy today.

The Haggadah

The Haggadah has been mentioned, but it deserves closer attention, for it plays a central role at the Seder.

The Haggadah is a kind of "guide book" for the celebration of Pesah. It has directions on how to conduct the Seder, explanations for the Pesah symbols, selections from Psalms (113-118), interesting stories, children's folk songs, riddles and prayers. Most important of all, it tells the story of why we celebrate Pesah.

The Haggadah has a long history. It is more than 2,000 years old. Even before it was written down, the father of the family would tell the story of Pesah at the Seder table. He was following the commandment in the Bible, "Thou shalt tell thy son in that day, saying: It is because of that which the Lord did for me when I came forth out of Egypt." The very term "Haggadah," as we have seen, comes from the Hebrew word "haged," which means "to tell."

As time went by, more parts were added to the Haggadah, which was still not written down—prayers, hymns, selections from the Mishnah. By the Middle Ages so much had been added that it was necessary to record the Haggadah. But even then the Haggadah was not a separate book, but a part of the prayer book. Soon after the Middle Ages the Haggadah became a book in its own right.

What the Haggadah Tells

It is in the Haggadah that we learn the use of the sacrificial lamb (Pesah), unleavened bread (matzah) and bitter herbs (maror). It interrupts the thanksgiving (Hallel) with the meal, and at last ends with the songs of Adir Hu and Had Gadya (An Only Kid).

One of the most stirring parts of the Haggadah is recited at the beginning of the Seder, beginning with *Ha-Lahma Anya*,

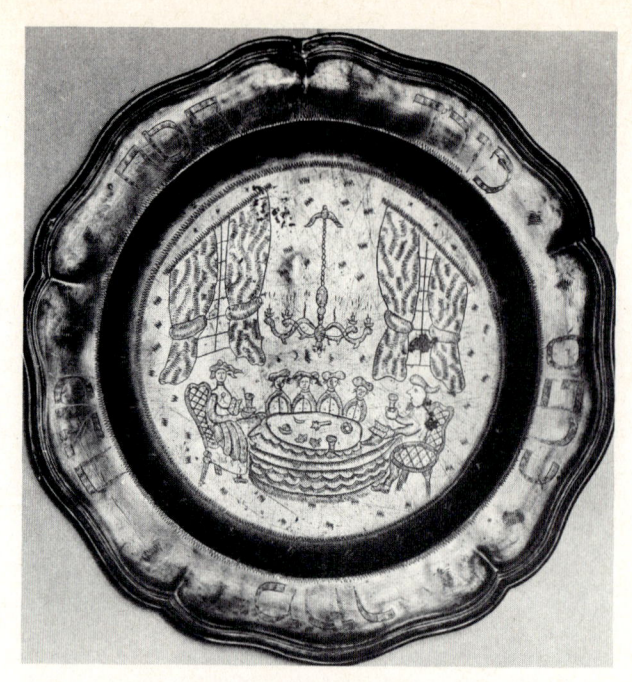

Pewter Seder plate; Europe, 18th century. Note the "four sons" who are described in the Haggadah.

"This is the bread of affliction." The head of the house rises, lifts the plate of matzah in his hands, and recites, "This is the bread of affliction which our fathers ate in the land of Egypt. Let all who are hungry come and eat. Let all who are in need come and celebrate Pesah with us. Now we are here. Next year may we be in the Land of Israel. Now we are slaves. Next year may we be free men."

Ha-Lahma Anya is one of the oldest sections in the Haggadah. It is written in Aramaic, a language spoken by our ancestors in Israel almost 2,000 years ago. It was once customary for the head of the house to step out into the street and recite Ha-Lahma Anya. Today the invitation to the poor is recited within the home—but the spirit of hospitality remains the same.

The Four Questions

Following Ha-Lahma Anya, the youngest child recites the Four Questions:

Why is this night different from all other nights?

1. On all other nights, we eat either leavened or unleavened bread. Why on this

Centuries have come and gone but never has a Passover gone by for over 3,000 years without a Seder somewhere on the face of the globe. This lad is asking the "four questions": "Why is this night different from all other nights?"

night do we eat only unleavened bread?

2. On all other nights we eat all kinds of herbs. Why on this night do we eat only bitter herbs?

3. On all other nights we do not dip the vegetables even once. Why on this night do we dip them twice? (First parsley in salt water, then bitter herbs in haroset.)

4. On all other nights we eat either in a sitting or a reclining position. Why on this night do we all recline?

Then comes the long story of the Exodus from Egypt followed by the passages about the four different kinds of sons a man may have—the wise, the wicked, the simple, and the son who asks no questions. The wise son eagerly asks about Pesah and why it is celebrated. He is given a full explanation. The wicked son scoffs at Pesah, and his father tells him that if he had lived in Egypt, he would not have been worthy of being saved. The simple son asks a simple question and gets a simple answer. The fourth son asks nothing, but his father does not neglect him. He, too, is told why we celebrate Pesah.

Here, in summary, is the order of the Seder ceremony, as outlined in the Haggadah:

1. Kiddush over wine, after which all drink the first of the four prescribed cups of wine.

2. Wash the hands, omitting the customary prayer.

Embroidered Passover towel; Alsace Lorraine, 1875.

95

3. Parsley or celery is dipped into salt water and a blessing is said.

4. The middle matzah is broken. Part of it is hidden (the afikomen) to be eaten later.

5. Reading from the Haggadah.

6. All wash hands and say the usual blessing.

7. The upper matzah is broken and eaten after the saying of the blessing.

8. A bitter vegetable (maror) is dipped in haroset and eaten.

9. A sandwich of matzah and bitter herb is eaten. (We thus follow a custom begun by the great scholar Hillel when the Temple stood in Jerusalem.)

10. The entire Passover meal is eaten.

11. The piece of matzah hidden earlier (afikomen) is distributed and eaten. No food is eaten after this.

12. Grace after meals is said (Birkhat Ha-mazon).

13. Parts of the Hallel (Psalms) and other selections from the Haggadah are recited or sung.

14. The Pesah service has proven acceptable to God and the Seder is over.

The Haggadah and Art

The Haggadah has played an important part in developing Jewish art. In the Haggadah, artists found many subjects they could illustrate—the four sons, the ten plagues, Jacob's ladder, the crossing of the Red Sea, the patriarchs, the baking of the matzah and many other things. The artists of the Haggadah all expressed themselves in their own way. Some preferred to draw the initial letters in an artistic way. There is a Spanish Haggadah of the fourteenth century which has many pictures of Seder scenes. This Haggadah even has a picture of a little boy asking his father the meaning of the festival. The Spanish Haggadot usually were in beautiful colors, with gold lettering and ornamentation.

In the seventeenth century, Amsterdam became a center of Jewish printing. In 1695, the famous Amsterdam Haggadah appeared "in the house and to the order" of Moses Wesel. This Haggadah was illustrated with copper engravings. On the title page are the words: "Formerly the pictures used to be cut in wood. That was not so beautiful. Now that they are engraved in copper, everyone will realize the difference, which is like that between light and dark." In a later Amsterdam Haggadah more pictures were added—borrowed from a woodcut Haggadah which had once appeared in Venice.

Rarer than the scarce copies of early printed Haggadot are those in "manuscript" —hand-written, painstakingly illustrated Seder guides—each of which is one-of-a-kind. Outstanding among these is the world-famous Darmstadt Haggadah.

The famous hand-written Darmstadt Haggadah, 14th century, has breath-taking illustrations and designs. Here the "four questions" (Mah Nishtanah) begin with a large "Mah" to attract the child who will read it aloud.

In Israel, each cooperative settlement celebrates Passover as a community festival. This little girl is about to spill a drop of wine at the recitation of the "ten plagues" in the Haggadah.

This Haggadah was written on parchment during the fourteenth century by Israel ben Meir of Heidelberg. Israel did only the lettering. One artist then painted in large gold and blue initials and decorated the borders; a second artist drew scenes of Jewish life, especially Seder scenes. Mingled among the Seder scenes are illustrations of wild life. Birds, bears, lions, and other animals abound on the pages.

Many Heidelberg Jews had come from France. In the Haggadah, they wear the lavish holiday dress of well-off French citizens. There is plenty of food on the Seder table, and the house must belong to a well-to-do merchant. Almost everyone in the illustration of the Seder table is holding a book. Even though it was before the days of Hebrew printing (which began in 1475) many Jewish homes had manuscript books.

The beautiful Darmstadt Haggadah belonged for centuries to German Jewish families. In 1780, a Baron Hopsch bought it for his collection. It then made its way into the Library of Darmstadt, Germany, where it has remained to this day.

When the Seder is ended, the Haggadot are closed. The questions have been answered and the story has been told. The children watched Elijah's goblet very carefully, and when they noticed the wine quiver, they knew that was the moment when the Prophet sipped it.

Faraway Customs

As we have followed *our* customs, so have our fellow Jews elsewhere followed their own. Would you like to hear a few interesting Passover customs of far-off lands?

There is the interesting ritual of the

Pilgrims to Mt. Zion are greeted by the sound of the shofar as they ascend the mountain on an annual Passover pilgrimage. Note the curved ram's horn, typical in Oriental Jewish communities.

Caucasian Jews of Southern Russia. They greet the Passover seated on the earth, dressed in their best clothes, with a spear, close at hand. This is their way of portraying the dangers that beset the Israelites in the hurried exodus from Egypt.

And in the Eastern provinces of Portugal, near the Spanish border, one finds this custom among several communities of Jews, descendants of the Marranos, who escaped Portugal when the Spanish Inquisition hounded them. Since the finding of a single matzah could mean death to the entire family, the only reminder of the Seder among these people is a picnic held in the country. Inquisitive strangers would think it only a spring outing. However, the Marranos are careful to say a special prayer in memory of the Seder service their ancestors enjoyed.

And—think of the Yemenite Jews and descendants of Bagdad families, who have their own way of performing the Seder. Among them a child holds the roasted bone in one hand and an egg in the other. Then he asks the Four Questions, answering each one himself.

Customs vary, but the Seder is observed wherever there are Jews, and for all of us the Haggadah is a universal guidebook. After the festive meal, which has been eaten very slowly, to symbolize that we are now a free people and no longer slaves who can be forced to hurry, traditional songs are sung by the whole family.

The family sings: "Who knows one? I know one! One is our God in heaven and on earth.... Who knows two? I know two—" and so on, up to thirteen, which is the number of the qualities of God.

The Little Kid

Then comes the final song for which the children have been waiting all evening. It is about a little goat that Father bought for two coins. It seems to have an endless number of verses, but at last it comes to a halt with:

> Then came God
> And smote the Angel of Death,
> Who slew the slaughterer,
> Who killed the ox,
> Who drank the water,
> That quenched the fire,
> That burned the stick,
> That beat the cat,
> That ate the little goat
> That father bought with two coins.

* * *

That is the story of Pesah—a heroic rebellion against oppression and of glorious freedom from slavery. No other people has a story more thrilling, not one that is as true today as it was thousands of years ago. Throughout the ages, Passover has symbolized freedom: whether it meant escape from Egypt, rescue from the Crusades of the Middle Ages, or liberation from the Nazis.

Just as we overcame our enemies in the land of Egypt, so will the Jewish people ever vanquish its oppressors. That is the message of Passover which must forever be kept alive in our hearts.

Silver kiddush cup for festivals; London, 1800. Passover Eve scene shows figures standing around table with Paschal Lamb as prescribed in *Exodus* 12:11.

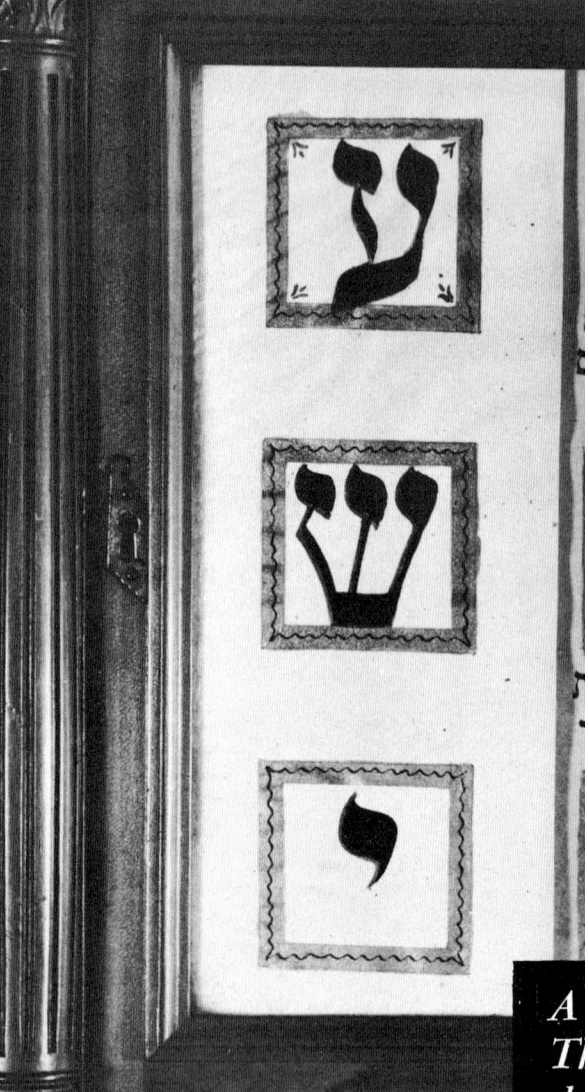

A 19th century European Omer calendar. The numbers, top to bottom, indicate that this is the 33rd day of the Omer (Lag Be-Omer), or 4 weeks and 5 days since the beginning of the seven-week period between Passover and Shavuot.

Lag Be-Omer

Lag Be-Omer, youngest of the Jewish festivals, arrives well in the spring, on the eighteenth day of the month of Iyar. Like many Jewish holidays, it tells of the Jewish people's fight for freedom against the dark forces of oppression.

Lag Be-Omer is a happy day; a day for weddings and for picnics and for outdoor sport. Bow-and-arrow games and other contests of skill are fitting for this holiday. And after the games are over, it is time to listen to the retelling of the story of Lag Be-Omer, the "scholars' holiday."

Reign of Terror

Long ago, nearly two thousand years ago, Palestine was conquered by the Roman general Titus. For many years, Palestine was ruled by governors appointed by the Roman emperor. The Roman governors did all they could to wipe out the love of independence which the Jews had always had. They taxed the people heavily and forbade them to study the Torah. The mighty Roman legions kept the Jews in constant terror.

Freedom's Call

At last a hero arose, determined to drive the Romans from the land. Bar Kochba, the people called him, Son of a Star. For Bar Kochba appeared to his countrymen like a heavenly messenger sent to restore freedom. About him Bar Kochba gathered a staunch and determined army of Jewish warriors. According to the legends that have grown up about Bar Kochba, he was able to root up a tree from the ground as he rode past it on his horse.

One of Bar Kochba's chief supporters was Rabbi Akiba. Akiba was one of the most beloved leaders of our people. Once an ignorant shepherd, he had married Rachel, daughter of a rich man. So enraged was Rachel's father with his daughter that he drove her from his house, and she and Akiba lived in poverty in a humble hut. But she encouraged her husband to go off to a *yeshiva* to study. He remained away for many years. But Rachel was happy that her husband was becoming a scholar, and when at last Rabbi Akiba returned to her, he was famed throughout the land for his wisdom and gentle ways.

Scholar and Soldier

Rabbi Akiba encouraged his students to join Bar Kochba's forces. For to Rabbi

A coin of the Bar Kochba period displaying a palm tree and a vine leaf. The ancient Hebrew reads: "First year of the redemption of Israel," and "Simon Nasi Yisrael."

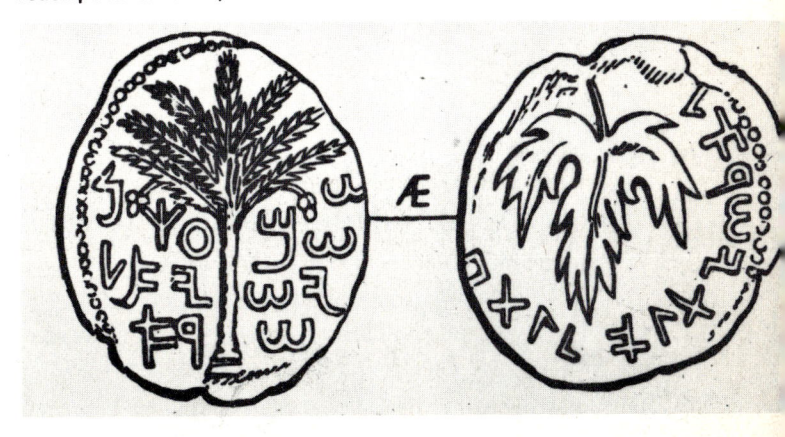

Tiberias, Israel, and the tomb of Rabbi Meir Baal Ha-Nes, second-century scholar, member of the Sanhedrin, and pupil of Rabbi Akiba. In the background: the Sea of Galilee.

Akiba freedom was the dearest possession man could have.

In fact, it was Rabbi Akiba who gave Bar Kochba his name. Akiba had been searching for a leader to spearhead the rebellion against the Romans. One day there came to him a man, fierce of visage, sturdy as a mighty boulder.

"My name is Simon Bar Kosiba," he said. "I am ready to strike the blow of vengeance. Will you bless me, great Akiba?"

And Akiba answered: "In the Book of Numbers of the Bible it is written: 'There shall step forth a star out of Jacob, and a scepter shall rise out of Israel and smite the corners of Moab and destroy the children of Seth.' You shall be the leader, and people will call you *Bar Kochba—Son of a Star.*"

Bar Kochba's army had little chance against the Roman forces. They were hopelessly outnumbered. Their weapons were inferior.

For three years they managed to withstand the attacks of the Romans. As a sign of their independence, the Jews struck new coins bearing the name of their hero, Bar Kochba. At last the Emperor Hadrian sent one of his fiercest generals, Julius Severus, to cope with the heroic rebels in Palestine.

Severus left Britain, where he was fighting for Rome, and hastened to Palestine. Like a giant steam-roller, his forces moved over the small land, crushing one stronghold after another.

The Last Stronghold

Bar Kochba was forced to retreat to Betar, the fortified city near Jerusalem. For one whole year, the Romans laid siege to the city. At last, in 135 C.E., the Romans broke through the gates and poured into the city and destroyed it. Bar Kochba fell fighting. Rabbi Akiba was put to a cruel death by the Roman governor of Judea.

The defeat of Bar Kochba's army was followed by even crueler persecution. Desperately the Romans tried to wipe out all desire for Jewish independence. They forbade the study of the Torah on pain of death. Many scholars followed the hard path taken by Rabbi Akiba and died mar-

At Meron, a town in Galilee, pilgrims still gather each year to celebrate Lag Be-Omer with prayer, song and dance. They pay homage to the memory of Rabbi Simeon Bar Yohai, buried in Meron.

Lag Be-Omer is celebrated with picnics and games because Rabbi Akiba's students carried bows and arrows as a disguise when they took to the woods to study Torah.

tyrs in the cause of freedom.

But despite all the Romans did, the torch of Jewish learning continued to burn. It was carried by Jewish exiles to other lands where they built schools and continued to teach the traditions of their people to their children. They celebrated the festivals which commemorated their life in Palestine and their battles for independence.

The Thirty-Third Day

Lag Be-Omer is one of these festivals. The name of the holiday means the thirty-third day of the *omer*, which was a measure the Palestinian farmers used for measuring their grain. The days between Passover and Shavuot were known to our farmer ancestors as omer days, for this was the time when the Jews gathered their harvest. They are also known as *sefirah*, or counting days. Having no calendar to guide them, the Jews counted the days from Passover to Shavuot to know when to celebrate the end of the harvest season.

The days between Passover and Shavuot are a solemn period on the Jewish calendar. They recall the suffering which the Jews endured under Roman persecution. No joyous celebrations, like weddings and parties, are held during the *sefirah* days. But Lag Be-Omer comes to break the series of solemn days. Lag Be-Omer is the one joyous day of the *sefirah* days. For according to folklore, Bar Kochba won a great victory on the thirty-third of the omer days. Another story tells that a plague which was raging among Akiba's students suddenly stopped on that day. For this reason, Lag Be-Omer is also called the Scholars' Holiday. In most countries Jewish children celebrate by holding picnics in forests and fields and shooting bows and arrows.

The bows and arrows are a reminder of the disguises worn by the students of Simeon Bar Yohai. Bar Yohai was a great scholar who went off to live in a cave when the Romans forbade him to study his sacred books. There he studied for many years, living on carob fruit (*bokser*) and other wild fruit, and drinking the waters of a spring that had appeared miraculously in the cave. When his students came to visit him, they disguised themselves as hunters to confuse the Romans, and carried bows and arrows.

Simeon Bar Yohai, before he died, asked his followers to celebrate rather than mourn his death. That is why the day he died is celebrated as a joyful outing, and bows and arrows are brought to the Lag Be-Omer picnics.

Festival at Meron

Israel has its own way of celebrating Lag Be-Omer. On that day the *hasidim* of the country visit the grave of Rabbi Simeon Bar Yohai, which is in Meron, near the town of Safed. It is night when the celebration at Meron begins. From every direction hundreds of men and women come streaming toward the grave of the scholar. Voices sing "Bar Yohai!" There are so many people that it is difficult to edge your way into the building which is built over the tombs. This building is a Bet Ha-Midrash. Thousands of candles and lamps are lit. People dance and sing. Arabs come to witness the celebration.

No one seems to walk. Everyone dances. Some sing, "Rabbi Akiba said . . ." and others respond, "Bar Yohai, happy art thou." Drums are beaten. Violins and flutes add their voices to the music coming from the throats of thousands of men and women. At last, at midnight, a huge bonfire is lit. Into it, men, women, and children throw fine embroidery work—lace handkerchiefs, silken scarves—as the flames shoot up. The singing grows louder. Only at dawn does the celebration end. Then mothers bring forward their young boys who have reached the age of three. The rabbi gives the children their first haircut. He cuts the hair, leaving only the side-locks.

The idea of celebrating Lag Be-Omer with a bonfire has spread to other parts of Israel. It is a field day for boys and girls. But in the evening, in Haifa, Jerusalem, Tel Aviv, and in many of the colonies, bonfires are lit. Around the burning flames stories are once more told about Bar Kochba, Rabbi Akiba, Bar Yohai—men who defied tyranny and carried forward the torch of Israel's hopes.

Simeon Bar Yohai ate of the fruit of the carob tree when he fled the Romans and hid in a cave.

Mount Sinai, wreathed in mist, rises majestically above the sands of the desert.

Shavuot

The holiday that follows hard on the heels of Lag Be-Omer, the youngest Jewish holiday, is Shavuot, one of the oldest of all Jewish festivals. "Shavuot" means "weeks" and it falls exactly seven weeks after the second day of Passover, on the sixth and seventh days of the month of Sivan. (Reform Jews observe only the first of the two days.) Another, non-Jewish, name for Shavuot is Pentecost, which in Greek means "fiftieth," because it takes place on the fiftieth day after the beginning of Passover.

Shavuot is a triple holiday, a three-fold celebration which commemorates

—the giving of the Torah on Mount Sinai
—the harvesting of wheat in Israel, and
—the ripening of the first fruit in the Holy Land.

The rabbis declared Shavuot to be the most pleasant of all Jewish holidays. In a way, it fits in very well with Passover and brings that great festival to a glorious conclusion. For on Passover the Jews were freed from slavery and on Shavuot the freed slaves were made into free men by the Ten Commandments.

In ancient days, two oxen yoked together helped the farmer harvest his crop.

A pewter plate made in Germany in the 19th century bears a design linking it with Shavuot.

A Torah Festival

As a Torah Festival, Shavuot is known as *Z'man Matan Toratenu*. This means "The Time of the Giving of Our Law." It was on Shavuot that God spoke to Moses atop Mount Sinai and gave the Israelites the Ten Commandments. As you know, the Ten Commandments are not only the foundation of the Jewish religion but the basis of the moral law of all civilized nations. If all the people on earth were to abide by the Ten Commandments, the world would be empty of evil and full of goodness.

 There would be no theft.
 There would be no murder or wars.
 There would be no adultery.
 There would be no falsehood.
 There would be no envy.
 There would be no idolatry.
 There would be no worship of false gods.
 There would be no taking the name of God in vain.
 There would be no slavery.
 There would be no false witness in the courts of justice.

It would, indeed, be a wonderful world in which to live.

Harvest Holiday, Too

Besides being a Festival of Torah, Shavuot is a Harvest Holiday. In ancient days, the cereal harvest was begun on the second day of Passover with the ripening of barley. On this day, an *omer* (a measure) of grain was brought to the Temple as Thanksgiving to God. The forty-nine days until Shavuot were counted, and this period is still called *Sefirat Ha-Omer* (counting the *omer*). A special prayer was, and is, recited each day at the end of the evening service. This prayer includes a special number for each day—"the first day of the omer ... the second day of the omer" and so on—so that an accurate count of the days elapsed can be kept.

After seven weeks of counting came the harvesting of wheat, the last cereal to ripen.

Thus Shavuot is also known as *Hag Ha-Katzir*—"Festival of the Harvest." A successful harvest meant prosperity for the coming year. Which is one more reason why Shavuot was a gay festival in ancient Palestine.

The grain was often stored in rough-hewn stone jugs like this one, unearthed in a cave in Galilee.

And Ripe, Ripe Fruits

Just about the time the wheat was harvested, the first fruits began to ripen on tree and vine in Israel. The Torah commanded every farmer to bring his first fruits as an offering of thanks to the Lord. In Jerusalem, at the Temple, our ancestors were grateful to God for a bountiful harvest.

The rabbis tell how the first ripe fruits were selected: "Upon visiting his field and seeing a fig, or a cluster of grapes, or a pomegranate that was ripe, the owner would tie a thread around the fruit, saying, 'This shall be among the *bikkurim.*'" *Bikkurim* means "first fruits," and one of the names for Shavuot is *Hag Ha-Bikkurim*.

Our Bible says: "For the Lord thy God bringeth thee into a good land, a land of brooks of water, of fountains in valleys and hills; a land of wheat and barley, and vines and fig-trees and pomegranates; a land of olive trees and honey" (*Deuteronomy 8:7*). Of these "*seven kinds*" every farmer was to bring his first fruits as a thanks-offering to God. That is why one name for Shavuot is *Hag Ha-Bikkurim*, the "Festival of First Fruits."

The 'Seven Kinds'

Each of these "first fruits" played an important part in our history and our Torah. Here's how:

Wheat and Barley. Israel's rainfall is heaviest during winter months, so the best crops are the winter crops of wheat and barley. Barley ripens about Pesah-time, and was brought to the Temple during Passover. Wheat needs more rainfall and ripens later. So important was the harvest that it was used to record events and dates. Ruth and Naomi, for example, came to Bethlehem at the beginning of the barley harvest. Samson used his famed flame-carrying pack of foxes during the wheat harvest.

Grapes. Grapes need plenty of rainfall for growth and lots of sunshine to allow the leaves and fruit clusters to develop. Israel has both. The first grapes ripen early in Sivan, in time for Shavuot. The messengers sent by Moses to the Land of Canaan brought back a cluster of grapes so heavy that "they bore it between two on a staff" (*Numbers 13:23*). The Bible says: "And Judah and Israel dwelt safely, every man under his vine and under his fig-tree..." (*I Kings 5:5*).

Figs. The fig-tree was originally found in Asia and then carried westward by desert tribes to Israel and the Mediterranean. The Torah has been likened to a fig—all fruits

In Israel, the tradition of bringing "first fruits" has been revived. Contributions often go to the Jewish National Fund.

109

From the palm tree come dates and the lulav. The Bible says: "Take on the first day of Sukkot the branches of palm trees . . . and dwell in booths seven days."

have some waste material, like seeds, pits, or rind; the entire fig, however, can be eaten, and so it is with every word in the Torah. The Talmud says: "When one sees a fig-tree, one should make a blessing: 'How pleasant is this fig-tree; blessed is God who created it!'"

Pomegranates. The messengers in the Bible, sent to examine Canaan, brought back pomegranates with them. Because it ripens in late summer, its blossoms were used to adorn the sheaves of grain brought on Shavuot to the Temple, and the fruit was brought after it had ripened. The farmer quenched his thirst with its juice, and the rind was used to make dyes and ink. The clothes of the Kohanim (priests) in the Temple were decorated with artistically-carved pomegranates, and some silver ornaments used to crown the Torah Scroll are still called *rimonim*, or pomegranates.

Olives. The olive tree is one of the most common in the Mediterranean climate. Its small leaves are covered with a thick, shiny coat and can well stand the scorching summer sun. The branch of the olive tree has become the symbol of peace. Noah's dove, sent from the Ark to find whether the flood had gone down, brought back an olive branch. Olive oil lit the Temple Menorah, and was one of the most important exports of ancient Israel.

Dates. During the picking season, dates are moist and juicy; later they are dried. The best area for dates in Israel is the Jordan valley. The date-palm is not planted by means of seeds, but with shoots which sprout from the roots of the date-palm. The Midrash says: "A righteous man will flourish like a date-palm—its dates are eaten, its branches used to thatch roofs, its fibres are made into ropes; so are the Children of Israel—some study Torah, some the Mishnah, some the Talmud."

The olive tree was well known in Bible days. God said: "Command the Children of Israel to bring pure olive oil to burn as an eternal light in your congregation."

110

Then—and Now

In ancient Israel, a long procession would wind its way through the streets of Jerusalem—men, women, and children—carrying baskets filled with these products of the soil to the Temple.

Today, in modern Israel, this custom has been revived. Long lines of children march with their baskets and guide beautifully decorated floats. The fruits are sold for the benefit of the Jewish National Fund.

What do *we* do on Shavuot? We decorate our homes and synagogues with plants and flowers. The greenery reminds us that this is a harvest festival and also that Mount Sinai was covered with green foliage when Moses ascended it to receive the Torah.

At Our Services: Ruth, Akdamut, Confirmation

In the synagogue, besides the regular holiday service, the Book of Ruth is read. The reason is that this beautiful story of faith and devotion took place during the harvest season. King David was descended from Ruth and it is believed that he was born and that he died on Shavuot.

A special prayer that is chanted in the synagogue on Shavuot is called *Akdamut*. This is a hymn of praise to God. It also thanks Him for giving us the Torah. There is a special melody for this prayer which over the years has become as definitely identified with Shavuot as the Kol Nidre chant has with Yom Kippur.

A Shavuot custom that has grown up in

In Jerusalem, children bring their offerings to the JNF building and enact a ceremony symbolic of the one performed by our forefathers who lived in the Holy Land in Temple days.

111

many Conservative and Reform synagogues is that of Confirmation. Because the Jewish people received the Torah on Shavuot, this holiday has become the season for the beautiful ceremony in which boys and girls are confirmed, or initiated, into the fellowship of our people. Youngsters who have been taught in religious schools and who have completed their course of study take part in this religious graduation exercise. They now consider themselves Bar Mitzvah and Bat Mitzvah—full-fledged sons and daughters of the Jewish faith who have become responsible Jews just as our ancestors were initiated into freedom and responsibility at Mount Sinai.

Shavuot Taste Treats

A final Shavuot touch appeals to our gastronomic sense—that is to say, to our hearty appetite. Shavuot calls for eating *blintzes* (a kind of fritter stuffed with cheese), cheese cake, and other dairy delicacies. This custom of eating dairy food symbolizes the fact that the Torah has been likened to "milk and honey." Another reason is that the Torah was given to Israel

In many synagogues, boys and girls who have completed a course of religious study participate in a confirmation ceremony on Shavuot, the holiday which is also known as *Z'man Matan Toratenu*, the "Time of the giving of our Law."

on the Sabbath. After the Jews received the Torah, they were no longer permitted to eat meat that was not slaughtered according to the rules set down in the Torah.

Since it is not permitted to slaughter animals on Shabbat, only dairy foods could be eaten.

* * *

And so, with Shavuot, the happy holiday season ticked off for us by the Jewish calendar comes to a close. The wheel has come full circle, and we can echo the words of King Solomon, who wrote in *Song of Songs:*

For lo, the winter is past
The rain is over and gone,
The flowers appear on the earth
The time of singing has come...

The cycle of Jewish holidays is over. Rosh Hashanah, Sukkot, Hanukkah, and all the others have come and gone, bringing in their train joy and solemnity, prayer and family fun. And perhaps the best aspect of each is the knowledge they leave behind that with the new calendar they will be with us once again, that they have not said "good-bye," but only—"so long for a while."

Two Tablets of the Law found in the caves at Bet Shearim, Israel. These carvings date back almost two thousand years.

All that remains of the ruined Second Temple is the Western Wall. It is to this day revered in the heart of every Jew.

Tishah Be-Av

Although Judaism is not a religion of excessive fasting and self-punishment, there are several days in the calendar which have been set aside to recall tragic events in the history of our people.

Of these, the chief one is Tishah Be-Av, which falls on the ninth day of the summer month of Av and which has a strange and tradition-filled background.

Series of Tragedies

According to the Talmud, many sad happenings took place on Tishah Be-Av. On that day it was decreed that the Israelites should wander through the wilderness for forty years. On that day the First Temple was destroyed in 586 B.C.E. by Nebuchadnezzar and the Second Temple in 70 C.E. by Titus. On that day the fortress city of Betar fell to the Romans in 135 C.E. And on that day, shortly afterwards, Bar Kochba and his men were massacred.

In the Middle Ages, on Tishah Be-Av, King Edward I of England signed the decree expelling Jews from England in 1290; they were not re-admitted until the seventeenth century. And on Tishah Be-Av in 1492, over 150,000 Jews were hounded from Spain, where they had lived peace-

A view of Betar today. In 135 C.E., the fortress city, which was Bar Kochba's last stronghold, was taken by the Romans, and Bar Kochba and his men were slaughtered.

Preparing to recite Lamentations, an aged Jew meditates in the solemn silence of the synagogue.

fully for centuries, by the cruel command of King Ferdinand and Queen Isabella.

To Remember, We Mourn

To commemorate the destruction of the two Temples, our rabbis ordered a day of mourning and of fasting on Tishah Be-Av. On Tishah Be-Av evening and on the following morning, passages of lamentation are read from the Book of Jeremiah, and mourning candles are lit. At morning services, neither Tallit nor Tefillin are worn, to show our deep sense of mourning. Instead they are put on for afternoon *(Minhah)* prayers. In the synagogue, shoes are taken off and the congregants seat themselves on the floor or on overturned chairs and benches. *Ekhah* is the first word of *Lamentations,* and they are said to the saddest chant in all of Jewish religious music. Towards the end of the services, poems by Yehudah Halevi, "sweet singer of Zion," are recited. These verses sing of the restoration of Zion, a hope that has been cherished by every generation of Jews.

And Close With Hope

The Sabbath following Tishah Be-Av is called *Shabbat Nahamu* and we read the fortieth chapter of Isaiah, which contains a dream of hope and comfort:

Comfort ye, comfort ye, my people,
Saith your God . . .

* * *

The fast days of Yom Kippur and Tishah Be-Av are observed from sunset of the previous evening. This is not the case with several minor fasts, when the fast begins at sunrise of the day itself. These include the Fast of Esther, already described in the chapter on Purim, as well as:

The Fast of the Seventeenth of Tamuz. On this day the walls of Jerusalem were broken into, leading to the destruction of the Second Temple in 70 C.E. According to tradition, on this day, too, the Tablets of the Ten Commandments were broken. The fast of the 17th of Tamuz begins the "three weeks" of mourning which conclude on the ninth of Av with Tishah Be-Av.

Tzom Gedaliah. This fast falls on the day after Rosh Hashanah. Gedaliah was a governor appointed by Nebuchadnezzar to rule the Jews of Palestine. On this day Gedaliah was assassinated, and wicked Nebuchadnezzar ordered cruel reprisals against the Jews.

Asarah Be-Tevet. On this, the tenth day of the winter month of Tevet, Nebuchadnezzar began his siege of fortified Jerusalem. Deprived of food supplies, the populace grew weaker and weaker, until at last Nebuchadnezzar was able to take the capital and destroy the First Temple in 586 B.C.E.

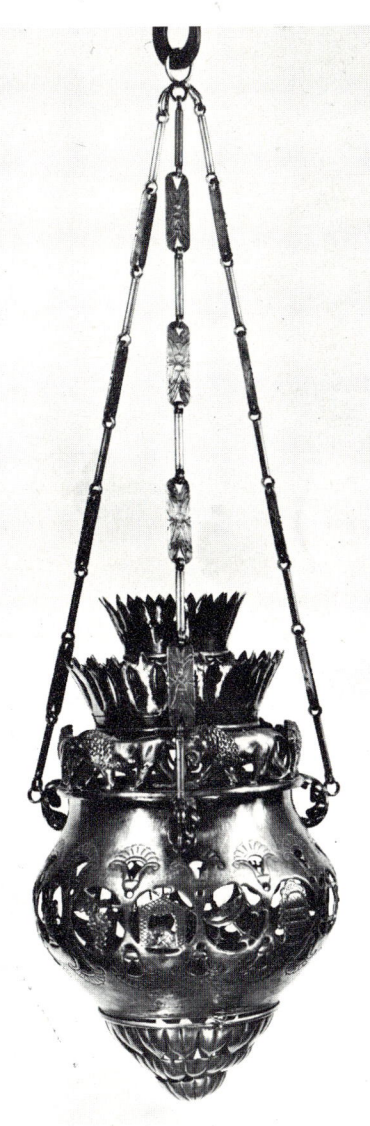

In every synagogue there is a Ner Tamid, or Eternal Light, which is never extinguished. The Eternal Light can be traced to the Bible, *Leviticus* 24:2—"Command the Children of Israel . . . to cause a lamp to burn continually."

Congregation Shearith Israel, New York (the Spanish and Portuguese Synagogue), was founded in 1654. It is the oldest congregation on the continent.

The Synagogue

Every festival and fast we have discussed relates itself in some way to the synagogue. It is time to focus our spotlight on our House of Worship. The best way to begin is to—

Walk into your synagogue. It may be a new building but it is the oldest of Jewish institutions. It was probably in Babylon, some 2,500 years ago, that the synagogue was born. Our ancestors were exiled from the Holy Land to Babylon in 586 B.C.E. The First Temple in Jerusalem was in flames, but did it mean the end of Jewish worship and prayer? The captives in Babylon did not think so. Though far from their native land, they gathered, perhaps first in private homes, to listen to words of encouragement from their leaders. They remembered the Temple ceremonies, and it may be that at one of these meetings the prophet Ezekiel spoke of the rebuilding of the Temple. At these assemblies, the exiles recited passages from the Torah or Prophets, observed the national feast and fast days, and perhaps sang the Psalms of David, which gave them hope for their return to Israel.

Center of Jewish Life

Each of these meetings was called *knesset*. The word was translated into Greek many years later as *synagogue*. The name *synagogue* means more than a "place of worship" It means a *house of assembly* for all Jewish activities—for prayer, for education, and for general communal welfare.

More than a half century after the first exile in 586 B.C.E., Persia conquered Babylon and allowed many of the Babylonian captives to return to Judea and to rebuild the Temple. This second Temple existed until the Roman General Titus destroyed it in 70 C.E. Yet, during these 600 years, known as the Second Commonwealth, the Judeans did not forsake the institution of the Synagogue which they had created.

So That All Might Take Part

The Temple indeed was the place of worship where sacrifices were offered daily, but in this sanctuary the priests or *kohanim* were in charge. Many plain people felt that they too should participate. It was therefore arranged that the Israelites (non-priests) in every town be divided into twenty-four divisions called *Ma'amadot*.

Ruins of this ancient synagogue at Capernaum (K'far Nahum), Israel, date back to the 2nd or 3rd century, C.E.

Relief of the Holy Ark, sculptured in rock, discovered in the ancient synagogue at Capernaum.

Each *Ma'amad* went to Jerusalem to take part in the Temple ceremonies for about two weeks of every year. Those who remained at home, however, gathered in a place in their town especially set aside for worship.

Originally, services may have been limited to the Sabbath, when work ceased. Next, they may have taken place on Mondays and Thursdays, the market days when the country folk came to town. Finally, services were held every day.

Philo, a Jewish philosopher of the first century, writes: "On the seventh day the Jews stop all work and proceed to sacred spots which they call synagogues. There, arranged in rows according to their ages, the younger below the elder, they sit quietly as befits the occasion, with attentive ears. Then one of them takes the books and reads aloud to the others...."

'When Ten Men Gather'

The Talmud often calls the synagogue "*bet am*," "*the house of the people.*" The rabbis declared: "Let a man but enter a synagogue, even stand behind a pillar (in any corner) and pray in a whisper, and the Holy One, blessed be He, hearkens to his prayer... When ten men assemble in prayer, the *Shekhinah*, the Divine presence, is there."

In the town of Betar there were 400 synagogues, with elementary teachers and schools. The holiness of the House of Worship was emphasized in Jewish law, which said that even if a synagogue were in ruins, one was not permitted to destroy it. The remains of such synagogues as the Dura-Europos synagogue in Syria of the 3rd century, which contains beautiful frescoes and inscriptions, is an example of this devotion.

'Miniature Temple'

When a Jewish traveler entered a city, the first place he sought was the synagogue. The synagogue therefore was called a *Mikdash M'aat*—"a miniature Temple."

One of the largest of synagogues of ancient times was in Alexandria. It had two rows of massive columns on either side of the great hall, and in the middle was a huge

Small synagogue in Rome, 5th century, C. E. (Based on a mosaic.) Note the Eternal Light, based on the biblical law found in Leviticus 6:6.

wooden platform, or *bimah*. The building was so big that the *hazzan* or reader had to give a signal by waving a cloth in order to have the congregation answer *Amen* to his prayers. In this same synagogue the congregants were always seated according to their trades: blacksmiths, goldsmiths, weavers, and so on, each in their section.

When the Second Temple at Jerusalem was destroyed in 70 C.E., numerous synagogues of Jerusalem went up in flames. By this time, hundreds of other synagogues existed wherever Jews lived, in Asia, Africa, and Europe. And, as Jewish merchant ships opened new roads of commerce, the construction of synagogues increased. They were built in countries as far east as China and as far west as Italy, Spain, France, and Germany. German Jews, fleeing from pogroms, brought the synagogue to Eastern Europe. Refugees from the Inquisition in Spain and Portugal came to Holland, and built houses of worship where they prayed in the Sephardic or Spanish tradition.

In the Middle Ages

In the Middle Ages, Jews were often forced to live in separate quarters of the town. These ghettos, as they were called, were generally gloomy places surrounded by high walls. But within the ghetto, Jews led a community life of their own which also had its happy side. And the most important institution in the Jewish community of those days was the synagogue.

The synagogue building stood in the center of the ghetto. Here people came for their religious services, for study and discussion, for celebrations and meetings.

The Three Names

The synagogue was known under three names: *Bet Ha-T'filah* or House of Worship, *Bet Ha-Midrash* or House of Study, and *Bet Ha-Knesset* or House of Assembly. Boys, by the way, had their rights in the synagogue long before they were Bar Mitzvah. They drank from the Kiddush cup. They held the Sefer Torah after the reading of the Sidrah, and, at the close of the Sabbath, they raised high the Havdalah candle.

On Sabbath and holiday afternoons, the rabbi of the community would speak. Teachers and preachers from foreign countries brought news from abroad. A *meshulah* or messenger from Palestine would sometimes bring news of the Holy Land to the community. The weary traveler came there to find lodging, and our custom of reciting the Kiddush on Friday night in the synagogue is a result of that age-old prac-

A "Jewish school" of days gone by. This drawing of a teacher and his pupil appears in a Bible written by hand in Germany over six centuries ago.

Model of a wooden synagogue in Pogrebnitz, Poland, first half of the 17th century. A fine example of the type of synagogue that was built by the entire community.

tice of hospitality. A child was given its name in the synagogue and a bridegroom came there to offer prayers on the Sabbath before his wedding. The custom still exists that sympathy is to be given to mourners by turning toward them with words of comfort as they enter the synagogue on Friday night.

Home of the Heder

The synagogue also housed the *heder,* or school for children, and the higher school of learning or *yeshiva.* Many a wandering student would sleep on the synagogue benches. The synagogue was a real community house, where town meetings were held, and charity was collected and distributed. The synagogue was a shelter for travelers as well as for students. When disputes arose, they were settled at trials in the synagogue. Friends met in the synagogue and used its library for reading and study. The officers of the synagogue were also the leaders in the community.

An interesting description of a visit to the synagogue in London in 1664 is recorded by Samuel Pepys, the famous English diarist. He happened to visit the synagogue on Simhat Torah and was amazed at the joyous spirit and dancing of the worshippers with the Torah. He thought this was the usual mode of conduct in the synagogue, not realizing that he had come precisely at the time when merriment was the order of the day. Only one who was unacquainted with the general practices in the synagogue could have made such a mistake.

When Tyranny Failed

As the Jewish people settled in various countries, officials often sought to curb Jewish life by issuing decrees against building new synagogues or making them higher than mosques or churches. The Emperor Justinian even tried to interfere in the worship by directing which Greek translation of the Bible was to be used.

The history of the Jewish people is portrayed in the role of the synagogue. Sometimes it even served as a fortress, as in

In the Old Country, pupils pose with their teacher before the *heder* in Tomashov, Poland.

122

The synagogue of the Ba'al Shem Tov, 18th-century founder of Hassidism, in Medziboz, Russia.

France and Germany during the Crusades or in Poland during the Chmielnicki pogroms of 1648. During the period of the Inquisition in Spain, the Marranos, who were forced to pretend that they were Christians, made their synagogues in cellars or caves, so that prayers should not be heard by spies.

Always the Same Purpose

With the dawn of modern times, the ghettos vanished and many Jewish communities built synagogues of beauty and grandeur. But the chief purpose of every synagogue, whether it was majestic or humble, was the same: to provide a place where men might worship God in democratic fashion.

The Synagogue in America

In the development of the synagogue among our people, the American synagogue is the youngest, for it cannot be older than the Jewish community in this country itself.

A little over three hundred years ago, a vessel containing twenty-three men, women, and children fleeing from persecution in South America sailed into what is today New York harbor. They settled in New Amsterdam, soon to be renamed New York. These twenty-three pioneers formed the first Jewish community in America.

First American Synagogue

Soon after they had landed, these early settlers formed a congregation named Shearith Israel, which means "Remnant of Israel." Peter Stuyvesant, the Dutch Governor, did not permit them to build a synagogue, so they held services under the trees, in homes, and in a rented one-room building in what is now the heart of New York's great financial district. A map of Manhattan Island of 1695 indicates a Jewish syna-

This Torah Ark of Cong. Beth Elohim, Charleston, S. C., is a replica of the one destroyed by fire in 1838. The original Ark was built in 1799.

Serving New Immigrants

In the meantime, however, other houses of worship were being built to meet the needs of new immigrants. In Newport, Rhode Island, where religious freedom was offered to all, the Touro Synagogue was dedicated in 1763. Jews came to Savannah, Georgia, in 1734, and organized a congregation in the very first month of their arrival. In 1745, religious services were first held in Philadelphia. Five years later, a synagogue was built in Charleston, South Carolina. And, in 1790, the sixth organized community took shape at Richmond, Virginia. To these congregations, President George Washington sent letters which are still quoted today because they so strongly champion tolerance and understanding.

An American Historic Shrine

The Touro Synagogue, mentioned just

Interior of the Touro Synagogue, Newport, R. I., showing the southwest corner. The colonial architecture blends with the style of Sephardic synagogues in this house of worship which is now a U. S. National Shrine.

gogue on the south side of Wall Street near Beaver Street. In 1730, the congregation built the first synagogue in North America, the Mill Street Synagogue, which remained in use for almost a century. Today, Congregation Shearith Israel, also known as the Spanish and Portuguese Synagogue, faces Central Park in Manhattan. It proudly observed its own three hundredth birthday during the American Jewish Tercentenary celebration.

That first synagogue on Mill Street was thirty-five feet square and twenty-one feet high. From 1730 to 1825 all New York Jewry worshipped in it. Until 1850, when the first synagogue was opened in the then independent city of Brooklyn, Jews would row across the East River to spend the Sabbath with their brethren in Manhattan.

above, deserves more extended comment, for it is today a United States National Shrine. It has a fascinating history.

In the year 1658 fifteen Jewish families of Spanish-Portuguese stock came to Newport. They were attracted to Rhode Island for in this colony founded by Roger Williams, all men, regardless of nationality or faith, were granted religious freedom. In Newport, the Jews felt they could live a fruitful life without fear of persecution.

For one hundred years the early Jewish settlers worshipped in private homes. In 1763 what is now the oldest synagogue building in the United States was dedicated.

Peter Harrison, a famous English architect, was chosen for the work. Reverend Isaac Touro, the father of the American Jewish philanthropist Judah Touro, was the rabbi of the Newport Congregation and dedicated the synagogue building which is today a national shrine.

The synagogue, a brick building, is at a sharp angle to the street, so that the Ark should face the East, towards Jerusalem. The bricks—196,715 in number—were imported from England. No nails at all were used in the structure, only wooden pegs, possibly because no iron tool was used in building the Temple in Jerusalem.

The inside is very impressive and dignified. Twelve columns of solid tree trunks representing the twelve tribes of Israel support the roof.

One of the prized possessions of the Touro Synagogue is a Torah which was brought from Amsterdam, Holland. It is at least 400 years old. The letters are as fresh and as clear as the day in which they were written. The silver bells which adorn the scrolls were made by the early American silversmith Myer Myers and are outstanding examples of craftsmanship.

A feature of great interest is the underground passage. The opening to the passage is in the floor of the *bimah*. At one time

This prayer room for Congress, the first in congressional history, was opened in 1955. The window's main panel shows George Washington praying for all America. Behind him, a verse from Psalm 16: "Preserve me O God, for in Thee do I put my trust."

the tunnel had an exit to the street at the side of the synagogue. The underground passage was probably built because the early settlers wished to have a symbol by which they could remind their children of the persecution they had suffered in Europe. Secret passageways were a feature of Marrano life in Spain. They served as a hiding place or as an escape exit in time of danger.

In 1780, a meeting of the General Assembly of Rhode Island was held in the synagogue. In 1790, George Washington wrote a letter to the warden of the synagogue, Moses Seixas, in which he stated "... happily the Government of the United States ... gives to bigotry no sanction, to persecution no assistance ..." A copy of this letter is on the west wall of the synagogue.

Since 1946, when the synagogue was designated a National Historic Shrine,

This is the nation's first "traveling synagogue." Rabbi Harold A. Friedman uses it to serve many small Jewish communities in North Carolina. Inside the bus are an Ark, Torah, and other ceremonial objects.

thousands of tourists from all parts of the United States and many foreign countries have visited it. During the winter months it is open for visitors on Sunday from 2:30 to 4:00 P.M., or by appointment, in the summer from 10:00 A.M. to 5:00 P.M. daily, except Saturday. Perhaps some day you will visit the Touro Synagogue. It will be an experience you will long remember.

The Cathedral in the Pines (Rindge, N. H.) attracts thousands of visitors of every faith. Here, preparations have been made for Jewish religious service. The Altar of the Nation, in background, contains stones from all the states.

Influx of Newcomers

Until 1815, most Jewish settlers who came to this country were descendants of Jews from Spain and Portugal. Then, as the American frontier swept westward and southward, as railroads spanned the country, as steamer passage across the Atlantic dwindled to nine or ten days, general population figures skyrocketed, and the Jewish population in the United States grew from 3,000 to 250,000. Most of these newcomers came from Germany, eager to flee the anti-Semitism that was widespread in that country in the beginning of the nineteenth century. In the United States, they laid the cornerstone of American Reform Judaism and founded many religious and philanthropic organizations.

America had firmly established itself as a symbol of freedom and equality. When the new waves of persecution battered the defenseless Jews of Eastern Europe—in Russia, Galicia, and Rumania—they turned to "the golden land" and America opened its heart to them. Among the immigrants who poured into eastern ports between 1880 and 1920 were two million Jews.

These three were the great periods of Jewish immigration to the United States—the Sefardic, the German, and the East European. Each group was different, and each brought its own Jewish traditions to the New World. The immigrants of three centuries were of all possible types—merchants, poor peddlers who traveled with packs on their backs, factory workers toiling in sweatshops. All of them contributed in their own way to America and to American Jewish life.

Building the Community

In the early years of American history, it was the synagogue that held the Jewish community together. The *shohet* who slaughtered meat according to Jewish ritual was paid by the congregation. Matzah-

The Jewish Theological Seminary of America is Conservative Judaism's highest institution of learning, training rabbis, teachers, and cantors, The J.T.S. conducts many projects for the advancement of Jewish scholarship and reseacrh.

The Hebrew Union College-Jewish Institute of Religion, with campuses in Cincinnati and New York, graduates the rabbis, teachers, and cantors who serve Reform temples all over America. H.U.C.-J.I.R. also has a pre-rabbinic school in Los Angeles. Shown here is the Cincinnati campus.

making was in the hands of the religious community. Every poor person, every needy widow and orphan was helped through the synagogue.

The Three Branches

As the country grew and as the Jewish population developed, the synagogue lost its control over many aspects of community life, but it remained a vital part of the American Jewish community. The Reform and Conservative movements grew up alongside of traditional Orthodoxy, and each branch of Jewish faith gathered followers and strength.

Jewish centers of learning such as Yeshiva University, the Jewish Theological Seminary of America, the Hebrew Union College-Jewish Institute of Religion, and others undertook the task of preparing American young men to be rabbis in our synagogues. Under their guidance, the synagogue has become more and more a center of Jewish activities and social life. It is the modern version of the *Bet Ha-Knesset* of old, offering religious services, a Jewish library, classes, and a place for family celebrations.

Yeshiva University, a center for Orthodox Judaism, has 17 schools and divisions, including a rabbinical seminary, Yeshiva college, Stern College for Women, teachers' and cantorial institutes, and the Albert Einstein College of Medicine. Students receive a Jewish and general education at Y. U. *Below:* the main academic center of Yeshiva.

Children in a Jewish school listen open-mouthed to a story of heroes who lived long ago.

In America today, the community has become truly synagogue-centered. The community center, always open, is a busy hive of activities. Recreation facilities enrich the daily lives of the members. What are some of the highlights of an American synagogue program today?

* Education—The synagogue is of course the home of Jewish education, for one of its names is *Bet Ha-Midrash* (House of Study). Today, we find more and more children in well-lit, airy synagogue classrooms. In America today, incidentally, there are more than 2,000 Jewish schools, many of them holding sessions in synagogues. There is the *Congregational School*, sponsored by the synagogue which it serves. There are two types of congregational school: the afternoon weekday school and the Sunday religious school. Other kinds of Jewish schools in America are: the *Yeshiva* or *All-Day School*, which is the fastest-growing type of school today; the *Talmud Torah*, supported by the community as a whole; and the *Yiddish School*. Education continues at the synagogue into the evening, for it is there that parents come to participate in Adult Education classes. The grown-ups study everything from Jewish history to arts and crafts, from Jewish literature to Jewish dance.

* Library and reading room—by buying books and publications, old and new, the synagogue library helps maintain the tradition of "the People of the Book." Jewish Book Month is a highlight of every synagogue program.

* Cultural events—concerts of Jewish

128

music explore the rich treasury of song, from Temple days through Eastern Europe to our own time. Music is a bond that links us to various periods in Jewish history.

* Athletics—the synagogue today is built to provide room and equipment for basketball, handball, ping-pong, even swimming. It's all part of the synagogue-as-Jewish-center idea.

* Parties—of breakfast clubs, ladies' teas, holiday festivities (such as the Purim Carnival and Hanukkah and Simhat Torah Parties). There are also testimonial parties to honor individual members of the community for outstanding achievements.

* Meetings—of men's clubs, of sisterhoods, of young married groups, of college clubs, of teenagers. Every synagogue has a "bulletin," and every bulletin has a meeting calendar; there's always a meeting for everyone in the family.

* Hobbies—there are clubs galore in the synagogue. Hikes, week-end excursions, stamps, newspaper and other publications, dramatics—all find a place in the program of the American synagogue.

* Community service—the synagogue today is host to many groups that foster neighborliness, good will, and patriotism. Jewish War Veterans, B'nai B'rith, Boy Scouts and Girl Scouts meet within its friendly walls. Fund drives support the Community Federation, the U.J.A., Israel Bond campaigns, and our rabbinical schools.

The Bevis Marks, oldest synagogue in London (1698) has a beam in its roof from a ship given by Queen Anne.

Thus the American synagogue today fulfills its ancient threefold calling: to be a House of Worship (*Bet Ha-T'filah*), a House of Study (*Bet Ha-Midrash*), and a House of Assembly (*Bet Ha-Knesset*).

Modern Design

As American Judaism developed a character all of its own from the blend of Sefardic, German, and East European immigrations, the American synagogue began to boast an architecture of its own. Throughout the nation, new synagogues are today combining Jewish traditional art forms with modern design. Beautiful stained glass windows, striking decorations and buildings capture the warmth of Jewish spirit in modern dress.

In the 1920s there was much discussion about the shape of the hall of worship. Should it be long or square? In an oblong room the people sitting in the back rows do not hear or see so well. It might be better to have a shorter room with longer rows of seats so that more people could be close to the Ark and pulpit. Perhaps place the seats in a curve and on a sloping floor? From these discussions came the horseshoe arrangement of the seats, as we know it from concert halls. The outer walls of the synagogue hall could form a square, a circle, or a many-sided figure. A very beautiful synagogue in a six-cornered shape is Temple Isaiah in Chicago, built in 1924. This type of synagogue needs a lot of free space all around. In Manhattan, where land is very expensive, space is limited. Therefore its synagogues are of the more oblong type.

With the expanding communal activities and a growing membership, more meeting space for educational and cultural activities was needed. The problem was how best to accommodate the assembly room, the various smaller meeting rooms, the classrooms, the rabbi's study, the library, the gym, the

Temple Emanu-El, an imposing sight on New York's Fifth Avenue, is built in an early Romanesque style.

offices, the kitchen, the storerooms and other facilities. In older synagogues with their simpler requirements the answer was the basement. Later a separate Synagogue House or Temple House was built adjoining the house of worship.

Wherever land was available social centers were added to the older synagogues. In New York a community center was added to the Park Avenue Synagogue on East 87th Street in 1954, and one to Shearith Israel on 70th Street in 1955. This was not a new solution, for B'nai Jeshurun on West 88th Street in 1918 had built its Social Center in the rear facing 89th Street and many other synagogues had a separate adjoining Community House.

Growth of the Suburbs

After the Second World War, as many people moved to the suburbs, the architects began to create new synagogues to meet new needs. The synagogue was built in a flexible way so that changes and additions could be made. Thus developed the synagogue hall with adjoining foyer and social hall, all three units connected with folding doors. Every unit could be used separately and when necessary as a whole with the three halls thrown together. In this way a small synagogue could serve an overflow audience on the High Holidays. The same space could be used for important social occasions.

Prayer and Assembly

Thus new ideas have affected synagogue architecture in every way. They have helped

Sixty-year-old German synagogue on outskirts of Berlin.

the house of worship fulfill its ancient mission—that of a *Bet Ha-Knesset*—a house of assembly for the whole community.

In the American synagogue today there is great understanding and feeling for the holiness of ceremonial objects. A meaningful piece of sculpture on a simple, bare front of a building can be very impressive. Nowadays, the architect himself, or professional painters, sculptors, and craftsmen are entrusted with the designing of the Eternal Light, the Menorah, the Ark curtain, and all the many things that are needed for the creation of a dignified and inspiring religious building. The members of the congregation are partners in the modern synagogue. It is discussed in the press and books have been written about it. It is a great satisfaction to see that the synagogue has become a challenge to the creative men and women of our time and more meaningful to us all.

Talking of Numbers

As new congregations are formed, they may join one of the three synagogue bodies. The membership rolls of these groups offer a picture of the synagogues in our land. The Union of Orthodox Jewish Congregations numbers 720 congregations; the United Synagogue of America (Conservative) has a membership of 600 congregations; the Union of American Hebrew Congregations (Reform) has 550 congregations. And there are many synagogues that do not officially belong to any of these bodies. All three groups are joined in the Synagogue Council of America which was formed in 1926 in order to help strengthen the American synagogue.

From that single hard-won synagogue in early New York have grown over 2,000 congregations. Within the borders of America, our synagogue has taken root and flourished as the heart of Jewish life in the United States.

Sacred Synagogue Objects

In our synagogues, we find ceremonial objects. They are symbols of our faith, hallowed by custom and tradition. They have graced our house of worship for many centuries. To know about them is to have more

Chinese Torah Ark from the Kai-Fung-Foo synagogue. The Ark dates from the 17th century.

respect for them and at the same time to increase our self-respect as members of a people with a great and glorious heritage. For they are a bond connecting us with our faith, our history, and our people.

Torah. What is the most precious object in every synagogue? The *Torah*, of course. Just as we have kept the *Torah* sacred for thousands of years, so has it kept the Jewish people alive during all that time. The *Torah* —which means "teaching" or "law"—is a scroll made of especially prepared parchment, and is the basis of the Jewish way of life. The five Books of Moses that it contains may be written only by hand and without punctuation or vowel points. For the purpose of Sabbath reading, the *Torah* has been divided into fifty-four *sidrot*, or portions.

In preparing a Sefer Torah, the scribe (sofer) sews the beginning and end sheets of parchment to two wooden rollers, each known as an Etz Hayyim (Tree of Life).

Writing a Sefer Torah

Incidentally, it is very interesting to know how a Sefer Torah is written. Just as the Torah is holy for what it contains, so is the Sefer Torah, the Scroll bearing the Five Books of Moses, itself a holy object. In our synagogues, we read from the Holy Scroll on Sabbaths and holidays, on Mondays and Thursdays, on festivals and fast days.

The Sefer Torah must always be written by hand. Today, as for countless past generations, the Holy Scroll is prepared with painstaking care by a Sofer, or scribe, especially trained in Jewish law and traditions for his sacred task.

Here are some of the main steps followed by a Sofer in writing a Sefer Torah:

1. For parchment, the Sofer may use only the hide of a clean animal (one that, according to the Torah, is kosher to eat). With a sharp point, he draws lines on the parchment, dividing each piece into 3 to 8 sections, with 42 to 72 lines for each section.

2. A Sefer Torah must be written in special black ink only. The pen is a feather of a clean (kosher) fowl, with the tip sliced off at an angle, and the point slit. This writing tool can shape thick or thin strokes, as required.

3. The Sofer uses a special script. He may not write even one word from memory and he must pronounce each word before writing it.

4. Only seven letters of the Aleph-Bet may have decorative little crowns called *Tagin*.

5. Some sections are written in a special form. The Song of the Red Sea (*Exodus 15*) is arranged like bricks in a wall, a reminder of how God split the waters so that our ancestors might pass unharmed. The last few lines of the Sefer Torah are left unfinished. They will be filled in at a synagogue ceremony called the "Completion of the Sefer Torah," the *Siyyum Ha-Sefer*.

6. The sheets are sewn together with sinews of animals (kosher), and woven into long threads. The sewing may not be visible on the face of the Sefer Torah.

7. The Scroll is attached to two wooden rollers, each called the "Tree of Life," the *Etz Hayyim*.

These tools are used in writing a Torah Scroll. Here you see the inkwell, the reeds and their case, quills, and sinews (of kosher animals) for sewing parchment sheets together.

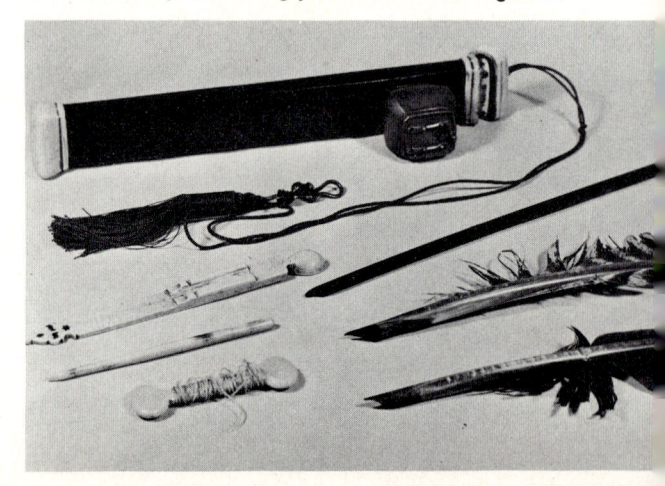

ואין מזהריך יככה יהוה מוערים ובעפלים
ובחרס ובחרש אשר לא תוכל להרפא יככה
יהוה בשגעון ובעורון ובתמהון לבב והיית
ממשש בצהרים כאשר ימשש העור באפלה
ולא תצליח את דרכיך והיית אך עשוק וגזול
כל הימים ואין מושיע אשה תארש ואיש אחר
ישגלנה בית תבנה ולא תשב בו כרם תטע ולא
תחללנו שורך טבוח לעיניך ולא תאכל ממנו
חמרך גזול מלפניך ולא ישוב לך צאנך נתנות

The *sofer* uses a special script. The decorative little crowns, called *tagin*, may be used on only seven letters of the Aleph Bet. The *sofer* may not write from memory and he must pronounce each word before writing it.

Keter Torah. Over the upper ends of the *Atzey Hayyim* we place the *Keter Torah*, the "crown of the Torah." It is usually wrought of silver and adorned with little bells, and is one of the scroll's chief ornaments.

The wooden rollers (the *Atzey Hayyim* or "trees of life") on which the scrolls of the *Torah* are wound are made of hard wood with handles of ivory and have flat round tops and bottoms to support the edges of the rolled-up scroll. The Torah, too, is called the *Etz Hayyim*, the "tree of life."

Mantle of the Law. The Mantle of the Law covers the holy scroll when it is not in use. Thus we protect the Torah from dust or injury. Shaped to slip over the Torah when it is rolled up, the mantle is open at the bottom and closed at the top, except for two round openings to allow the scroll handles to pass through. It is made of embroidered silk or satin which has never been used for any other purpose before. Old worn-out mantles, like the Scroll and all objects associated with it, are stored away, for they are too sacred to be discarded or used for anything else.

Hoshen. When the Torah is taken out of the Ark, we see its beautiful breastplate suspended by a chain from the top of the rollers. Lions, eagles, flags, and the Magen David are its chief decorations. In the center

Lavishly decorated Ark of the Torah in the Forest Hills (N. Y.) Jewish Center. Designed by Arthur Szyk.

of the breastplate there is frequently a tiny Ark whose doors are in the form of the two tablets of the Law. The lower part of the breastplate has a place where small plates may be inserted. The name of one of the Jewish festivals is engraved on each plate, to be displayed on the holiday or Sabbath on which the scroll is used.

Aron Ha-Kodesh. We keep the scrolls of the *Torah* in the *Aron Ha-Kodesh*, or "holy ark." This chest or closet is named after the *Aron Ha-Brit*, the Ark of the Covenant, which held the Tablets of the Ten Commandments when our ancestors crossed the desert. The Aron Ha-Kodesh is placed against the wall of the synagogue facing east or toward Jerusalem. It is often made of costly carved wood or marble, and it is crowned by the tablets of the Law.

Parokhet. Just as the Children of Israel while wandering in the desert hung a curtain

A silver-gilt Torah crown (keter Torah) made in Breslau, Germany, in 1750, showing biblical scenes.

before the Ark of the Covenant, so do we follow their ancient example in many of our synagogues today. The *Parokhet*, or curtain, is made of satin, velvet, or other fine material, and is richly embroidered, usually with the Ten Commandments.

Ner Tamid. Up above the Aron Ha-Kodesh hangs a light which is never permitted to go out. This is the *Ner Tamid*, the "eternal light," a symbol of the presence of God among us, of happiness, of the light that the synagogue gives. In the days of the Temple, a lamp containing pure olive oil burned continually before the Ark, thus illuminating at all times the Aron containing the Ten Commandments. When a new synagogue is dedicated, the most important ceremonies are the placing of the Torah scrolls in the Ark and the lighting of the Ner Tamid.

Siddur and Mahzor. The Siddur is the prayer book for weekdays and Sabbath; the Mahzor is used for festivals. The prayer book contains passages from the Bible and from the Talmud as well as selections written by rabbis and poets through the Middle Ages. The Siddur is mostly in Hebrew, but some of its prayers are in Aramaic, the language Jews used in everyday life in Babylonia. The Kaddish, for example, which is a hymn of praise to God and is said as a prayer for the dead, is still repeated in the ancient Aramaic. Prayers such as the *Shema* and the *Shmoneh Esrey*, and beloved hymns like *Adon Olam* and *Yigdal* are found in the pages of our prayer book.

Tallit. The Tallit is the prayer shawl worn by men and by boys in morning prayers on weekdays, Sabbaths, and festivals. It recalls the style of the upper garment worn in ancient Palestine. In those days the rabbis wore special robes as a sign of distinction. When Jews went to other lands, the Tallit came to be used for religious services. The Tallit is fringed at each of the four corners in accordance with instructions in the Bible: "make a fringe upon

A pair of Torah headpieces (rimmonim) made of silver and cast in Amsterdam, Holland, in the early 17th century. The use of bells is based on the biblical description of the garb of the High Priest: "A golden bell and a pomegranate (rimmon) upon the skirts of the robe" (Exodus 28:34).

Torah pointers (one of wood, two of silver), with motif of a dolphin head and hand, made in Eastern Europe in the early 19th century. The pointer (yad) is used because one should not touch the Scroll with the bare fingers.

the corners of your garments so that you may look upon it and remember the commandments of the Lord" (*Numbers 15:38*).

Ten Commandments. Above the Ark are the Two Tablets with Hebrew letters on them, usually abbreviations of the Ten Commandments, which are found in *Exodus 20:2-14* and *Deut. 5:6-18*. The Ten Commandments tell us how to worship God and be kind and honest to one another. They are the highest laws in Judaism and the basis of the moral law of most of mankind.

Menorah. The Menorah reminds us of the golden seven-branched candelabrum that was in the Holy Temple. The light that it sheds stands for the brightness of Torah.

Bimah. This is the raised platform on which the desk stands for the reading of the weekly portion from the Torah and from the Prophets. The Bimah is often placed in the center of the synagogue where it represents the Altar that once stood in the middle compartment of the Temple.

Yad. The pointer of silver or olive wood which is used to guide the reading of the Torah is called the *Yad,* or "hand." Shaped like a staff, its end is narrow and in the form of a closed fist with the forefinger outstretched. When the Torah is rolled, the Yad is hung by a chain over the Atzey Hay-

The Torah breastplate is related to the *hoshen,* the breastplate of the biblical High Priest, which was studded with twelve stones for the Twelve Tribes of Israel.

yim, and rests on the silver breastplate.

Tzedakah Box. The Temple in Jerusalem had a Charity Box. Contributions were used for Temple repairs and to help the poor. The custom has remained with us, for we all know giving charity is one of the finest things we can do. Often a charity box in a synagogue will bear a note stating the purpose for which the money is to be used. It may be for clothing the poor, extending loans to the needy, or for some other worthwhile cause or institution.

Synagogue Duties

Over the centuries, certain synagogue duties have been performed by persons specially trained in Jewish law, in customs and traditions. Here are a few of the offices of the synagogue and brief descriptions of their history and the role they play today.

Types of the "B'nai Israel", a native Jewish tribe in India, presumed to descend from the Lost Ten Tribes of Israel.

Rabbi. This title, which means "my teacher," is given to a religious leader and teacher. The title was first used during the time of the destruction of the Second Temple (70 C.E.). Today, a rabbi is ordained by the rabbinical seminary from which he graduates. His duties are to serve as religious leader of his congregation; make decisions on practical questions of Jewish law; conduct services and preach on Sabbaths, holy days, and festivals; teach Judaism, to children and to adult groups; officiate at important events in the life of his congregants (such as circumcision, marriage, and burial). Many rabbis have distinguished themselves as scholars. Some have been gifted orators and communal leaders.

Hazzan. In the days of the Mishnah and Talmud, the hazzan was a caretaker of the synagogue and an official at religious ceremonies. Today the term hazzan, or cantor, is used to describe one who chants the religious services in the synagogue.

Shammash. The shammash, or sexton, has had a role in synagogue life for many centuries. In early times and in the medieval period, he stood ready to carry out official synagogue decisions. He was the superintendent of the synagogue, and in East European towns, would call the congregants to services when dawn broke. Sometimes, the duties of the shammash were so numerous that he was given assistants to help in his work. In many synagogues today, the shammash is well-versed in Jewish learning and often does the reading from the Torah.

A crowd of worshippers gathers in Tel Aviv's Great Synagogue to listen to Israel's Chief Rabbi.

136

At the conclusion of the Torah reading, the Scroll is held aloft for all to see and to pronounce a blessing.

Baal Kore. The "master reader" chants the fixed portions *(sidrot)* from the Torah. Long ago, this was one of the functions of the hazzan, and later, of the shammash. When the duties of the shammash became too heavy, he had the right to hire a baal kore to help him.

Gabbai. His title comes from the Hebrew word for "to raise" or "to collect," and in medieval times he was a very important congregational offical, for he was the treasurer of the synagogue. Today, the gabbai is often a congregant who is given certain synagogue duties to perform, such as maintaining order during services, collecting dues, keeping records, and the like.

Baal Tokea (or Baal Tokiya). He is the "master blower" whose honor it is to blow the shofar when synagogue services require it.

Ba'al Tefilah. This title designates the person (other than the hazzan) who leads the congregation in prayer. When he leads in the morning service, he is the Baal Shaharit; the leader of the additional service is known as the Baal Musaf.

* * *

This is our synagogue, its background, its role, the meaning of its ceremonial objects. No one can deny that the history of the synagogue truly records the preservation of our people. Without this ancient institution, we could not have endured hardship and suffering, nor continued our devotion to Torah, to learning, and to social justice. The synagogue remains the echo of the past and the sounding board of today.

Silver yad (Torah pointer). Germany, 19th century.

בסימנא טבא
ובמזלא מעליא להתנא
ולכלתא ולכל ישראל
אמן כן יהי רצון

מצא אשה
מצא טוב ויפק
רצון מיי:

בששי בשבת ארבעה עשר יום לחדש תשרי שנת חמשת אלפים מאורית
ותש״יך ושמונה לבריאת עולם למנין שאנו מנן כאן סינגאליא מתא
דיתבא על כיף ימא ועל נהרי ניבולא פיננא וציסאנו הבחור כמר ישראל
רפאי יצ״ו בן הזקן המנוח כמר צפעה מונטיבארוציו נע אמר לה לבחירה בתולה כבודה
וצנועה מרת ויטוריא מבת בת היכר כמר חיסאלמונה יצ״ו הוי לי לאנתו כדת משה וישראל
ואנא בסייעתא דשמיא אפלח ואוקיר ואזון ואפרנס ואכסה יתיכי כהלכת גוברין
יהודאין דפלחין ומוקרין וזנין ומפרנסין לנשיהון בקושטא ויהיבנא ליכי מהר בתולייכי
כסף זוזי מאתן דחזו ליכי ומזוניכי וכסותייכי וספוקייכי מיעל לותיכי כאורח כל ארעא
וצביאת מרת ויטוריא מבת הנל כלתא בתולתא דא והוות ליה לבחר ישראל רפאל חתן
דנן יצו הנל לאנתו ודן נדוניא דהנעלת ליה מבי אבוה עשרין ליטרין של בסף
צרוף וצבי הבחר ישראל רפאל חתן דנן יצו הנל והוסיף לה מן דיליה וממונה על המהר
הנל עשרין ליטרין של כסף צרוף כנל נמצא סכום כתובתא דא בין נדוניא ותוספא
ארבעין ליטרין של כסף צרוף כנל כמבואר בשטר נצרי שעשו ביניהם לבד ממארון
זוזי דחזו לה דאינון עיקר הכתובה וכך אמר לנא כהר ישראל רפאל חתן דנן יצו הנל
אחריות כתובתא דא ותוספת דא קבילית עלי ועל ירתאי בתראי להתפרעא מן כל
שפר ארג נבסין וקנינין דאית לי תחות כל שמיא דקנאתי ודעתיד אנא למקנה נבסין
דאית להון אחריות ודלית להון אחריות כלהון יהון אחראין וערבאין עלי לפרוע
מנהון כתובתא דא ותוספת דא עד גמירא ואפילו מן גלימא דעל כתפאי בחיי ולבתר
חיי בן יומא דנן ולעלם ויקבל עליו כהר ישראל רפאל חתן דנן יצו הנל חמיר שטר
כתובתא דא כחמר כל שטרי כתובות די נהיגין בבנת ישראל הנתולות הצנועות
והכשרות העשויין כתקון חזל דלא כאסמכתא ודלא כטופסי דשטרי וקנא
אנן סהדי די חתימנן להתא מן כהר ישראל מר כהר ישראל רפאי יצו הנל בן הזקן המנוח כמר
צפעה מונטיבארוצו
דוד סאלמונה יצו הנל
במנא דכשרי לב...

זתים סביב
לשלחנך

A Ketubah (marriage contract), written in Italy, 1838. This document contains the obligations of the bridegroom toward his bride, is written in Aramaic, and must bear the signatures of two witnesses.

The Cycle of Jewish Life

From birth to death we are wrapped in Jewish custom and tradition. For, as has often been said, Judaism is more than a religion. It is a way of life. Because it is that, a wealth of observances have clustered round the great events of birth, Bar Mitzvah, education, marriage, and death of a Jew and Jewess.

A Child Is Born

In ancient days, a large family was considered a great blessing. The Bible says: "Be fruitful and multiply." When a son was born, a messenger was sent at once to bring the news to the father. "A man-child is born unto you!" he would cry, and there would be great rejoicing.

In biblical days, a child was given a name that had a definite idea behind it. Joseph was so named because his name is derived from the Hebrew word meaning "to add," and his mother said, "The Lord add to me another son." Sometimes a child was named for a living creature or a plant. "Deborah" means a bee; "Tamar" means a palm-tree.

Today, a Jewish child is usually named after a dear one who is dead, in order to keep the name alive and remembered within the family.

Circumcision

On the eighth day after his birth, a baby boy undergoes the rite of circumcision, or *Brit Milah*. A symbol of Jewish allegiance, *Brit Milah* has been practiced by our people for some four thousand years.

It began in the days of Abraham. The Book of Genesis tells us: "This is My Covenant, which you shall keep, between Me and you and thy seed after thee. Every male among you shall be circumcized... And Abraham was ninety years old and nine, when he was circumcised in the flesh of his foreskin."

The Torah tells us when a Jewish male shall be circumcized: "And in the eighth day the flesh of his foreskin shall be circumcized."

A circumcision bench, made in Italy about 1650. The embroidery at top shows the craftsman's conception of a circumcision ceremony.

Although today circumcision is recognized as healthful practice, since it lessens the possibility of infection and even of dread cancer, circumcision is kept up by our people as a sign of belonging to a great and ancient nation. When a father and mother have their new-born boy circumcized on the eighth day, it shows they are proud to be Jews.

Naturally, if it is medically necessary, circumcision is postponed until the baby is strong and healthy.

Just before the child is circumcized, he is placed upon a seat reserved for the Prophet Elijah, and called Elijah's Chair. Tradition says that this is to make the child develop into a healthy grown-up.

At the ceremony, the boy is named. A girl receives her name in the synagogue, when her father is called to the Torah on the Sabbath following birth.

Brass plate used for the Pidyon Ha-Ben ("redemption of the first-born") ceremony, Eastern Europe, 18th century.

Pidyon Ha-Ben

At the end of his first month of life, a first-born boy takes part in yet another ceremony, that of *Pidyon Ha-Ben,* or "redemption of the first-born male." The reason for this custom is that in olden days first-born males were dedicated to the service of God, to act as priests, musicians, and servants in the Temple. Later, the tribe of Levi was appointed to officiate in the Temple. The Book of Numbers tells us: "And I, behold, have taken the Levites instead of every first-born; and the Levites shall be mine." Thus every first-born male child was freed, or redeemed, from service by paying the amount of five shekalim (about $2.50) to the Kohen or Levite who served for him.

Today a Kohen, or descendant of the priestly tribe, is invited to the Pidyon Ha-Ben ceremony. After receiving the five shekalim, he usually turns the money over to a charitable Jewish cause.

Bar Mitzvah and Bat Mitzvah

The customs and traditions of Bar Mitzvah have already been fully discussed above in the chapter devoted to this great event in a Jew's life. The Bat Mitzvah ceremony was described in the chapter on Shavuot.

Marriage

The Jewish boy and girl have grown up and are now ready to take the most important step in their collective lives—marriage.

Because this is such a decisive moment in the life of any individual, many laws, customs, and traditions have been handed down to Jewish parents and to their children who are about to take the holy vow of matrimony.

Our first guide, as usual, is the Bible. There we find a description of the first known Jewish wedding, that of Isaac and Rebekah. What does that wonderful story teach us? For one thing, we learn that even in those days, so far-off that they are dimmed by the mist of history, a Jew took a wife from among his own people. For a second, we learn that a young man asked the girl of his choice for her consent before

English wedding tray, 1769. The inscription reads (in Hebrew): "Let God rejoice over you as a bridegroom rejoices over his bride."

he sought the approval of her parents. For a third, we learn that first and foremost, the young couple looked for signs of good character in their prospective mates before "taking the plunge."

In Jewish tradition, the engagement played a very serious role. There was held —as is also true today—an engagement party, at which the betrothal or engagement (*Airusin*) was declared. A document bearing the formal terms of the forthcoming wedding (*Tenaim*) was signed (and in Orthodox families still is) and the approximate date of the marriage was set. Then it was time for a toast of *L'Hayyim!* and *Mazal Tov!* to the future bride and groom, and for merrymaking by all the guests.

Today, in most cases, the formalities of the betrothal are disposed of at or immediately before the wedding ceremony itself.

June Brides

Jewish weddings may not be held between Passover and Shavuot (except on Lag Be-Omer and Rosh Hodesh Sivan) for these are days of mourning. Nor may a marriage be solemnized during the "Three Weeks" before Tishah Be-Av, nor on Sabbaths and holidays. Any other time is considered a fine time for a wedding, though the month of June is an all-time favorite with brides everywhere.

On the Sabbath before the wedding, the bridegroom or *Hatan*, is called to the Torah in the synagogue. If possible, the bride's family is present at this happy occasion. There is an interesting reason for this tradition of "calling-up" or *oifruf* as it is known in Yiddish. The Talmud tells us:

> King Solomon had a special gate for bridegrooms built in the Temple, where the inhabitants of Jerusalem would gather on the Sabbath to congratulate the fortunate young men. After the destruction of the Temple, it was ordained by the sages that the bridegrooms should go to the synagogue so that the local residents might see them and congratulate them.

Silver headdress for a bride, set with precious gems. Persia, early 18th century.

A Bokharan wedding ceremony in Israel. Under the tallit-canopy, East meets West in the dress of bride and groom.

'Harey At Mekudeshet...

The day of the wedding is here. Invitations have been sent, replies have been received, arrangements are complete. On the wedding day, until after the ceremony, the bride and groom fast, so that all their sins may be forgiven and they may enter their life of "togetherness" in the bliss of innocence.

The wedding may take place in a synagogue, in a hotel ballroom, or in the quiet of a rabbi's study. It is the solemnity and sacredness of the event that counts, not the surroundings. The bride and groom stand under the *Huppah,* or marriage canopy, which represents the litter in which the bride was transported in long-forgotten days. The bride wears white, a symbol of purity and, according to tradition, a touch of mourning (for white is the color of a burial shroud) for the destruction of the Temple. For this last reason, a groom sometimes wears a white robe (a *Kittel*) under the Huppah.

The groom is led under the Huppah by his parents, followed by the bride escorted by her father and mother. The assembled guests hear the blessing over wine and, if they are close enough, observe the groom slip the wedding ring (which must be smooth with no ornamentation, to insure a smooth and unbroken married life!) on the forefinger of the bride's right hand. As he performs this act he recites the ancient vow.

"Harey at mekudeshet li betabaat zu kedat Mosheh ve'Yisrael."

("You are hereby betrothed to me by token of this ring in accordance with the law of Moses and Israel.")

Following this, the *Ketubah*, or marriage contract is read aloud. The Ketubah, written in Aramaic, details the rights and responsibilities of husband to wife in wedded life. It is the duty of the wife to preserve this document. In the very late Middle Ages and in early modern times, many beautifully illuminated and decorated and illustrated Ketubot were prepared for wealthy families, and they still may be seen in museums and private collections.

The "seven blessings" are then recited. One of these, translated into English, follows:

Silver wedding cup made in Germany, late 19th century.

A wedding ceremony exhibit at the Jewish Museum in New York. The huppah (canopy) is supported by four poles. At right: bench for bride (made in Danzig, 1838), used during the veiling ceremony.

Blessed be thou, O Lord, our God, King of the universe, who hast created joy and gladness, bridegroom and bride, mirth and exultation, pleasure and delight, love, brotherhood, peace and fellowship. Soon may there be heard in the cities of Judah and in the streets of Jerusalem, the voice of joy and gladness, the voice of the bridegroom and the voice of the bride, the jubilant voice of bridegrooms from their canopy, and of youths from their feast of song. Blessed be thou, O Lord, who makes the bridegroom to rejoice with the bride.

The ceremony closes with the crushing of the wine-glass under the bridegroom's heel. The reason is to provide still another reminder of the destruction of the Temple in Jerusalem, thus demonstrating that even in times of greatest personal happiness, we pause for a moment to recall the sorrows of our people.

With the stamp of the shoe and the crunch of the glass, the wedding ceremony is over. The new husband-and-wife retreat from under the Huppah to cries of Mazal Tov! and the guests are welcomed to the wedding feast.

These are the essentials of a Jewish wedding. The other customs that you may see—the best man, maid of honor, ushers and bridesmaids—are all customs borrowed from our non-Jewish neighbors. While they are familiar sights to all of us, it is well to remember that they are not basic to a Jewish marriage ceremony. The age-old customs and traditions *are* basic, and they have served to maintain the solidity and unity of our people throughout the centuries.

Tzedakah

Tzedakah is not an event or occasion in the life of a Jew. Yet it is so much a part of our collective and personal existence and has permeated the consciousness of our people to such an extent, that a discussion of the cycle of Jewish living would be incomplete without it.

To be a Jew means to understand the concept or idea of Tzedakah, to support it, to pass it along to our children. It is a golden thread in the rich fabric of our heritage. It is part and parcel of Jewish life.

From earliest times, Tzedakah has meant the act of sharing what we have, being kind to the poor, and doing good deeds. The best one-word translation of Tzedakah is "righteousness," and that is what it has signified throughout the ages.

The golden thread of Tzedakah can be traced through Jewish pathways for thousands of years. It makes its first appearance in the Bible. Afterwards, the strand of Tzedakah is taken up by the Rabbis of the Talmud and those who followed. Still later, Tzedakah played a vital part in the life of the Jewish community in Europe. And now, in our own day, we find that it has grown more important and meaningful than ever before.

Tzedakah In Bible Days

The Bible gives us our first lessons in Tzedakah. Abraham was practicing righteousness when he invited the three strangers

Every Jewish community in Europe had its own *Hakhnasat Orhim*, or lodging-house for the weary wayfarer.

to come in out of the midday sun and break bread with him. He was not giving charity; he was sharing what was his with those who possessed less.

Because our ancestors were a farming nation, the Bible gave them many special regulations so that they might perform deeds of Tzedakah in the daily routine of living. When the harvest was reaped, a portion had to be left for the unfortunate. The corners of the field and the fruit and grain which the farmer forgot were to be left untouched after the harvest. "Thou shalt leave them for the poor and for the stranger," says the Bible.

Each seventh year was called *Shemitah*, and for those twelve months the land was to lie fallow, or unworked. Whatever happened to grow of itself during that year belonged to the needy—the stranger, the fatherless, the widow.

Tzedakah in the Talmudic Period

The people that had been given the Torah carried its teachings everywhere. When we had our Temple in Jerusalem, there was a room known as the *Lishkat Hashaim* (chamber of Tzedakah). It was purposely kept very dark so that well-to-do persons might leave donations unobserved and the poor might take as much as they needed without being seen. The earliest synagogues adopted the practice and had similar private rooms.

Leaders of the community were chosen to be in charge of relief work. There were *Gabbay Tzedakah* who collected and distributed funds to the poor. They followed a Tzedakah system that had been used in the days of the Second Temple. Every town had a community-chest or *Kuppah*. Each Friday, the poor would receive money for meals for the whole week for clothing. There was also a charity-bowl in which food was kept for the hungry, a clothing fund, and a burial fund. The Rabbis said that a city that had no charity-box was not worth living in.

The most important rule our ancestors followed was that *no man should be put to shame by receiving Tzedakah.* For that reason it was a custom to cast charity into the homes of the poor, and to set aside special buildings open on all four sides, where the poor might enter and eat their fill without begging.

The Community in Europe

When the Jewish people was driven into exile, there was more need than ever for deeds of kindness. Many Jews wandered from place to place, unable to establish a permanent home. Community life often had to be built in an atmosphere of persecution and intolerance. The Jewish family had to care for its own, for no one else would undertake the task.

The tradition of G'milut Hasadim (free loans) is an ancient and honorable one. G'milut Hesed means "doing kindness."

In the Middle Ages, Tzedakah societies existed all over Europe. They undertook many important assignments. They supported and clothed the poor; they educated the children of the poor and contributed to wedding funds for poor girls; they educated orphans, visited the sick, sheltered the aged, and provided burials for those who could

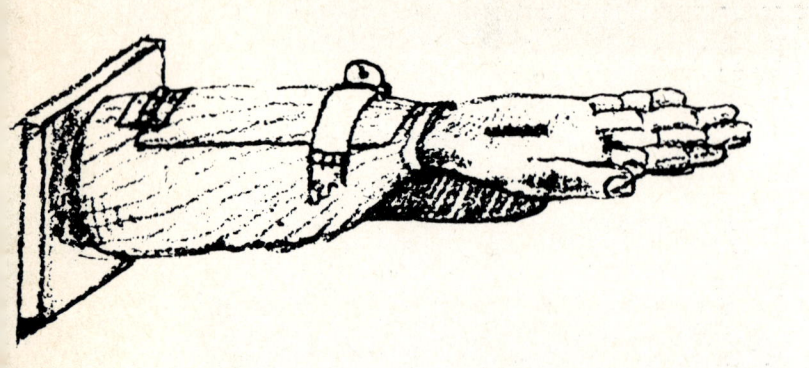

Drawing of a charity box in a German synagogue.

not afford it. They ransomed prisoners who had been kidnapped for the purpose of extorting money. This last mission, *Pidyon Shevuim*, was one of the most vital acts of Tzedakah in medieval times.

During the centuries of Jewish life in Europe, many customs arose which were designed to mask the face of charity and make it appear like anything *but* that. So that the poor would not be embarrassed, messengers were sent from house to house with a sack. Those who could, put something *into* the sack; those who needed aid helped themselves *from* the sack, and no one was the wiser.

In the days of the great Yeshivot in Europe, the practice of *essen teg* (eating days) flourished in every town that boasted an academy of learning. Students knew that on each day of the week they would be welcome at another person's home. They were expected to come; they did not need to *ask* for food.

As means of communication developed, one city was able to learn of the achievements of another, and communities taught each other new ways to practice Tzedakah. In our grandparents' times there was no Jewish settlement without a *Hakhnasat Orhim*, or lodging-house for the wayfarer. This institution exists to our very own day.

In fact, wherever there was a synagogue, no man had to go hungry. There he could obtain money for food, find a place to rest, even be put up overnight. And which well-to-do *Ba'al Ha-Bayit,* or head of a family, would not bring with him a poor stranger on Friday night when he returned home from the synagogue? When parents blessed their children, they would add: "And may you have a hospitable table, and extend a warm welcome to the needy . . ."

Tzedakah Today

Our great tradition of righteousness, of Tzedakah, stands us in good stead today. For never has Tzedakah been so important as in our own times. And never has it been needed on so large a scale.

In our own community, we are called upon to practice Tzedakah all the time. When we contribute to the Community Chest we are aiding those less fortunate than we. That is Tzedakah. When we pro-

When we support the United Jewish Appeal, we are fulfilling a mission of Tzedakah. Here you see new arrivals, young and old, being helped as they disembark at Haifa. They came from Rumania; the UJA made a new life in the land of their forefathers possible for them.

146

That is how we of the twentieth century fulfill an age-old, time-honored mission. In these ways we practice Tzedakah, a mitzvah as old as the Jewish people itself.

The Meaning of Death

All living things—human beings, beasts, insects, flowers—must one day die. To be alive means to bear within oneself the seeds of death. To avoid death means not to have lived at all.

The Jewish religion teaches us to face this final event in the cycle of life with strength and fortitude. Our sages have pondered the meaning of death and have taught us the lesson of continuing to live and to serve God and humanity despite the loss of our loved ones.

The age-old tradition of Tzedakah is practiced in many ways today. These youngsters, at Kfar Abraham, Israel, for example, are helped by us through the Joint Distribution Committee. They are among the 30,000 students in 500 ORT Schools located in 20 countries. ORT stands for "Organization for Rehabilitation Through Training." Founded in 1880, ORT has given job-training to many thousands.

By contributing to our local Federation, we nourish all the agencies on the Federation roster. Thus we aid Jewish education, hospitals, the poor and the aged, summer camps, and many other causes. This photo was taken at the 92nd Street Y in N.Y., largest and most famous community center in the world and a member agency of N.Y.'s Federation of Jewish Philanthropies.

vide the Jewish Federation in our community with the means to support Jewish education, to cure the sick, assist the aged, and protect the homeless—that is Tzedakah in its finest form.

Although our Tzedakah begins at home, it does not end there. When World War II wiped out 6,000,000 Jews, we who were more fortunate were faced with the staggering task of helping those who survived rebuild their lives. Through such agencies as the American Joint Distribution Committee, the United Jewish Appeal, and the United Palestine Appeal, we have done—and must continue to do—our utmost to help the remnant of European Jewry regain its strength and to create a strong and flourishing State of Israel.

The customs of Jewish burial vary the world over. In Cochin, India, a small community of Jews retains the customs of their forefathers. In the Cochin Jewish cemetery, the burial vaults are all above ground.

Judaism teaches us first to honor and respect our parents when they are alive—it is so written in the Ten Commandments. Only after we have attended to this mitzvah can we honestly revere the memory of dear ones when they are dead.

Reverence for the dead was displayed by our forefather Abraham when he bought a burial place for his wife Sarah. The Cave of Machpelah became the burial ground for Abraham and Sarah, Isaac and Rebekah, Jacob and Leah.

This attitude of respect and reverence has been handed down from generation to generation. Today we still observe annual memorial days (*Yahrzeit*), hold memorial services (*Yizkor*) in the synagogue on major holidays, and visit graves of loved ones at certain seasons of the year.

All the Jewish rites and traditions surrounding death, burial, and mourning are designed to honor the memory of the departed and to help those who remain behind to carry on their lives with dignity and courage.

When a person dies, the first words said by those who hear the news are *Barukh Dayan Emet*—"Blessed be the true judge." For, while death is tragic, we accept it as the decree of an all-wise and all-understanding God who rules His world in mercy and wisdom. Close relatives make a slight tear in their clothing—*Keriah*—a symbol of mourning which they will display for one month.

The funeral procession is simple and dignified. No flowers are permitted. The procession halts briefly at the synagogue which the deceased attended, where a prayer is recited. The burial takes place in a Jewish cemetery, often called the *Bet Hayyim*, the House of Eternal Life. Often a little sack of Israel soil is placed in the grave, for our forefathers considered it a great mitzvah to live and die in Eretz Yisrael, and if they could not do so, at least they might have a bit of Holy Land soil with them on the final journey.

When the coffin has been covered with earth—spaded in by family and friends—the famous prayer *Kel Male Rahamim* ("O God, full of mercy") is recited and then the *Kaddish* by the sons of the deceased. The Kaddish speaks of the greatness of God, of everlasting peace when the Messiah will come.

When the mourners return home, they are given a hard-boiled egg, symbol of life in the midst of death. The bereaved sit on low stools for seven days of mourning. During this period known as *Shivah* (or "seven") relatives and friends come to visit and to console the mourners. Services are conducted in the home during this week and Kaddish is recited by the sons of the deceased at each service, as it will be for the next eleven months. For the first year, the mourners will refrain from pleasures and amusements.

About one year after the death of the loved one, a tombstone is unveiled and relatives and friends assemble once again to pay honor to the dead.

Every year thereafter, the death anniversary is observed at home and in the synagogue. A memorial candle—usually set within a glass—is lit at sunset; it will not go out until the next sunset. Kaddish is recited in the synagogue. Many visit the grave on that day. This day is *Yahrzeit* and is one of the most widely observed Jewish customs in the world, crossing the barriers of Reform, Orthodoxy, and Conservatism.

Aside from Yahrzeit, memorial services are also held for *all* Jewish dead on certain holidays: Yom Kippur, Shemini Atzeret, the last day of Passover, and the second day of Shavuot. Each person reads silently several prayers into which he inserts the names of the deceased.

A Final Word

These customs, while they vary from land to land, from community to community, and even from family to family, all serve a three-fold purpose: to fill our lives with the dignity and self-respect of honorable human beings; to show our attachment to our faith and our people; and to express our belief in the goodness and wisdom of an Eternal, All-Knowing God.

In truth, that is the purpose underlying all our holidays, customs, and ceremonies.

And, by knowing and learning these things, are we not indeed earning our Jewish heritage?

Pewter wall lamp for yahrzeit light; Germany, 18th century.

Being called to the Torah to chant the Benediction marks the high point of the Bar Mitzvah ceremony.

Bar Mitzvah

Bar Mitzvah is a great moment in the life of every Jewish boy. It means that he has become "a son of commandments." The celebration, the excitement, the joy that surround the ceremony of Bar Mitzvah live on forever in the boy's memory. The study and preparation, reading from the Torah and the Prophets, putting on the Tallit, or prayer shawl, on Sabbath and holidays, and putting on a Tallit and Tefillin on weekdays—all of these begin when a boy reaches this shining milestone on the road of life.

What are some of the words that are closely connected with this ceremony? When we know their meaning, we will be prepared to appreciate the values symbolized by the event and the objects associated with it.

Tefillin. When a Jewish boy reaches the age of thirteen, he is expected to put on Tefillin, or phylacteries, during morning weekday prayers. The custom arises from the biblical commandment: "And thou shalt bind them for a sign upon thy arm, for frontlets (or headgarments) between thine eyes."

Each of the two Tefillin is a little square box made of parchment with a long strap, or *Retzuah*, attached. One box, called the "Shel Rosh," is worn above the forehead, and the other, the "Shel Yad," is worn on the left arm. Both contain hand-written strips of parchment on which are inscribed passages from the Bible. The head-piece has the letter *Shin* stamped on it; the knot of the arm-piece forms the letter *Yud*. The strap of the head phylactery is tied in back

Silver Tefillin cases made in Warsaw in the 19th century. *Right:* the hand phylactery case; the four sides are engraved with text and animals mentioned in *Ethics of the Fathers:* "Be strong as a leopard, light as an eagle, fleet as a hart, and strong as a lion to do the will of thy Father who is in Heaven" (5:23). *Left:* case for phylactery for the head. Inscription: "O my dove, that art in the clefts of the rock" *(Song of Songs, 2:14)*. On opposite side: three sheep under a tree, with text "Israel is a scattered sheep" *(Jeremiah 50:17)*.

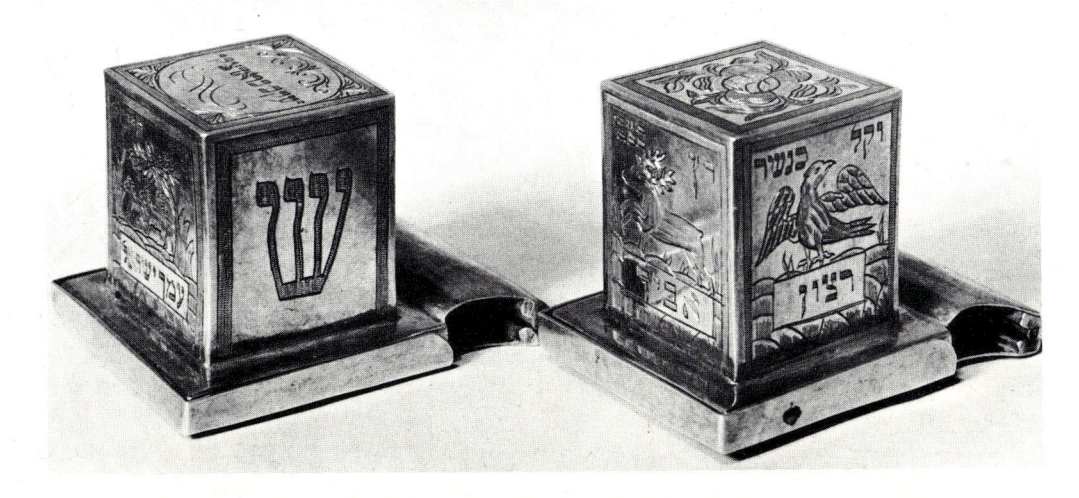

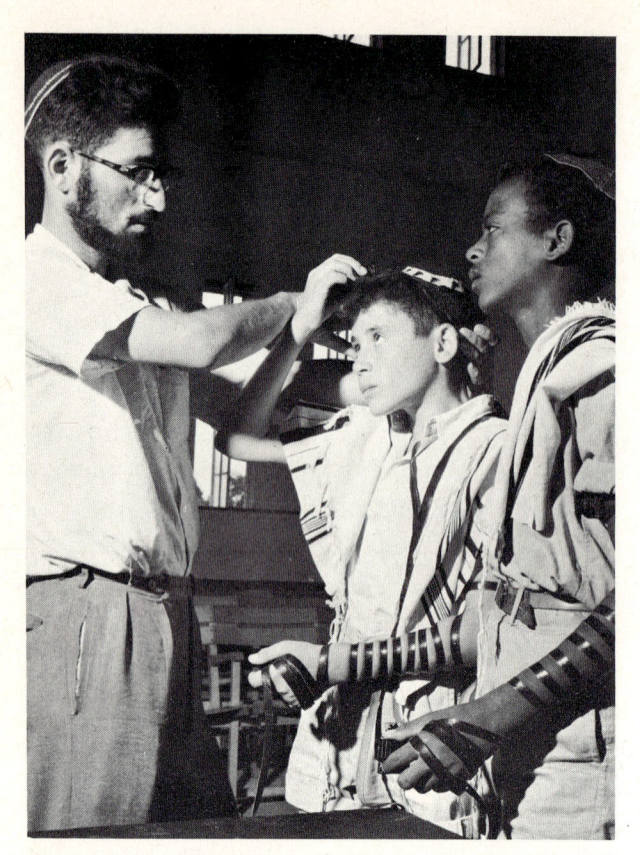

In Israel, boys who are about to become Bar Mitzvah practice putting on the Tefillin. At right is a young Ethiopian Falasha, member of a tribe of black Jews who claim descent from King Solomon and the Queen of Sheba.

into a knot shaped like a *Daled*. The three Hebrew letters spell *Shaddai*, Almighty.

Tallit. The prayer shawl (as was noted in the last chapter) recalls the style of the upper garment worn in ancient Palestine. In those days the rabbis wore special robes as a sign of distinction. When Jews spread to other lands, the Tallit came to be used for religious services.

The Bible tells us: "Make a fringe upon the corners of your garments... that ye may look upon it and remember the commandments of the Lord." In olden times, these fringes were worn on the outer garments in daily use. The Tallit is worn by men and boys in morning prayers on weekdays, Sabbaths, and festivals.

The Drashah (Discourse or Speech). The speech, or *drashah*, which some boys deliver at their Bar Mitzvah celebration, is an old Jewish custom dating back to the learned oration on some topic from the Talmud, which a yeshiva student would present at his Bar Mitzvah and at his wedding. The drashah would show that even in moments of great joy and celebration our thoughts turn to Torah and Jewish learning.

Maftir and Haftarah. Bar Mitzvah means that a child is entering the period of youth. To mark this change with an appropriate ceremony, the boy is called up to the Torah when the last section of the portion of the week, the maftir, is read from the Holy Scroll. Afterwards, he chants the Haftarah, or selection from the Prophets. From his Bar Mitzvah Sabbath on, a boy may enjoy the privilege of being called to the Torah at any time.

Cantillation. When we read the Torah we use a special chant based on musical notes. These notes are called the "Trop" or Ta'ame N'ginah. According to tradition, we follow this system in order to read the Scriptures as they were read in the days of Ezra and Nehemiah.

These are the names of the *Ta'ame N'ginah*, the special notes used in the chanting of the Torah.

שְׁמוֹת הַטְּעָמִים.
Names of the accents.
מֻנַּח זַרְקָא מֻנַּח סֶגּוֹל מֻנַּח ׀
מֻנַּח רְבִיעִי מַהְפָּךְ פַּשְׁטָא זָקֵף־
קָטֹן זָקֵף־גָּדוֹל מֵרְכָא טִפְחָא מֻנַּח
אֶתְנַחְתָּא פָּזֵר תְּלִישָׁא־קְטַנָּה
תְּלִישָׁא־גְדוֹלָה קַדְמָא וְאַזְלָא
אַזְלָא־גֵרֶשׁ גֵּרְשַׁיִם דַּרְגָּא תְּבִיר
יְתִיב פָּסֵק ׃ סוֹף־פָּסוּק ׃ שַׁלְשֶׁלֶת
קַרְנֵי־פָרָה מֵרְכָא־כְפוּלָה יֶרַח
בֶּן־יוֹמוֹ.

At the Age of Thirteen

When we think of Bar Mitzvah, we think of the age of thirteen. How this precise age was fixed is not quite certain. Probably, it goes back to a passage in that great and popular Jewish classic *Ethics of the Fathers*, in which it is written: "At five a child is brought to the Bible, at ten to the Mishnah, at thirteen to Commandments."

This was taken to mean that from the age of thirteen on, a boy was himself *responsible* for the observance of Jewish law. Until now, his father had been responsible for the boy's deeds. But now the lad was considered old enough to judge right from wrong and to act accordingly.

Two *mitzvot*, or religious practices, became especially associated with Bar Mitzvah. One was the placing on the head and binding round the arm of the Tefillin during the morning prayer, except on Sabbath and holidays. The other was the privilege of being called to the Torah in the presence of the congregation and reciting the prayer thanking God "Who has chosen us from among all nations and given us His Law."

Bar Mitzvah on Thursday

In olden days (and rarely today) the Bar Mitzvah ceremony would often occur on a Monday or Thursday morning, when the Torah was also read at services. Thus the boy could perform both mitzvot, the donning of the Tefillin and the blessing at the Torah, at one and the same time. Later, the ceremony took place most often on Saturday, when the congregation was in greater attendance.

Originally, every person who was called to the Torah was expected to be able to read his own portion. Later, this task was taken over by the Official Reader, in order not to embarrass those who were less learned. However, the older custom was preserved in the case of the Bar Mitzvah, and even today, a Bar Mitzvah boy will chant his own portion and sometimes even the entire Sidrah of the week.

Oriental type of Torah case, made of silver in 1860. The Holy Scroll was made of deerskin in the 17th century.

How Old Is Bar Mitzvah?

How old is the Bar Mitzvah ceremony? It used to be thought that it only went back to fourteenth-century Germany. Scholars have shown, however, that some form of ritual existed as early as the sixth century in Palestine. One source tells us that a great Babylonian sage rose to his feet when his son was called to the Torah for the first time and recited the benediction: "Blessed be He Who has relieved me of the responsibility for this child."

Much later, in the Middle Ages, the Bar Mitzvah ceremony became quite elaborate.

At the close of the Bar Mitzvah ceremony, the rabbi blesses the boy and reminds him of the honor and the responsibilities which are now his, for after this day, the lad will be considered a "son of the commandment."

The boy, who by now had been studying Jewish subjects intensively for several years, was expected to deliver a *drashah*, a lecture on a difficult point in the Talmud or other rabbinic learning. This would take place most often not in the synagogue but at home, during a rich and festive banquet.

Thus Bar Mitzvah grew to become one of the great occasions in Jewish life. As the observance spread, it took on different forms and features in accordance with the native culture of the lands in which it was adopted. Here are some unusual Bar Mitzvah customs practiced in faraway lands.

Unusual Bar Mitzvah Customs

Morocco. When a boy reaches twelve, his father or teacher prepares him to deliver a talmudic lecture with rabbinical commentaries. The boy reviews the lesson every night until he knows it by heart.

When the boy becomes thirteen, the *hakhamim*, or scholars, examine him at length. After the examination they all go to the family feast in honor of the Bar Mitzvah. Invited are the rabbi, the heads of the community, relatives and friends.

On Thursday morning all congregate at

A special volume called a *Tikkun* is used to practice reading the Torah correctly. In the *Tikkun* the right column includes vowel points and cantillation notes. In the left column the same section is printed just as it appears in the Torah. The word *Tikkun* means "correction."

the home of the Bar Mitzvah for morning prayer. The rabbi binds the Tefillin arm-piece on the arm of the boy and the father the head-piece. This is done to the accompaniment of song and choir. The Bar Mitzvah is called to the Torah.

Soon after the Torah is returned to the Ark, the Bar Mitzvah delivers his speech, translating it himself into Arabic so that the women too may understand. When he finishes, the hakhamin engage him in questions and discussions. Afterwards, the listeners congratulate the boy, saying: "Be strong and blessed! May you grow up to spread and strengthen Torah." On the following Sabbath the Bar Mitzvah is called on to chant the Haftarah in the synagogue.

Other North African Countries. On the Sabbath before the Bar Mitzvah, which is called Sabbath Tefillin, the relatives gather for a party which lasts until early Sunday morning. That afternoon the womenfolk, dressed in holiday clothes, visit friends, acquaintances, even the boy's playmates, and invite them to the celebration held in the evening of the same day. When they all gather together they bring along a barber who cuts the hair of the Bar Mitzvah. Those who are present contribute a coin to the barber in payment for his work.

Monday morning, the hakham and teacher proceed to the home of the parents. They wrap the Bar Mitzvah boy in a Tallit and crown him with Tefillin. Then they lead him to synagogue in a candlelight procession to the accompaniment of appropriate songs.

In the synagogue, the father, members of the family and the Bar Mitzvah are called up to the Torah. The hakham blesses the boy who then presents his address. This is followed by the distribution of charity to the poor by the members of the family.

After the service all present accompany the boy to his home where the guests are wined. In the afternoon the Bar Mitzvah,

In the Old Country, a child began his Jewish studies at a tender age. By the time a boy reached Bar Mitzvah age, he was ready to spend many hours a day poring over the problems found in the pages of the Talmud.

The Tallit, or prayer shawl, is donned by adult males during the morning (and additional) prayers (on Tishah Be-Av in the afternoon, and on Yom Kippur at all services). It is a four-cornered garment, usually made of wool, upon the corners of which *Tzitzit* have been knotted in accordance with the biblical rules *(Numbers 15:37-41).*

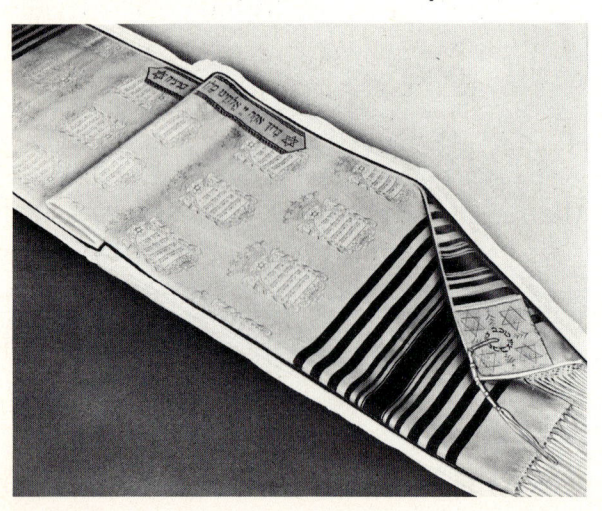

wearing Tallit and Tefillin, and accompanied by his friends, calls on the womenfolk of the family. Every relative unwinds once the Tefillin straps from around his arm and presents him with a coin.

In Some Sephardic Communities. Among Sephardic Jews, boys begin to put on Tefillin a year (in the case of an orphan, two years) before the age of thirteen and the parents hold a big family feast.

On his thirteenth birthday, the Bar Mitzvah boy carries his Tallit and Tefillin all through the day. At the family festivities the boy is permitted to invite his friends and playmates to a feast. On the following Sabbath, the Bar Mitzvah is privileged to go around the synagogue carrying the

Torah. He is followed by boys of his age who snap their fingers in rhythm.

Yemen. Since in Yemen even children who are not of Bar Mitzvah age are called up to the Torah, the calling up to the Torah is not as special a ceremony as elsewhere.

On the morning of his Bar Mitzvah day the son accompanies his father to the synagogue where he puts on the Tefillin under the supervision of his teacher. The Bar Mitzvah chants the Torah portion of the week before the congregation. After the service the boy is led home like a bridegroom, with song and dance. At home a big feast awaits the company.

* * *

Although Bar Mitzvah has gone through many changes in its development through the centuries, and has often indeed been vulgarized, those who stop to think will bear in mind its original meaning. That meaning is simple and beautiful. On this day, the boy who has come into possession of this religious heritage of his people has for the first time the right to lead a congregation at services, the duty to recite a passage when called to the Torah, the privilege of being counted as a member of a *minyan*, and the opportunity to thank God for being a member of the Jewish people.

Bar Mitzvah boy reading the Torah.

A 17th-century Mizrah made in Italy. Once this Mizrah (meaning "east"), decorated with the Ten Commandments and biblical scenes, hung in a synagogue to indicate, for purposes of prayer, the direction of Jerusalem.

The Jewish Home

The Jewish home has kept our people alive through the ages. In most cases, you can look at a Jewish home and tell what kind of Jewish adults will emerge from it.

It is at home that we practice the customs and ceremonies we learn in school. In the home we drink in ideas which will mold our thinking, our attitudes, and actions.

When ours is a warm Jewish home, our feelings toward Judaism and all it stands for will be positive and strong. The happy Jewish home means a happy family; it means a center of love and cooperation; it means a place where the Fifth Commandment "Honor thy father and thy mother" is always obeyed.

What makes a Jewish home? That cannot be answered in a simple way, for it depends on many elements, and when one deals with human beings, mathematical accuracy is well-nigh impossible.

But it can be said with certainty that one of the basic ingredients is a collection of Jewish objects and the observance of certain customs. For all Jews celebrate the same holidays and cherish the same Torah. Despite differences in personality, in cultural climate, in temperament, these things provide a common bond. When they are ours, they give us a sense of unity not only with fellow Jews in other lands, but with the generations of Jews who have preceded us on this earth.

What are some of the objects and observances which we may expect to find in the Jewish home? Here are a few of the outstanding ones. They make our home a richer, brighter place to live in. When we have them and honor them through proper use, we add a link to the golden chain of tradition forged by our ancestors.

Mezuzah

When we move into a new home, the first thing we do is fasten a *mezuzah* to the upper part of the right doorpost of each room. By doing this we announce that we are proud members of the Jewish people and aware of our long and honorable heritage. Mezuzah is Hebrew for "doorpost," and it

The *Shema Yisrael* ("Hear O Israel") is Judaism's confession of faith, proclaiming the absolute unity of God. Recited twice in daily worship, it consists of three quotations from the Bible: *Deut.* 6:4-9; 11:13-21; *Num.* 15:37-41.

שמע ישראל יהוה אלהינו יהוה אחד ואהבת את
יהוה אלהיך בכל לבבך ובכל נפשך ובכל מאדך והיו
הדברים האלה אשר אנכי מצוך היום על לבבך ושננתם
לבניך ודברת בם בשבתך בביתך ובלכתך בדרך
ובשכבך ובקומך וקשרתם לאות על ידך והיו לטטפת
בין עיניך וכתבתם על מזזות ביתך ובשעריך
והיה אם שמע תשמעו אל מצותי אשר אנכי
מצוה אתכם היום לאהבה את יהוה אלהיכם ולעבדו
בכל לבבכם ובכל נפשכם ונתתי מטר ארצכם בעתו
יורה ומלקוש ואספת דגנך ותירשך ויצהרך ונתתי
עשב בשדך לבהמתך ואכלת ושבעת השמרו לכם
פן יפתה לבבכם וסרתם ועבדתם אלהים אחרים
והשתחויתם להם וחרה אף יהוה בכם ועצר את
השמים ולא יהיה מטר והאדמה לא תתן את יבולה
ואבדתם מהרה מעל הארץ הטבה אשר יהוה נתן לכם
ושמתם את דברי אלה על לבבכם ועל נפשכם וקשרתם
אתם לאות על ידכם והיו לטוטפת בין עיניכם ולמדתם
אתם את בניכם לדבר בם בשבתך בביתך ובלכתך
בדרך ובשכבך ובקומך וכתבתם על מזוזות ביתך
ובשעריך כמען ירבו ימיכם וימי בניכם על האדמה
אשר נשבע יהוה לאבתיכם לתת להם כימי השמים
על הארץ

159

The *Mezuzah* ("doorpost") is a parchment scroll placed in a container and nailed to the doorpost. On the scroll is written *Deut.* 6:4-9 and 11:13-21. The silver *Mezuzah* shown here was made in Germany, about 1805.

consists of a small case of metal or wood containing a roll of parchment. Upon the tiny scroll we find two passages from Deuteronomy: 6:4-9 and 11:13-21. They are in Hebrew, written in the manner of Torah script. The first is the famous passage which begins: HEAR, O ISRAEL, THE LORD OUR GOD, THE LORD IS ONE.

Through a small opening in the upper part of the mezuzah case is seen the Hebrew word, *Shaddai*, Almighty.

Mizrah

As you know, we face east when we pray in order to remind ourselves of the importance of Palestine in our spiritual history. And that is why our Jewish home has a plaque with the word *mizrah* on it on a wall facing east. It is decorated with beautiful flowers and designs. The members of our household turn toward it when they pray, so that they may face the Land of Israel, the ancient home of the Jewish people, and its capital, Jerusalem, where the Temple stood.

Siddur

Our Siddur or prayer book means *order* of the service in Hebrew. It was written by many authors over many ages. Most of its prayers are from the Bible, particularly from Psalms; some are taken from the Talmud; some were written by rabbis of a later period.

Although the Siddur is mostly in Hebrew, some of its prayers are in Aramaic, the language Jews used in everyday life in Baby-

Jewish books, religious objects grace a Jewish home.

lonia. The *Kaddish*, for example, which praises God and is said as a prayer for the dead, is still repeated in the ancient Aramaic.

Prayers such as the *Shema* and the *Shmoney Esrey,* and beloved hymns, like *Adon Olams* and *Yigdal,* are found in the pages of our Jewish Prayer Book.

The Siddur is the prayer book for weekday and Sabbath; the prayer book we use on festivals is called a *Mahzor.*

Tallit

The prayer shawl, as we have seen in the chapter on Bar Mitzvah, recalls the style of the upper garment worn in ancient Palestine. In those days the rabbis wore special robes as a sign of distinction. When Jews spread to other lands, the Tallit came to be used for religious services.

The Bible tells us: "make a fringe upon the corners of your garments...that ye may look upon it and remember the commandments of the Lord." In olden times, these fringes were worn on the outer garments in daily use.

Tefillin are two black leather boxes, fastened to leather straps, containing four portions of the Bible written on parchment (Ex. 13:1-10; 11-16; Deut. 6:4-9; 11:13-21).

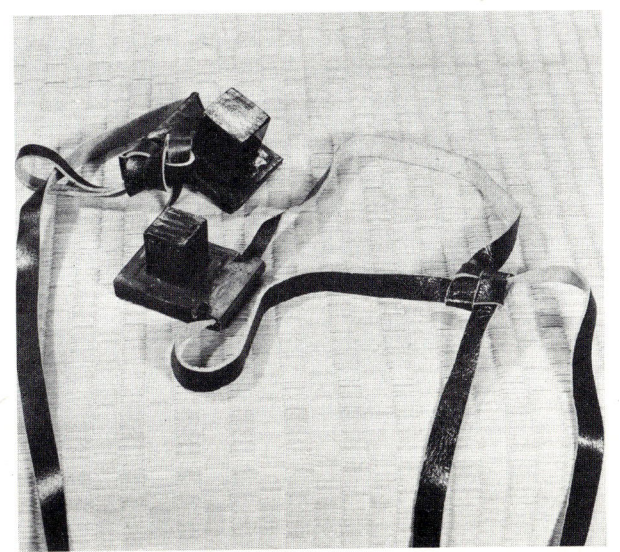

Tefillin

When a Jewish boy reaches the age of thirteen, he is expected to put on Tefillin, or phylacteries, during morning weekday prayers. The custom arises from the biblical commandment: "And thou shalt bind them for a sign upon thy arm, for frontlets (or head-garments) between thine eyes."

Each of the two *tefillin* is a little square box made of parchment with a long strap, or Retzuah, attached. One box, called the "Shel Rosh," is worn above the forehead, and the other, the "Shel Yad," is worn on the left arm. Both contain strips of parchment on which are inscribed passages from the Bible. The headpiece has the letter *Shin* stamped on it; the knot of the armpiece forms the letter *Yud*. The strap of the head phylactery is tied in the back into a knot shaped like a *Daled*. The three Hebrew letters spell *Shaddai*, Almighty.

Sabbath Candles

Of all the many lovely Jewish customs, one of the most beautiful is the lighting of the Sabbath candles. When Mother says the blessing over the glowing candles, she covers her eyes, so that she may concentrate on the prayer and also that she may not see the candles' light until she has finished the prayer. Before the ceremony, the children drop coins in the *Tzedakah*, or charity, box. Afterwards, Father blesses the children and prays to God that they may grow strong and healthy and wise.

Wine Cup

Our beautiful silver wine cup is used on the eve of Sabbath and other holidays, except fast days, to usher in the festival. The *Kiddush* began to be said at the synagogue because wayfarers were lodged in the house of prayer. Thus they were given the opportunity to hear the blessing over wine. The wine cup is also used at the *Havdalah* service.

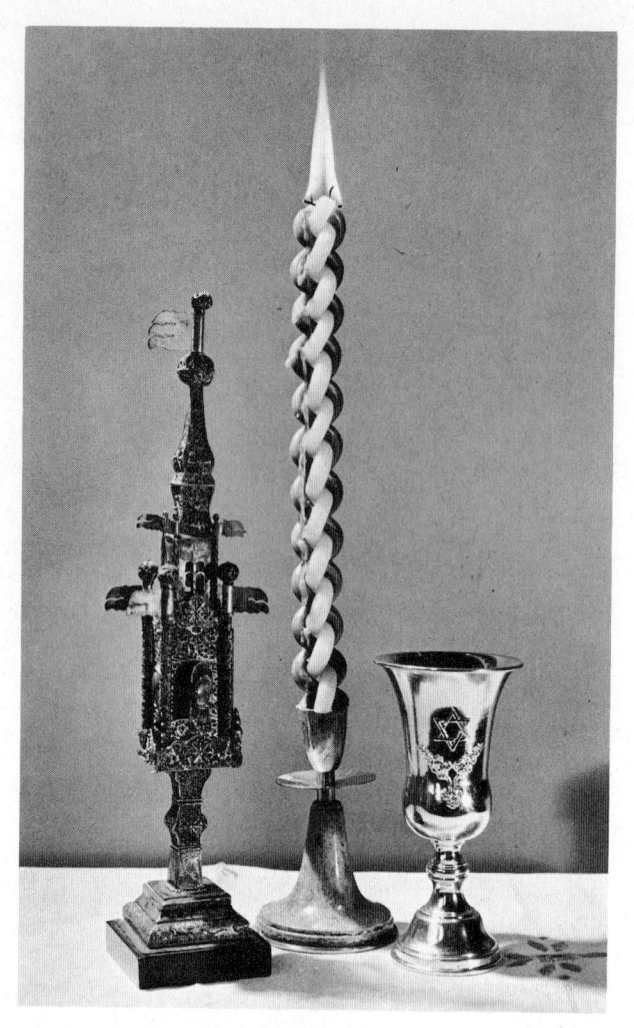

The Havdalah ("distinction") ceremony consists of blessings over wine, spices, and flame. The main blessing refers to the separation between the holy and profane, between light and darkness, and between the day of rest and the six working days of the week.

Havdalah Candle

When three stars appear in the sky it is time for the *Havdalah* service marking the close of a Sabbath or festival. *Havdalah* means separation, and the ceremony emphasizes the difference between the holy day and the week-day. Father says a blessing over wine, spices, and light. He pronounces the blessing over the light to remind us that light was the first thing God created.

Spicebox

The box containing *besamim*, or sweet-smelling spices, is used during the *Havdalah* service. The spices have replaced the burning of incense which was customary on festive occasions. Spice boxes are made of gold, silver, or fine wood, in many shapes. Often they are made to resemble towers. These are called by the Hebrew word for tower—*migdal*.

Menorah

The Hanukkah menorah waits from Kislev to Kislev to be put into use. It is the "star" of the Hanukkah celebration, but it adorns our home with equal grace the rest of the year. Today, many Hanukkah menorahs come from Israel. The menorah may be modern or traditional in style, of brass, silver, or of modest chromium plate. It is not the material of which it is made that is important, but what it stands for. When we see it, we know that here is a home in which

Cast brass Hanukkah menorah made in Galicia, Poland, in the 18th century.

This silver Passover plate (Austria, 1807), has three compartments for the three matzot. Decorations: Figures of Moses, Aaron, and Miriam, and three groups of men, carrying small dishes for symbolic Seder foods.

the brave spirit of the Maccabees is proudly remembered; here is a home proud of the traditions of our people.

Seder Plate

The Seder plate is used but twice a year, on the first and second nights of Passover. On these occasions it adorns the rich Seder table. Sometimes, the Seder plate itself, through inscriptions and decorations, tells the story of Passover. It is the duty of the Seder plate to bear the foods that symbolize the sorrow and joys of Passover. Usually it is divided into sections, and each section is marked in accordance with the food that is to be placed into it: Matzot, Shankbone, Roasted Egg, Bitter Herbs, Haroset, Karpas.

Jewish Books

Every Jewish home has a Jewish library, for your bookshelf shows that you accept our people's age-old ideal of learning. Your library should contain the Bible, the prayer book, books on Jewish history, and story and poetry books by famous Jewish authors. The works of Peretz, of Sholom Aleichem, of Mendele Mokher Seforim, of Bialik, of Ahad Ha-Am are among the books we treasure in our home. There are also many books of Jewish paintings, and volumes especially written for boys and girls which deserve a place on your Jewish bookshelf.

The Dietary Laws

Judaism is a religion which has often been described as "a way of life." This means that it embraces all aspects of Jewish life.

One important area of our religion is that of the dietary laws. The Bible contains the basis of our regulations about food. The

On the Seder table stands the wine cup of the Prophet Elijah, symbolically awaiting the forerunner of the Messianic age. On this 18th-century Russian cup, the Messiah is seen, riding on a donkey, preceded by Elijah blowing a shofar. Inscribed on the base: the blessing over wine.

Shehitah ("slaughtering") of animals is carried out in accordance with humane Jewish laws. Only a properly qualified person called a *shohet* may perform *shehitah*. The meat is then inspected and certified as "kosher." The "kosher" stamps shown here were used in a European Jewish community in the 19th century.

laws in the Bible were discussed, explained, and expanded by the Talmud, the writings of Maimonides, the Shulhan Arukh, and other books.

Why Are These Laws Important?

According to the Bible, we were given dietary laws to make us pure and holy. The Bible lists those animals, fowl, and fish which we may eat, and those which are forbidden. Maimonides said that *Kashrut* (observing dietary laws) teaches us that eating and drinking are not the goals of man's existence.

Adherence to dietary laws has been a mark of Jewish loyalty over the centuries. Many Jews gave up their lives rather than allow themselves to be forced to eat forbidden food. It is interesting to note that many people who do not claim to be Orthodox nonetheless observe dietary laws, for they feel that they are continuing and strengthening Jewish preservation in doing so.

What Is Permitted and What Is Forbidden

All fruits and vegetables may be eaten and all dairy food, as long as the milk is from a kosher animal.

Winged insects and creeping things are forbidden to be eaten.

Kosher fish must have fins and scales. All shellfish are forbidden.

Mammals which have cloven hoofs and chew the cud are permitted. The hoof must be completely cloven; this excludes the camel, which has a pad or cushion at the base of its hoof.

The Bible enumerates all the fowl which may not be eaten. Most forbidden animals and birds are creatures that prey on other creatures.

Dairy and Meat

Mixing meat and dairy foods is strictly forbidden by Jewish religious law. The Bible says: "Thou shalt not seethe the kid in its mother's milk." This regulation was applied to all manner of meat and dairy products. It was extended to utensils, and every kosher home has two sets of dishes, pots, and other food utensils. In order to make the distinction between meat and dairy clear, observant Jews wait six hours after eating meat before eating dairy food.

Kashrut and Shehitah

Kosher meat must be carefully supervised from the moment the animal is slaughtered to the time it reaches the table. Only a *Shohet,* a man learned and pious, and trained in the laws of his calling, may slaughter the kosher animal.

The act of slaughter is a religious rite; the rules must be observed strictly. To do so means that the animal will be caused no needless suffering. Maimonides said: "Since the need of obtaining food makes it necessary to slay animals, the law tells us to make death of the animal the easiest possible." When an animal is slaughtered by means of *Shehitah*, the Jewish ritual method, unconsciousness is immediate. The knife (*Haleff*) must be razor-sharp, so that there will be no unnecessary suffering whatsoever.

After Shehitah, the Shohet examines the animal carefully, to see that it has no disease or other flaw which would render it unfit. The carcass is inspected by a *mashgiah*, who stamps it with an official seal. The kosher retail meat markets are supervised by a mashgiah, too, to insure proper handling and care all the way.

Before the meat is sold to the housewife, certain ligaments must be removed. Since the ligaments in the hind-quarters are very difficult to remove, kosher butcher stores in America sell only the fore-quarters.

There is one final step: the total draining of blood. The Bible forbids the eating of blood, and even though Shehitah removes most of the blood, the meat we eat must be soaked in water for half an hour, kept in salt for a full hour, and then thoroughly rinsed. Some meat may be broiled without this special treatment.

These, then, are the principal laws of Kashrut. They have been considered a foundation-stone of Jewish religion for centuries upon centuries. They are still observed with scrupulous attention by a large portion of our people. Those who maintain Kashrut feel that they are living by a regimen which is divinely inspired, and which has served as a binding and preserving element for Judaism and the Jewish people.

Hanukat Ha-Bayit

Because the home is such a vital center of Jewish life, we cannot leave it without mention of another charming custom, that of the Hanukat Ha-Bayit ("dedication of the home" or "house-warming"). When we move into a new dwelling, we invite relatives and friends to celebrate the occasion. The ceremony begins with the fastening of the Mezuzah on the door-post. At the same time the benediction is said: "Blessed art Thou, our God, King of the universe, Who hast made us holy with His Mitzvot and commanded us to fasten the Mezuzah."

This is often followed with the recitation of psalms and prayers. One of these prayers says in part:

"Master of the universe, look down from Thy holy habitation and accept in mercy and favor the prayer of Thy children who are gathered here to dedicate this dwelling and to offer their thanksgiving... Grant them that they may live in their homes in brotherhood and friendship."

Bread and salt, ancient symbols of life and happiness, are brought into the house. Refreshments and good cheer are, of course, the order of the day. The *Hanukat Ha-Bayit* is actually a prayer dressed as a pleasant ceremony, a prayer to God for good health and good life under a new roof.

At the *Hanukat Ha-Bayit* ("dedication of a new home") the Mezuzah is affixed to the right doorpost. A benediction is said, asking the Almighty to bless the house and all those who dwell in it.

Studying the Book of Books. For the Jew, the Bible has been the source of life, of growth, and of survival.

Jewish Books

For centuries we have been known as "The People of the Book."

True, this phrase refers to the Bible, our Book of Books, but we can take the expression to indicate our love for books in general.

From the days when books were "published" in manuscript form and were considered rare treasures, until our own time, the Jewish book has been one of our dearest possessions.

An old legend tells us: "When Adam was driven from Eden, he was sorrowful. God pitied him and said: 'The Tree of Knowledge did not make Man wise, nor did he eat his fill of the Tree of Life. What shall be his fate?' And God created the book and said to it: 'Go forth and accompany Man. Be a friend and companion to him, comfort him, teach him, and gladden his heart.'"

Importance of Books

Can you imagine life without books? Would there be schools, or libraries, or teachers, or physicians? Would there be any learning without books?

When you think about it even for a moment, you will agree that books have always played such an important part that, without them, man would still be a savage rubbing sticks together to light a fire in some dim and misty cave.

For *our* people, as for every other, books have been a vital force for growth.

In the very beginning, the Jewish people came into existence because of a book. The Bible tells us that before Moses died, he "wrote the words of this Torah in a book."

The Origin of 'Book'

When we use the word "book," we mean a printed volume, made up of a number of sheets printed on both sides and bound together and provided with a cover.

In ancient times, however, "book" meant any single work. It was only after the introduction of printing, in the fifteenth century, that the word "book" came to mean a printed volume. In the middle of the fif-

In the spring of 1947, ancient biblical manuscripts were found in a cave on the shore of the Dead Sea. The Dead Sea Scrolls, one of the greatest archaeological discoveries of all time, cast new light on Bible days.

Torah Scroll, Germany, 1700. The Scroll is opened to the Song of the Red Sea, traditionally written in the form of interlocking bricks, symbolic of the walls of water into which the Lord divided the sea.

much like the Torah Scrolls in our synagogues.

Since each scroll had to be written by hand, books were extremely scarce, and most of the early books were either read aloud or recited from memory to whole groups of people by wandering story-tellers. A book in ancient times was to be "heard" rather than to be read silently to oneself.

Thus the Bible tells us that King Josiah of Judah called "all the men of Judah and all the inhabitants of Jerusalem with him, and the priests, and the prophets, and all the people, both small and great: and he read in their ears all the words of the book of the covenant which was found in the house of the Lord."

Rare edition of the Five Books of Moses, Paris 1543.

teenth century, movable type was invented. This is the dividing line in the history of books. Before this time all books were in manuscript (which means hand-written); after this time all books were printed.

Two Manuscript Periods

The manuscript period is also divided into two: 1) the period when such forms as clay tablets and papyrus rolls were used, and 2) the period when manuscripts began to look like modern books.

Earliest Jewish records do not tell of clay tablet "books" or of papyrus rolls, such as other nations used. Instead, they speak of scrolls written on the skins of animals. These hides were not bound together like books of today but were laid end-to-end and rolled up into a scroll—looking very

When a scribe (sofer), writes a Torah Scroll, he rules guide lines with the blunt edge of a knife, and divides each parchment sheet into sections. Every Torah Scroll must be entirely hand-written.

Later, when the Jews returned to Israel from their exile in Babylon, their leader, Ezra, read them the book of the law, or Torah.

As time went on, however, more and more books were written and circulated among the common people. We know, for example, that messages from the Prophets and government proclamations were recopied by hand and distributed among the people.

And of course the Torah, which became more and more important in the synagogue service, was constantly copied and recopied. To this day, the Torah Scrolls found in our synagogues must be written by hand on animal skins according to a rule made by the Rabbis in still another Jewish book—the Talmud.

The famous Dead Sea Scrolls, discovered in Palestine in 1947, consist in part of biblical books copied down by an unknown Jewish scribe for use in study.

Changes Are Made

In time, wooden rollers were placed on the ends of some of the larger scrolls to make them easier to handle. The Torah, usually a large and bulky scroll, has wooden rollers (each is called an *Etz Hayyim,* or "tree of life") even today, while the Megillah of Esther, which is read on Purim and is much smaller, does not have these rollers.

Soon, other changes came into use. Paper replaced parchment as writing material and then someone came up with a brand new idea—putting the pages of a manuscript one on top of the other and binding them together in modern book form instead of rolling them up into a scroll.

By the Middle Ages most Jewish books were in modern form, and only those used in the synagogue service were still in scrolls.

The early manuscripts in modern book form were extremely large as compared with our present-day books. Some of them were so big, in fact, that it took two people to handle them. The reason for this was that books were still scarce, and, by making

The first page of *Genesis*, with Rashi's commentary, in a very rare edition published by the Hebrew printer, Gershom Kohen, in Prague, 1518. Only two copies of this volume exist. One is in the library of the Jewish Theological Seminary of America, the other at Oxford University.

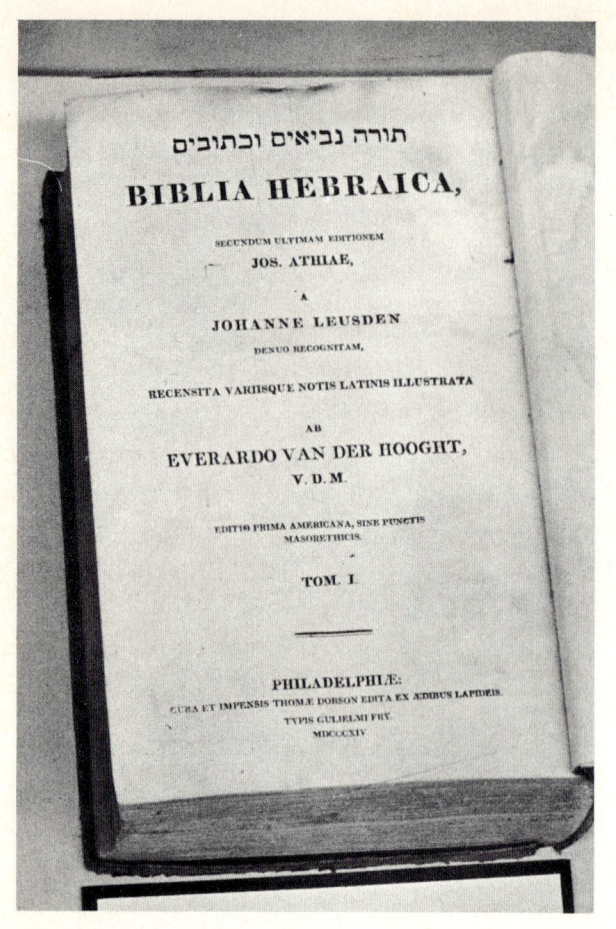

The first Hebrew Bible printed in America. Philadelphia, 1814. It contains the twenty-four books.

them large, a whole group of people could read them at the same time.

Illustrations In Books

Since they were written by hand, many of the early books were works of art as well as literature. The scribes who copied the books would often illustrate them richly and in many colors. Since the rabbis forbade any illustration of the Torah, scribes would save some of their richest illustrations for the Passover Haggadah. This practice has lived on to this day, and the Haggadah you used for Passover is probably full of such rich illustrations.

The Invention of Printing

Late in the fifteenth century the invention of printing changed the form of the Jewish book for all time.

The first Jewish book to come off a printing press was an edition of Rashi's commentary on the Bible, printed in Italy in 1475. From Italy, the art of Hebrew printing spread to Spain and Portugal. After the Spanish Inquisition in 1492, the art moved, along with the Spanish Jews, to all the countries of the world in which Jews lived.

The introduction of printing had a powerful effect on Jewish life. Although books were still scarce, there were more of them than before. They came down in price, and very soon, many persons could have a book. After a while, everyone could have a prayerbook of his own. Now a copy of the Bible could be found not only among the rich but in practically every Jewish home.

The books most frequently printed by Jews at first were, of course, religious books. As time went on, however, storybooks, books of legend, schoolbooks, and books only meant for entertainment, were widely circulated among Jews. Everywhere, Jews were hungry for the printed word and for the learning, enjoyment and comfort that can be found only in books.

More and more Jewish books were printed every year, and the quality of the printing, which had been poor at first, became better as the years went by. By the nineteenth century, Jewish books written in Hebrew, Yiddish, or other languages, were published and distributed on a worldwide scale.

The Greatest Jewish Books

Of the many volumes on the Jewish bookshelf the greatest of all are three: the *Bible*, the *Talmud*, and the *Siddur*. Without the first, there would be no Jewish people; without the second, there would be a vast gap in Jewish scholarship and learning; without the third, there would be no bridge of prayer uniting many centuries of Jewish happiness and despair, fears and hopes.

The Bible

Our most cherished possession, the Bible, has been translated from Hebrew into over a thousand tongues; it continues today, as in ages past, to help people lead a good and righteous life. The Bible tells us that there is One God; it teaches us to honor our parents; it urges us to tell only the truth. The Bible contains the world's most wonderful stories—of heroes like Moses, Joshua, and Samson; of thrilling events like the Flood and the Exodus; of stirring prophecies like those of Isaiah and Jeremiah.

For us, the Bible—our Torah—has been the very center of Jewish spiritual life. Study it over and over again, said the Rabbis, for all knowledge and wisdom may be found in it.

The Bible consists of twenty-four books divided into three sections: The *Torah*, the *Prophets*, and the *Writings*.

The Five Books of Moses

1) The *Torah* consists of the Five Books of Moses (although the word *Torah* also means the *whole* Bible). The Five Books

Some say that the Mosque of Omar was built at the summit of Mt. Moriah, where the Temple once stood.

begin with Genesis and the creation of the world, and end with Deuteronomy and the death of Moses.

The Five Books are Genesis, Exodus, Leviticus, Numbers, and Deuteronomy.

Genesis discusses many subjects. How did the world begin? Why do men have to work so hard to earn a living? How did murder enter the world to mar God's beautiful plan? When did the idea of wearing clothes begin? Where did man get the idea of fashioning tools and instruments with his hands? The Book of Genesis answers these questions in the language and thought of long ago. It is not a "Book of Knowledge," however; its chief purpose is to tell us *how* God wants us to live in His world. It makes clear that the Jewish way of life leads to happiness. The Hebrew name for Genesis is *B'rayshis* and comes from the first word of the book which means "in the beginning."

Exodus tells us about the hardship of the Israelites in Egypt and their escape from slavery under the guidance of Moses. The Book of Exodus tells us how the Israelites became slaves, how they won their freedom,

Today, a Moslem mosque covers the Cave of Machpelah, which Abraham bought for a burial place (Genesis 23).

A solitary camel and his master cross the Sinai Desert, unchanged by the passage of centuries. Here the Israelites encamped as they marched to the promised land.

what kind of man Moses was, how the disunited Israelites became One People. The Book of Exodus describes how the Jewish people received the Ten Commandments on Mount Sinai. It pictures the very first Passover celebration. Step by step, it details the building of the Sanctuary. Most of all, the Book of Exodus sings the praises of freedom and reminds us that God wants all men to have and enjoy freedom. Exodus, the second Book of Moses, receives its name from the departure, or exodus, of the Israelites from Egypt. Its Hebrew name is *Shemot* (Names), because it begins with a list of the names of Israel's sons in Egypt.

Leviticus takes up many important matters dealing with Jewish nationhood. What kind of judges and courts were to be established? What provisions were to be made against the possibility of war? Also discussed in Leviticus are: the proper attitude of a Jew toward his parents, his duties toward charity, the poor, the widow, and the orphan; festivals and fasts; dietary laws. Leviticus, the third Book of Moses, is called in Hebrew *Va-Yikra*, the word with which it begins, meaning "And He called (to Moses)."

Numbers tells what happened to the Israelites from the time they left Mount Sinai until they reached the borders of Canaan. The trials of the pioneers is described and problems of their new freedom are analyzed. After forty years of wandering, the Jewish people were now prepared to enter the Promised Land. Numbers is the fourth Book of Moses. It is named in Hebrew *Be-Midbar,* from its first important word meaning "In the Wilderness." In English we call it "Numbers," because it begins with the numbering, or census, of the Israelites as they began their journey toward Palestine.

Deuteronomy reviews the history and the laws contained in the Books of Exodus, Leviticus, and Numbers. It closes with the great song and blessing of Moses just before that teacher and leader died. The Hebrew name of Deuteronomy is *Debarim*, or

On the heights of craggy Mt. Sinai, Moses received the Law.

172

The remains of a Canaanite tower provide proof of the historical truth of battles described in the Bible.

"Words," and comes from its first verse which reads, "And these are the *words* which Moses spoke."

2) The *Prophets* include nineteen books, four of which continue the history of the Jewish people after the death of Moses. The remaining fifteen are named for the Prophets, from Isaiah to Malachi.

The earlier *Prophets* are Joshua, Judges, First Samuel, Second Samuel, First Kings, and Second Kings. The later *Prophets* include Isaiah, Jeremiah, and Ezekiel, and a book called "The Twelve," which contains the prophecies of Hosea, Nahum, Joel, Habakkuk, Amos, Zephaniah, Obadiah, Haggai, Jonah, Zachariah, Micah, and Malachi.

Joshua tells of the wars and conquests of Joshua, son of Nun, the lieutenant of Moses, after he came to the Promised Land. Many small, warlike peoples lived in Palestine, in cities surrounded by high walls. To gain the land that was "flowing with milk and honey," the Israelites had to conquer the nations opposing them. This they did under the leadership of Joshua, who had been one of the "twelve spies" who scouted the country and who now bore the mantle of leadership inherited from Moses.

Judges reports the event that occurred after Joshua's death. Stalwart warriors of Israel, the Judges were leaders who subdued individual enemy tribes. During this period Israel was not yet a united nation.

First Samuel and *Second Samuel* tell how the first Jewish kingdom was established. One chief enemy remained: the Philistines. A great Jewish leader emerged who was both judge and prophet. His name was Samuel and his goal was to unite the tribes of Israel. He called upon the Jewish people to worship God, and under his direction Saul and David became the first two kings of Israel.

First Kings and *Second Kings*. Through the reigns of David and his son Solomon, the kingdom remained united. But when

Gideon's Fountain is named for the biblical Judge who served Israel for forty years and refused the kingship out of loyalty to the principle that God is king of Israel.

173

Solomon's son, Rehoboam, ascended the throne, civil war broke out in Israel. The northern kingdom was known as Israel and the southern kingdom was known as Judah. This division made for weakness. At last Israel was defeated by the Assyrians; afterwards Judah was conquered by the Babylonians. Its capital, Jerusalem, was burned and its people were exiled to distant Babylonia.

Isaiah. Known as the prophet-statesman, Isaiah, son of Amoz, lived in Judah, the southern kingdom. He was a great preacher who lived in times of tremendous national crises. He had seen the destruction of Israel, the northern kingdom, by Assyria and feared that the same fate might befall Judah and his beloved Jerusalem. His counsel to Judah for some forty years (740-700 B.C.E.) was chiefly to steer clear of alliances with foreign powers like Assyria and Egypt. So strong was Isaiah's belief in God that, in an age of corruption and evil, he dared dream of a Golden Age, when men would "beat their swords into plowshares" and peace would reign in the world. Isaiah dreamed heroic dreams for Zion, for Israel, for all of mankind. Today his words envisioning peace on earth are graven on a great wall facing UN Headquarters in New York.

Jeremiah. He came from a priestly family and studied the prophecies of Amos,

The Tomb of David on Mt. Zion. Since 1948 this hill is the only part of ancient Jerusalem in the possession of Israel.

God. For this he was flogged in public. His prophecies came true and he saw Judah destroyed by its enemies. He finally died in a foreign land.

Ezekiel. Unlike the other Hebrew prophets, he was active in Babylon during the Exile. He was thus the first to prophecy outside of Palestine. His great task was to teach the people that they could worship God even outside the Land of Israel. Like Jeremiah, he believed that Nebuchadnezzar was God's agent to punish Judah. Because of his message and the place in which he found himself, he became the builder of the

House of Naaman in Damascus. A 9th-century (B.C.E.) general of Damascus, Naaman went to Israel to consult the Prophet Elisha, who cured Naaman of leprosy.

Tower of Jezebel in Jezreel. Wife of King Ahab, Jezebel angered Elijah by introducing idol-worship into Israel.

Isaiah, and Micah. Torn between the desire to save his people and the duty to tell them of the doom that lay in store for them at the hands of Babylonia, he was hated and despised. He advised submission to Babylon, for he believed that only thus would Judah find peace. This was an unpopular policy. He also attacked the emptiness of temple worship without sincere belief in

Castle of Sennacherib at Mosul, Iraq. King of Assyria, Sennacherib invaded Judah in 701 B.C.E., captured forty-six cities and many prisoners.

first religious Jewish community in the Exile. He helped his people face the uncertain future.

Hosea. This book forms the first of the twelve Minor Prophets, known as Trey Asar, "the Twelve." These books were gathered into one collection because they are so short. Hosea lived after Amos in the eighth century B.C.E., and he prophesied in the kingdom of Israel. He was still alive

175

Pool of Hezekiah in Old City of Jerusalem. King of Judah, 720-692 B.C.E., he fortified Jerusalem and built the Siloam tunnel to improve the city's water supply.

when the Assyrians destroyed the kingdom of Israel in 721 B.C.E. He spoke in a time when the people had fallen back into their ancient sin of idol-worship. Nor were the priests fulfilling their duties. They kept silent while evil raged in the land. Hosea, who had seen much personal suffering, was a tender and kind man. He did not threaten, but pleaded with Israel to repent so that God might show His mercy and love. He was not listened to. Israel was exiled from Palestine and forever disappeared, to become known as the "ten lost tribes of Israel."

Joel. We know next to nothing about Joel, whose book consists of only three chapters. He tells us in very descriptive language of a plague of locusts sweeping over Judah and destroying its fields and vineyards. He calls upon the people to fast in repentance, and promises that one day Judah will be glorious again, blessed with abundance by the Almighty.

Amos. This prophet came from the village of Tekoa, near Jerusalem. He lived in the mid-eighth century, B.C.E. and he left his native Judah to warn the kingdom of Israel against wickedness, evil-doing, and falseness in religion. Israel was prosperous, yet most of its people lived in terrible poverty. Amos believed that Israel should set an example for other nations and he saw that God would use Assyria as a weapon to punish the wickedness of Israel and the other nations. Amos was the first of the prophets to write his words down and they have been preserved to this day.

Obadiah. With its one chapter of twenty-one verses, Obadiah is the shortest of all the books in the Bible. The prophet predicts doom for the Edomites for their cruel treatment of Israel, and for gloating over the people of Judah on the day of their disaster.

Jonah. Jonah is not actually a prophecy but a short story about a prophet written, according to tradition, by one of the "Men

Gateway to Nebuchadnezzar's palace. He captured Judea in 586 B.C.E., destroyed the Temple, and exiled the entire population to Babylonia.

176

of the Great Assembly" who lived during the days when the Jews returned from the Babylonian exile. The Book of Jonah teaches us that kindness and a spirit of repentance may be found among all men. Jonah did not want to bring God's promise of forgiveness to the city of Nineveh. He did not think its evil citizens could learn to be good. So Jonah had to be taught the lesson of God's love for all of mankind. Jonah's being swallowed by the great fish has been interpreted as Israel's captivity. His being brought forth to safety represents Israel's deliverance by God. The Book of Jonah is read in all synagogues on the afternoon of the Day of Atonement, for it preaches God's mercy and goodness to all who atone.

Micah. Like Isaiah, Micah dreamed of a future when nations would be at peace with each other. From Micah comes one of the most famous and beautiful expressions in the Bible: "The Lord requires of thee only to do justly, to love mercy, and to walk humbly with thy God."

Nahum. In three superb chapters, which comprise the entire Book of Nahum, the prophet describes the downfall of the Assyrian empire. The account of the destruction of Nineveh (capital of Assyria, in 612 B.C.E.) is one of the most dramatic recitals in ancient writings. He portrays the panic-stricken palace, the fainting hearts, the preparations for the siege. Nahum's book is so sharp in its details that it must have been written during or shortly after this historic event.

Habakkuk. Only three chapters in length, the Book of Habakkuk is laden with deep and poetic thought. The prophet wonders why the cruel oppressor constantly seems to be rewarded with happiness and victory. He stations himself on an imaginary tower and waits for an answer from God. The reply comes: it is that evil will one day be banished from the earth.

Excavating the ruins of Ahab's magnificent palace at Samaria. He ruled Israel from 876-853 B.C.E.

Zephaniah. Here is another book of only three chapters, portraying the Scythian invasion which began the closing chapter of the Assyrian empire. Zephaniah, who came of royal blood, lived in Jerusalem and cried out against the customs of their Assyrian conquerors. The prophet ends on a note of hope, for he predicts that one day Jerusalem will regain her lost glory.

Haggai. This prophet had a special mission. In 520 B.C.E., eighteen years. after King Cyrus had permitted the Babylonian exiles to return to Judah, very little work had been done on the rebuilding of the Temple. The unfriendly Samaritans had interfered with the work and the Israelites had lost their courage and determination. Haggai urged the returning exiles to be of good cheer and to build the Temple anew. His words gave spirit to flagging souls and the weary exiles bent their energies to the task.

Zechariah. In fourteen chapters, Zecha-

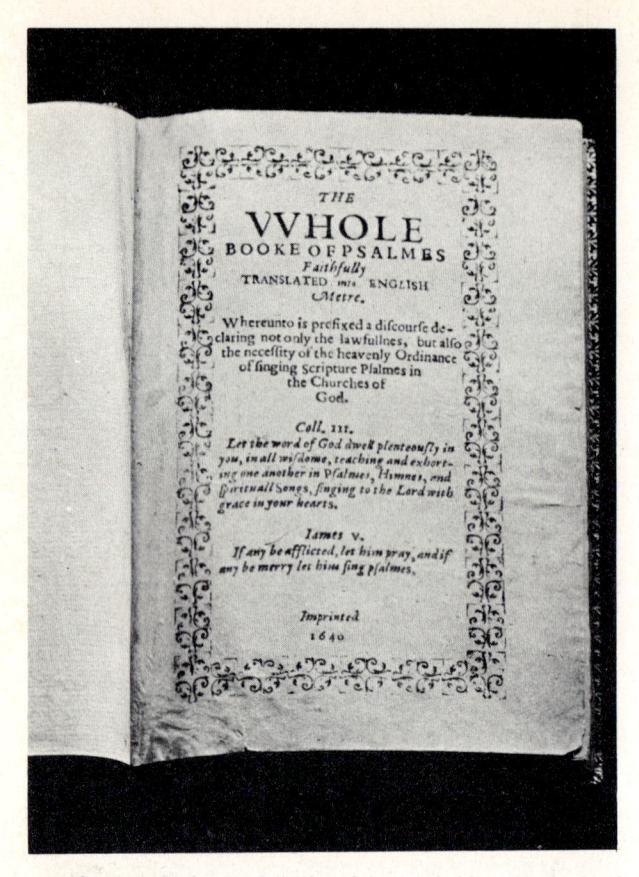

The Bay Psalm Book, printed in Cambridge, Mass., in the year 1640, was the first book to be set in type and produced in America. It also marked the first time Hebrew printed letters appeared in America.

riah assures his people that the Lord will restore them to their greatness as of old, and prophesies about the end of days, when the Messiah will bring an everlasting victory to our people. Then will peace reign supreme.

Malachi. In a series of questions and answers, the Book of Malachi deals with the problems all of us face in life. "Malachi" means "my messenger" and is taken from a verse in Chapter Three which reads: "Behold, I will send my messenger." We do not know the real name of this prophet, who lived in the fifth century B.C.E., but his words have left a strong impress in our thoughts. "Have we not all one Father? Has not one God created us?" These are two of the many questions posed by Malachi.

3) The *Writings* include: Psalms, Proverbs, Job, The Song of Songs, Ruth, Lamentations, Ecclesiastes, Esther, Daniel, Ezra, Nehemiah, First Chronicles, Second Chronicles. Among the Writings are King David's beautiful psalms (... "The Lord is my shepherd, I shall not want..." is one of them), the wise proverbs of King Solomon, and the tender story of Ruth.

Psalms. The first of the books of the Bible known as The Writings, *Psalms* contains 150 hymns which stress the importance of an understanding heart, of good deeds and of faith in God. The name *psalm* comes from the Greek word *psalmos* which means the music of stringed instruments. Originally, the psalms were sung to the accompaniment of instruments in the Temple. Some of the psalms have been famous throughout the world for centuries. Surely you know the one which begins: "The Lord is my shepherd; I shall not want." That is the first line of Psalm 23. One psalm describes a violent storm at sea; another portrays the glory of God as revealed in the forces of nature. Almost every experience, every joy and suffering of man—is mirrored in *Psalms*. These poems have brought confidence and solace to countless generations. Who wrote the Book of Psalms? According to tradition, they come from the pen of David, who was not only a doughty warrior and wise statesman, but an inspired poet as well.

Proverbs. A proverb is a nugget of wisdom. It expresses much in a few words. We often use proverbs in everyday life. A well-known one is: "Speech is silver; silence is golden." Another is: "Don't count your chickens before they hatch." One of the greatest collections of proverbs is the Book of Proverbs, written according to Jewish tradition by that wisest of all kings, Solomon. Here you may find rules and hints about every aspect of life—about parents and children, about wealth and poverty, about wisdom and folly. "Go to the ant, lazy one; look at her ways and learn wisdom." That is from the Book of Proverbs. There are many, many others, all strung like bright pearls on a necklace.

Job. In forty-two brilliant chapters, Job explores the deep problem of human suffering. Why is it that good people are often unhappy? Why is it that the wicked often seem to achieve success? These are the central questions in Job. Job was a man who was beset by many evils, yet who remained faithful to God. His story teaches us that we cannot understand God's ways. Belief in divine justice brings comfort in sorrow and strength in times of anguish. In Chapter 31, Job lists the virtues a person should possess: a blameless family life, consideration for the poor and weak, charity, modesty, generosity, hospitality to strangers, and honesty. The Book of Job is one of the most deeply religious ever set down by man.

The Song of Songs. Tradition states that King Solomon, who was the author of 1,005 songs, composed the delicate and lovely lyrics that make up the Song of Songs. Nowhere in the Bible is nature more charmingly described; nowhere is such a simple and sincere love story to be found. Our rabbis say that this book is an allegory, which means a story in which the words say one thing, but actually mean another. The Beloved represents God and Shulamit stands for the bride, Israel. Thus, the Song of Songs tells of God's deep love for the Jewish people. We read the Song of Songs in the synagogue on Passover, a fitting combination, for the book's description of spring goes well with the springtime spirit of the Festival of Freedom. The Song of

Solomon's Book of Proverbs in an early Italian translation.

An 8th-century B.C.E. seal. The act of sealing documents is mentioned frequently in the Bible.

Songs is the first of the five *Megillot*, or Scrolls.

Ruth. The drama of the Book of Ruth is played against the background of the period of the Judges. A beautiful story of friendship and devotion, it takes its name from Ruth who refuses to leave her mother-in-law Naomi though her husband is dead. Ruth's words have echoed in the halls of history: "Beg me not to leave you; for wherever you go, I will go, and wherever you lodge, there will I lodge. Your people shall be my people, and your God my God." At the end of this book, Naomi finds a suitable husband for Ruth in the person of Boaz, and we are told that from this union will descend David, King of Israel. The Book of Ruth is read in the synagogue on Shavuot, the harvest festival commemorating the giving of the Torah, because Ruth and Boaz met in a harvest field, because Ruth was a Moabitess who embraced Judaism and the Torah, and because King David is said to have died on Shavuot.

Lamentations. The Book of Lamentations consists of five sad poems describing the sorrows suffered by the Jewish people when the mighty Babylonian armies swooped down upon Jerusalem in 586 B.C.E., destroyed the Temple, and sent the mourning citizens into the Babylonian Exile. Thus was Solomon's Temple laid waste after it had been in existence for 410 years. The Book of Lamentations is read in the Synagogue on Tisha Be-Av, the day on which both the First and Second Temples were destroyed.

Ecclesiastes. In Hebrew, Ecclesiastes is known as Kohelet, or "Preacher." King Solomon is said to have written it when he was an old man. It is a book full of ripe wisdom, of questions and answers about life. It advises patience and courage. Make the most of life while it is yours, says Kohelet. *Ecclesiastes* is read in the synagogue on Sukkot.

Esther. This book combines a captivating tale with a very important message. It tells of Esther, the beautiful maiden who saved her people from destruction. It also warns the world against the ills that prejudice and intolerance can bring. When the Jews were exiled from Judah to Babylonia, they formed new communities there. Later, Persia conquered Babylonia, and the Jews became loyal subjects of the King of Persia. For many years they lived peacefully until, in the reign of King Ahasuerus, an enemy named Haman rose to plot their destruction. Rescued by Queen Esther and her guardian Mordecai, the Jewish people established the Feast of Purim, on which the Book of Esther is read in the synagogue.

Daniel. In the book of Daniel we learn of the sacrifices made by this hero and his three friends in order to remain true to their religion. Daniel was the only one able to explain the strange dream of Nebuchadnezzar, king of Babylonia. He said that it meant that soon God would take away the ruling power of proud Babylonia. Daniel's three friends refused to worship the king's golden image, so they were thrown into a fiery furnace, only to emerge unharmed. Then Belshazzar ruled and Daniel explained the strange handwriting the king saw on the wall—Belshazzar would go the way of all tyrants. As a final test, Daniel

Ruins of Babylon, to which Nebuchadnezzar exiled the Jews after his conquest of Judah.

was thrown into a den of hungry lions. But the beasts did not harm a single hair of Daniel's head. From that day on, Daniel lived in happiness and safety.

Ezra. The books of Ezra and Nehemiah are often counted as a single book because they deal with one period. Ezra tells about the scribe who replaced the prophet after the return to Palestine from the Babylonian exile. The scribes carefully copied the Torah and taught it to the people. Ezra came to Jerusalem about 450 B.C.E. He wanted the Jewish people to remember their ancestry and nobility. He insisted that the laws of the Torah be strictly observed in the new Jewish Commonwealth. According to tradition, Ezra was the founder of the Great Assembly, the leaders who followed the last of the prophets and who were in the forefront of those who kept alive the Torah and its teachings.

Nehemiah. A cupbearer of the Persian king Artaxerxes, Nehemiah came to Palestine soon after Ezra arrived. A representative of the king, he built the wall around Jerusalem. Constantly he warned the people to beware against enemies who sought to destroy them. He kept a kind of diary

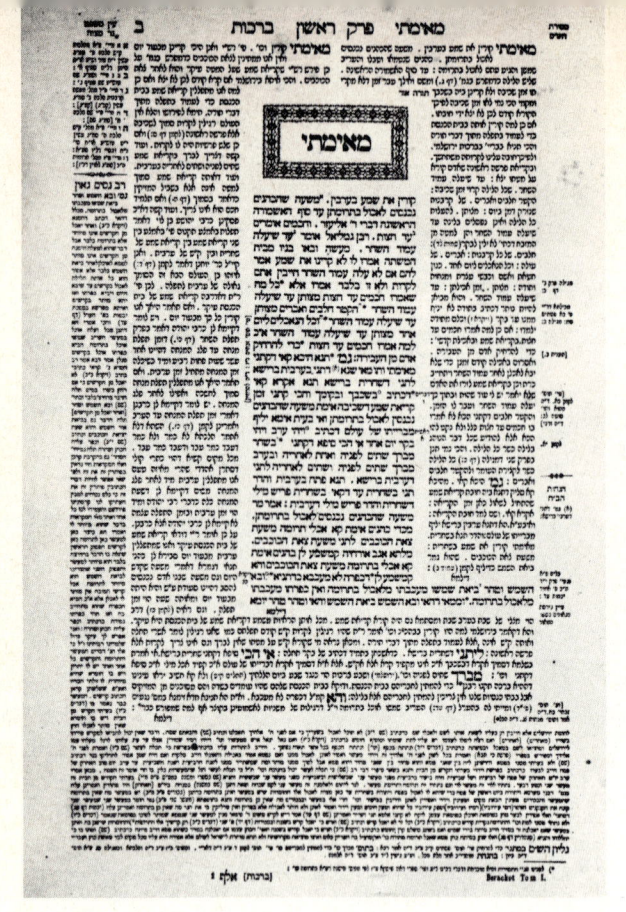

A page of the Babylonian Talmud. The portion of the Mishnah and Gemara *(center)* is flanked by commentaries, including Rashi *(right)*, the Tosafot *(left)* and additional notes *(far right and bottom)*.

and his book is written chiefly in the first person singular. He gives us a detailed, eye-witness account of the building of Jerusalem's wall. From his memoirs we can see that he was an upright, honest, and efficient leader.

Chronicles. In two books, Chronicles retells the history of the Jewish people from the creation of the world to the end of the Babylonian exile. When it reaches the period of the two kingdoms in Palestine, it tells only the story of Judah and says nothing about the northern kingdom of Israel. Chronicles emphasizes that God rules the world and that history is created by Providence and does not happen by accident.

With Chronicles we have come to the end of the Writings, the third and final division of the Books of the Bible.

The Talmud

Honi ha-Meaggel once saw an old man planting a carob tree. He asked him when he thought the tree would bear fruit. "After seventy years," was the reply.

"Do you expect to live seventy years and eat the fruit of your labor?"

"I did not find the world empty when I entered it," said the old man, "and as my fathers planted for me before I was born, so do I plant for those who will come after me."

* * *

This legend, which you read earlier in connection with *Tu Bi-Shevat,* is taken from the Talmud and is one of the hundreds of stories to be found in its pages; yet no one would call the Talmud a story-book. The Talmud contains all our religious laws; but it is more than a law book. It tells us much about our history; still, it is certainly not a history text.

The Talmud (from the Hebrew *lomed,* or study) has often been called "a sea of learning." This is an apt comparison: like a sea, it has boundaries which we can measure; and yet, like a sea, it has depths which have never been completely plumbed.

The Oral Law

When our forefathers were exiled from the Holy Land after the destruction of the First Temple in 576 B.C.E., they lived in Babylonia. The Torah they had brought with them was the Law. Although the Jewish people was soon afterward permitted to return to Zion, many stayed on in Babylon where they built flourishing communities. The Torah remained their Law, but as generations passed, explanations of biblical law developed. This wealth of matter, plus the oral traditions that had been handed down from the time of the giving of the Law on Mt. Sinai, was called *Torah she'be'al peh,* the Oral Law. In the course of time the Oral Law, written in many volumes, was to become known as the Talmud.

The Talmud consists of two separate parts. One part is the Mishnah, which comes from *shanah*, to repeat, or study. The Mishnah contains all the Jewish laws that had been handed down since the time of the Bible. The other part is the Gemara, from the Aramaic *gemar*, meaning study or teaching) which is an explanation of the Mishnah.

The Mishnah

The Mishnah was written down in Hebrew by its editor and compiler, Rabbi Judah the Prince (Yehudah ha-Nasi), about 1,800 years ago, and comprised the first Jewish code of laws since the Torah. A very compact work, it is divided into six parts, dealing with such matters as agricultural laws, fasts and festivals, ceremonial and ritual laws, marriage, and criminal laws.

The Mishnah was a milestone in our history. It explained many passages in the Torah in the light of daily problems of living. But the compact style of the Mishnah needed interpretation and expansion. That task was undertaken by the Gemara.

The Gemara

There are two Gemaras. One was completed about 1,500 years ago by Jewish scholars in Babylonia, the other a hundred years earlier by scholars in Palestine. The Mishnah plus the Babylonian Gemara is called the Babylonian Talmud (the *Talmud Bavli*); the Mishnah together with the Palestinian Gemara is known as the Palestinian Talmud (the *Talmud Yerushalmi*).

The Palestinian Talmud is about one-third the length of the other. From the beginning, it was never used as much as the Babylonian Talmud. That was chiefly because Babylonia was the real center of Jewish life at the time and it lasted as such much longer than the community in Palestine, from which we were exiled again in 70 C.E. When the name Talmud is mentioned, the Babylonian Talmud is meant.

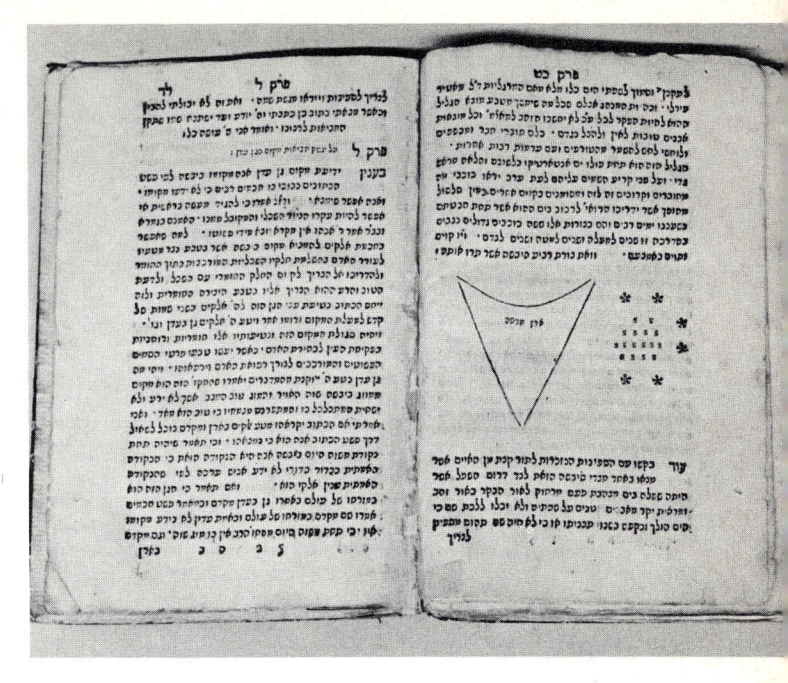

A map of the New World, the first to appear in a Hebrew book, was published in *Iggeret Orhot Olam*, by Abraham Farissol, Venice, 1586. The words in the "map" are *Eretz Hadashah*, "new country."

The Babylonian Talmud was written in Aramaic, the language used in Babylonia. It was created slowly, layer upon layer, by the sages who sought to interpret the Mishnah.

The men who created the Talmud were not professional scholars solely, like most university professors today. They came instead from every walk of life. Rabbi Meir was a writer of scrolls. Samuel was a well-known astronomer. Huna was a field laborer. Yokhanan Ha-Sandlar was called that because he was a cobbler, or sandal-maker. These men became experts in special fields. For example, those who worked on the Jewish calendar learned astronomy. Others specialized in medicine, geology, and biology. Thus the Talmud was truly a creation of all the Jewish people. According to tradition, the scholar Ashi, who died in 427 C.E., began the tremendous task of writing down all that had been said. Rabina bar Huna filled in the gaps, and when he died in 499 C.E., the great Talmud was closed.

Because books and the study of books have always played such an important role in Jewish life, typesetting was a very honorable trade among craftsmen in the Old Country. Here you see a compositor in Bratislava, Slovakia, carefully selecting type to be set by hand.

The Aggadah

The men who compiled the Talmud were reporting the minutes of important legal discussions. As the day progressed and minds wearied, one of the rabbis might tell an anecdote to lighten the atmosphere, or to illustrate a point. These anecdotes and stories, one of which you read at the beginning of this article, were written into the Talmud. Thus the dry matter of law, which is called Halakhah, was broken up with history, traditions, and legends; with proverbs and sayings; with mathematics, astronomy, and psychology. This material is called "Aggadah", the Aggadah makes up about one-third of the entire Talmud.

The forty-odd volumes of the Talmud contain no punctuation. One word may express the meaning of a whole sentence. There are no question marks to guide the pupil. The Talmud has remained an open book to the studious because of the commentaries on its text.

All of these—the Mishnah, the Gemara, and the commentaries—make up the Talmud as we know it today. The two million five hundred thousand words of the Babylonian Talmud are one of the greatest achievements of the Jewish people. Its 6,000 pages, containing the contributions of over 2,000 scholars, form an encyclopedia of Jewish culture. Built upon the solid foundation of our Torah, the Talmud sums up a thousand years of religious and social thought of the Jewish people.

Generations of our forefathers were nourished on its wisdom; thousands upon thousands of Jewish youths pored over its leaves; to become a rabbi and spiritual leader, a Jew must still, as in days past, devote himself to the study of the Talmud.

Whenever persecution lashed at us, the Talmud too suffered the fury of the persecutors and was burned. However, like the Jewish people itself, it always survived the foe. Today, it enriches our institutions of learning and libraries as well as many Jewish homes and continues to cast its light into every corner of every Jewish community in the world.

To acquire the knowledge of the Talmud is no easy task. But to those who are ready and willing to prepare themselves for its study, it offers a rich reward of the finest wisdom of our sages and a deep understanding of our golden Jewish heritage.

The trend today is toward making study a year-round activity. These young people are participating in the annual Teen-Age Torah Leadership Seminar sponsored by Yeshiva University. In an atmosphere that combines religious education with camping fun, leaders are trained for synagogue youth groups.

This Yom Kippur Mahzor, or prayer book, was a mute witness to the cruel period of the Inquisition in Spain and Portugal. It was designed in this elongated shape for a special purpose. In case of a surprise "visit" by officers of the government, Marrano Jews (who pretended to be Christians but who practiced Judaism secretly) would drop the prayer book into their wide sleeves and thus escape detection.

The Siddur

Our prayer book, or Siddur, is like a skyscraper of the spirit which was built very slowly, brick by brick. Gradually, over the centuries, the prayers in the Siddur changed and were added to. At last the Siddur became a rich collection of Jewish literature. Its passages show the development of Jewish life—the Shema Yisrael of the Bible, the Hallel from King David's Psalms, the Ani Ma'amin of Maimonides. The Siddur also contains the religious poetry and prayers of known and unknown authors. Their words so touched the hearts of our people that they found their way into the Siddur. For over 1,000 years, the Siddur has graced Jewish homes in every corner of the globe.

These eternal masterworks of Jewish learning and literature have helped us survive hardships and persecution and to stay united as a people. They are our *Three Greatest Books*.

Other Great Jewish Books

There are many, many other great Jewish books and great Jewish authors. In the following pages, you will meet but a few. Each, however, has had enormous influence upon Jewish life and literature.

Works of Maimonides

Rabbi Moses ben Maimon, usually called Maimonides or *Rambam* (from the initials of his name) lived from 1135-1204. He spent much of his early life wandering from place to place because of religious persecution. At last he settled in Cairo, Egypt, and became the court physician of the Sultan Saladin. He had a brilliant mind and, despite hardships, studied Talmud, logic, mathematics, medicine, astronomy and the

A 19th-century prayer book with beautiful binding of silver gilt with metal embroidery set with pearls. In the center, priestly hands are raised in blessing.

other natural sciences known in his day. He wrote works which have influenced Judaism to our own day. His commentary on the Mishnah was written between the ages of twenty-three and thirty-three. He spent ten years writing his code of Jewish laws and ethics, the Mishneh Torah. This great work is a summary of material in the Bible, the two Talmuds, and the legal writings of the Rabbis up to the Rambam's day. Here we find Maimonides' famous "Eight Degrees of Charity."

As a leader of the Jewish community, Maimonides knew that people are often embarrassed when they need assistance and receive it publicly. To guide his fellow Jews in the practice of Tzedakah, he formulated a "ladder" known as the "Eight Degrees of Charity." The first degree is the best way to give charity; the second is the next best, and so on. Here are the top, middle, and lowest rungs on the ladder of Tzedakah:

Facsimile of an autograph letter by Maimonides (1173). Maimonides was well-known in every Jewish community, and to his home in Egypt came many requests for medical advice and counsel.

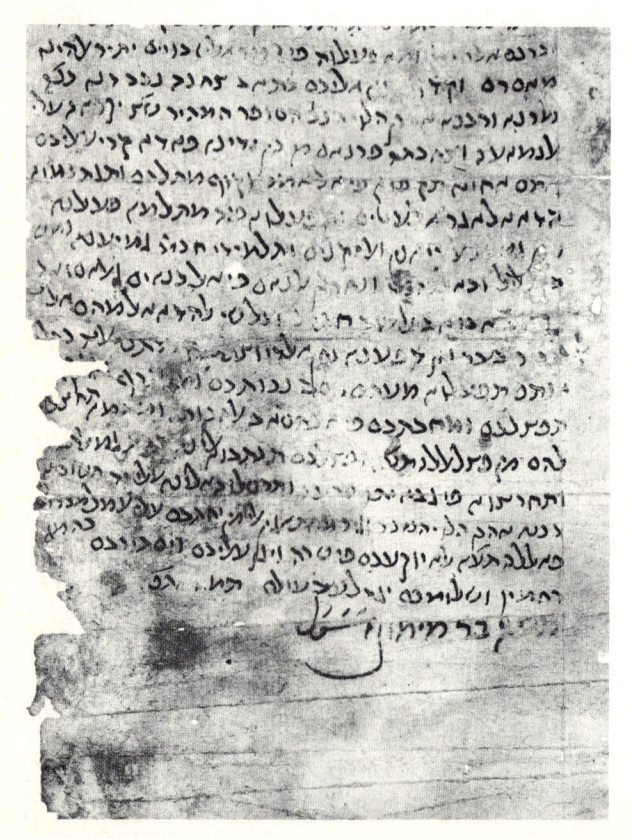

Traditional portrait of Maimonides (Rabbi Moses ben Maimon). This picture is a hypothetical likeness, for no contemporary portrait exists.

First Degree: "Help a Person Help Himself." We can prevent poverty by giving someone a loan or gift or finding work for him so that he will not need to appeal for help. (This is the top rung of Tzedakah's ladder.)

Fourth Degree: "Giver Does Not Know Receiver." By this method the poor man knows from whom he takes but the giver does not know the receiver. For example, there were men who tied money in the corners of their cloaks, so that the poor might help themselves without being seen. (This is a middle rung.)

Eighth Degree: "Gives Unwillingly." Lowest on the ladder is the man who helps others only because he is forced to do so. This is the gift of the hand but not of the heart (and the least respected way of giving Tzedakah).

Another of Maimonides' works is the *Guide for the Perplexed,* an original treatise which gave the Rambam a highly respected place among the philosophers of world history. Maimonides—scholar, rabbi, philosopher, and physician—was one of the remarkable men of all time.

Rashi's Commentaries

Rabbi Shlomo Itzhaki, better known as Rashi (an abbreviation of his name) was born in Troyes, France in 1040 and died in his native city in 1105. As a young man he felt that not enough people understood the meaning of the Bible, and he decided to write a new explanation. Throughout his life, he wrote commentaries on nearly all the books of the Bible and on most of the Talmud. His commentary on the Torah was the first Hebrew book to be printed (in 1475). And on his own work, more than a hundred commentaries have been written. Rashi's greatness lay in his ability to open the difficult books of the Bible and Talmud to everyone who wanted to drink of their wisdom. To explain the things he discussed, Rashi studied the subjects thoroughly. When he dealt with talmudic laws concerning illness, he studied medicine; he also learned the craft of the shoemaker, the smith, and the shipwright. The rabbis of the Middle Ages honored Rashi by calling him Parshandata—"Interpreter of the Law." He made our ancient heritage live, not for the scholar alone, but for the Jewish people as a whole.

The Shulhan Arukh

In 1492, when Joseph Karo was four, his family fled the Spanish Inquisition, taking the lad to Portugal. When Joseph was eight, his family was driven out of Portugal; this time they arrived in Constantinople. Young Karo studied there and moved on; in 1536 he settled in Safed, Palestine. His fame rests on his Shulhan Arukh (which means The

The title page of the tenth book of Maimonides' Mishneh Torah, handwritten in Cologne, 1296, with an illustration of the sacrifice of Isaac at the foot of the page. This great Jewish law-book was copied by scribes in many lands.

Prepared Table) published in Venice in 1565. This work is a guide for the observance of traditional Judaism. (Karo's book was popularized by an abridgment known as the *Kitzur Shulhan Arukh,* written by Rabbi Solomon Ganzfried in the nineteenth

The first Hebrew book to appear in print was Rashi's commentary on the Torah, printed in Italy, 1475. This type face became known as "Rashi script."

century.) The author of the Shulhan Arukh studied all the discussions of problems of Jewish law and presented the decision. In the Shulhan Arukh we learn the laws about benedictions (blessings), about charity, about building a family, about judges and courts, and so on. There was no problem of religious Jewish life up to his time that the Shulhan Arukh does not touch on. In many Jewish homes, the shorter version (the Kitzur) came third, after the Siddur and the Humash (Five Books of Moses).

Yehudah Halevi

Yehudah Halevi was the greatest Hebrew poet between biblical and modern times. Born in Spain about 1085, he was a physician by profession, and wrote in both Hebrew and Arabic. In the Book of the Kusari, Yehudah recalls an event of some 400 years before his day, when the King of the Khazars was converted to Judaism along with his whole people. In the Kusari, the author-poet defends the Jewish religion against its attackers. And, asks Yehudah Halevi, where can the promises made by the Prophets come true? Only in the Holy Land. Thus did Yehudah sound the call for the return to Zion, and earn for himself the name "Sweet Singer of Zion." The chord struck by the Kusari echoed through the ages, and was hearkened to by the pioneers in Israel. According to legend, when Yehudah came to Jerusalem himself (about 1140) a passing Arab horseman rode him down and killed him.

Ahad Ha-Am

Ahad Ha-Am, whose real name was Asher Ginzberg, hoped that Palestine would one day be the source and center of all Jewish culture. Born in Russia in 1856, he spent his childhood in a very pious atmosphere. He wanted more than a religious education, and he began to study Russian and other

Ahad Ha-Am (Asher Ginsberg), 1856-1927, a leading thinker and essayist in Hebrew literature, was the philosopher of cultural or "spiritual" Zionism.

languages. In the 1880's he wrote an essay called "This Is Not the Way," in which he said that pioneers (*halutzim*) must be trained to face hardships *before* they went to Palestine. He signed the essay "Ahad Ha-Am" (*One of the People*); overnight Asher Ginzberg, shy book-lover, became Ahad Ha-Am, champion of Zionism. He thought of Palestine as a creative center of Jewish writing, music, dance; there, too, the Jewish ideals of righteousness and learning might flourish best. He died in 1927 in Tel Aviv. The hopes we have for Israel today were dreamed of more than half a century ago by Ahad Ha-Am.

Mendele Mokher Seforim

Sholom Jacob Abramovich's pen-name means "Mendele the Bookseller." Born in 1835 in Russia, he became known as the grandfather of modern Yiddish and Hebrew literature. He remembered everyone he met

188

This photo of a group of famous Jewish writers and intellectuals was taken in Odessa, Russia, in 1906. Seated, (l. to r.): Hayyim Tchernowitz, M. L. Lillienblum, J. C. Ravnitzky, Ahad Ha-Am, Mendele Mokher Seforim, A. L. Levinsky. Standing (l. to r.): A. M. Borochov, Joseph Klausner, Chaim Nachman Bialik.

and sooner or later they all appeared in his writings. Impatient with his fellow-Jews, he scolded them and mocked them and tried to rouse them to lead a more modern life. That is why he portrayed Tuneyadevka, the place of the poor, and Grupsk—the place of the fools. He died in 1917, and will always be remembered as the first of the three classic writers (Peretz and Sholom Aleichem are the other two) who laid the cornerstone of modern Hebrew and Yiddish literature. But to Mendele alone belongs the honor of raising Yiddish—the language of the people —to the level of a literary language.

Peretz

Isaac Leib Peretz, the second of the great founders of modern Yiddish literature, wrote for the new generation, for those who had studied in up-to-date classrooms in larger communities. Born in Poland in 1852, he read widely in every period of Jewish history. The stories, dramas, essays and poetry that flowed from his pen breathed life into a whole gallery of heroic figures, of brave and righteous people. The stories he set down about the distant past were really a gift to the future. Perhaps you have read Peretz's "Three Gifts." If so, you will remember the tortured soul who faces death instead of giving up the last symbol of Judaism in his possession—his skull cap. This incident teaches us a lesson. It tells us to

Isaac Leib Peretz (1852-1915) was a pioneer and great stylist in modern Hebrew and Yiddish literature. He was also one of the first major writers to depict the beauty and moral strength of the Hassidic way of life.

lead our own lives in an honest and upright fashion. Peretz also tried to teach as well as entertain. That is why his work lives on and why his mighty spirit will always be with us.

Sholom Aleichem

Sholom Aleichem brought laughter into countless Jewish homes and captured in immortal words the folkways of our people. His real name was Sholom Rabinowitz; he was born in Russia in 1859 and died in New York in 1916. His pen-name means "peace unto you," or "how do you do?" or just plain "hello." The gayest and jolliest of all great Jewish writers, Sholom Aleichem was always saying "howdy" to millions of readers. In his works he described Jewish character-types of Eastern Europe. He wrote of great

Sholom Aleichem (Sholom Rabinowitz), 1859-1916, enriched Yiddish literature by mirroring Jewish life of the small towns of Eastern Europe. In his tales he reflected Jewish wit and wisdom. Many of his works have been translated into English.

Sholom Aleichem wanted to be remembered as a simple man. He had said: "Let me be buried among the poor, so that their grave may illumine mine, and mine theirs." He died on Saturday, May 13, 1916, and was buried in Brooklyn. His tombstone in translation reads:
"Life to him was but a jest,
 He poked fun at all that mattered;
When other men were happiest,
 His heart alone was bruised and shattered."

scholars and simple folk, of Tevye the Dairyman, Menachem Mendel, Mottel the cantor's son, children in the *heder,* Methusaleh the horse, Rabchick the dog, and many others. He showed the bravery of the Jewish people—they could poke fun at themselves even when the skies seemed darkest. The world Sholom Aleichem wrote about formed a wonderful chapter in Jewish history, and we should never forget it.

Bialik

Hayyim Nahman Bialik (1873-1934) is the greatest Hebrew poet of modern times. Born in a little Russian town, Chaim was brought up in the religious home of his grandfather. In 1892, he published his first poem, "To the Bird." The last period of his life was spent in Palestine, where he lived on Bialik Street—a street named for him—in Tel Aviv. His poetry sings of God and of the Jewish people. It cries out for freedom and justice. It protests against the cruelty suffered by his people and calls upon them to throw off their chains of oppression. His pen-pictures of the European yeshiva student, of the city of Kishinev after Jews were massacred there, and of the house of prayer, have never been excelled. His Book of

Chaim Nachman Bialik (1873-1934), the greatest Hebrew poet of modern times, created poems, essays, and stories. Like the prophets, he rebuked his people in fiery verses.

Legends drew the most fascinating stories from the Talmud and cast them into unforgettable language. He wrote nature poems and songs for children. Although he died less than a generation ago, the writings of Bialik have already become part of our lasting literature.

Graetz's 'History'

Heinrich Graetz (1817-1891) taught at the Jewish Theological Seminary of Breslau, Germany and at the University of Breslau, but at night he labored on his History of the Jews. It took him twenty-two years to complete this eleven-volume work (six in English translation). It was translated from German into many languages, including English, Hebrew, Yiddish, French, Polish, Russian and Hungarian. Graetz surpassed all previous Jewish history writers because of his tireless and painstaking research, his scientific approach, his warm manner, and his clear style. He was never dry. He searched through the Talmud to find out about the history of that time. The historical characters stand before you as heroes or villains. Although today we see that he made certain errors, the History continues to be both popular and a classic.

Heinrich Graetz knew how to make the past speak to the present in clear and ringing tones.

Herzl's 'The Jewish State'

Israel was founded on Iyar 5, 5708, but the dream of a Jewish State was born over half a century before in the mind of Theodor Herzl. "I do not know when I shall die," said the founder of modern Zionism, "but Zionism will never die. The Jewish State will come into being in its own country." The son of a prosperous merchant, Herzl was the Paris correspondent of a Viennese newspaper when the Dreyfus case in 1904 awakened him to anti-Semitism and other pressing Jewish problems. In 1896 he wrote the famous book, *The Jewish State* (Judenstaat). The rest of his life was spent in stirring his fellow Jews to mass action for a Jewish homeland and in interesting political leaders—kings, emperors, sultans, prime

Heinrich Graetz (1817-1891), Jewish historian, wrote the monumental *History of the Jews*, a work that is still a basic source of information about the Jewish past.

ministers—in the ideal of a Jewish homeland. Overworked, he died at forty-four in Vienna; only recently his remains were reburied in Jerusalem. Because it expressed the new and daring philosophy of twentieth-century Zionism, *The Jewish State* captured the imagination of the Jewish people and became one of the most influential and moving of modern Jewish books.

David Pinski

Wherever Yiddish is spoken or read, the name of David Pinski is a household word. Born in Russia in 1872, he met Peretz in Warsaw when he was in his twenties, and determined to make the Yiddish language a powerful tool for creative writing. A second goal would be to use Yiddish to educate the poorer ranks of the Jewish workers. He was invited to New York where he edited a Yiddish newspaper. Then he began to write plays, several of which were produced in English translation on Broadway. Some of his best-known plays are *The Eternal*

S. J. Agnon (1888-1959), noted Hebrew novelist, based his works chiefly upon traditional Jewish life in Europe. His stories are rich in Hasidic lore and legend.

Theodor Herzl (1860-1904), the founder of political Zionism, proposed the creation of a Jewish State as a solution to anti-Semitism. This photo was taken in Basle, Switzerland, during the First Zionist Congress, 1897.

Jew, The Treasure, Shlomo Molcho, and *Sabbatai Zevi.* From the theatre, Pinski turned to novel-writing and the Zionist cause; for a time he was editor of *Der Kemfer,* a Labor Zionist weekly magazine. Much of his finest work was done in New York. Today David Pinski lives in Haifa, Israel.

S. J. Agnon

Samuel Joseph Agnon, one of the foremost living Hebrew novelists, is noted for his novels dealing with the life of the Jews of Eastern Europe, and for his writings about the pioneers in Israel. Born in Galicia in 1880, he has been living in Israel, except for a few years in Germany, since 1907. His best-known work, translated into English as *The Bridal Canopy,* tells of the strange adventures of Reb Yudel, a simple Jewish scholar of the nineteenth century, who travels far and wide to find bridegrooms for his three daughters. He has written many other books and stories about Jewish life. In 1936, Agnon received the honorary degree of Doctor of Hebrew Letters from the Jewish Theological Seminary of America; the following year he received the Bialik Prize for Literature for the novel *The Bridal Canopy*. His works have been translated into fifteen languages. Today, S. J. Agnon lives in Jerusalem.

Zalman Shneur

Learning the mystic and inspiring lore of the Hassidim filled the boyhood hours of this famous Hebrew and Yiddish poet and novelist. He was born in Russia in 1888, and his father, a jewelry dealer of a distinguished Hassidic family, gave Zalman a *heder* education. At night he would tell him stories of his Hassidic ancestors. At the age of thirteen, Zalman left home and wandered to Odessa. There he was hailed as a literary child prodigy by such giants as Bialik and Mendele Mokher Seforim. He produced a wealth of writings, much of it still unpublished. If all his Hebrew and Yiddish works were to be printed, they would fill some fifty volumes. A favorite theme in Shneur's poetry is the clash between nature and civilization. He called himself a poet of "rebellion and strife," and he has been praised everywhere for the strength and beauty of his work. An honorary member of the international Mark Twain Society, he received the Bialik Prize. Shneur died in 1959.

Rare Treasures

Most old Jewish books—including some rare and ancient editions—have come down to us because Jews have always loved and treasured books. Jews were among the first people in the world to collect books and form their own private libraries. Such libraries were formed all over the world, and old books were saved so that we might have and enjoy them today.

Zalman Shneur (1887-1959), Hebrew and Yiddish poet and novelist, wrote novels of life in Eastern Europe which ranked with the classic works of Mendele Mokher Seforim and Sholom Aleichem. He was also recognized as one of the most powerful poets in modern Jewish literature.

A manuscript fragment from the writings of Ben Sira, a sage who lived in the 2nd century, B.C.E. The original Hebrew text was lost for centuries, but fragments covering most of the work were found in the Cairo Genizah in 1896.

The Bible, translated into a thousand tongues, is today also available in Braille. Sightless persons can now avail themselves of the opportunity to read the Book of Books unaided.

As for old holy books, they have come down to us because of an ancient Jewish law which forbids the destruction of any book that has the name of God in it.

Therefore, when such books grew worn and old, they were not thrown away but were stored in a special section of the synagogue called a "Genizah." By searching these old storehouses of books, archaeologists have been able to come away with some rare finds.

During World War II, the great Jewish publishing centers of Europe were either destroyed or damaged beyond repair. The Nazis, who hated the freedom that the Jewish book represents, held public book-burnings at which they destroyed books that Jews had treasured for centuries.

Books Today

Although there are still many Jewish books published in Europe today, the United States, Israel, and Argentina have become the Jewish book publishing capitals of the world. Thousands of books dealing with Jewish history, religion, public affairs, and literature are published in this country every year. Some of these books are written in Hebrew or Yiddish, while most are in English or in a host of other languages.

Today, with thousands of years of Jewish literature behind us, with the upbuilding of the Jewish community in the United States, Israel, and elsewhere, we may look forward to yet another golden age of Jewish writing. And today every one of us can do easily what our ancestors could only dream of doing—we can read and own many books.

By this time, you may know why an ancient Jewish sage once said: "The book is a good companion."

Among our people it was always felt that nothing could add more to the beauty and warmth of a home than a collection of Jewish books, carefully chosen and always increasing. Moses ben Jacob Ibn Ezra, a famed Jewish poet and philosopher of twelfth-century Spain, declared:

"A book is the most delightful companion. If you wish entertainment, its witty sayings will amuse you; if you want advice, its words of wisdom will gladden you. Within its covers it holds everything: what is first and what is last, what is gone and what still is. Although it is not alive, it talks about things both dead and living.

"A true friend, it brings out your inner accomplishments. In the whole world, there is no friend more faithful, no companion more bending, no teacher more instructive, than a book. It is a friend that will cause you no harm and deny you no favor. If you fall on evil days, it will be a friend in your loneliness, a companion in your exile, a light in darkness, good cheer in your sorrow. It will bestow upon you whatever it can, asking no favor in return. It gives all, it takes nothing."

Is it any wonder that we have been called —"The People of the Book"?

The ancient Temple was used as a printer's mark by Antonio Giustiniani in Venice in the 16th century.

INDEX

A

Aaron, 88
Abraham, 28, 31, 139, 144, 148
Abramovich, Sholom Jacob, 188-189
A.D., 6
Adam, 64, 69, 167
Adar, 5, 7, 8, 71, 73, 76, 80, 81
Adar Sheni, 5, 81
Adir Hu, 94, 99
Adloyada Carnival, Israel, 78, 80-81
Adon Olam, 134, 161
Afikomen, 85, 93, 96
Agag, 23, 73, 80
Aggadah, 184
Agnon, Samuel Joseph, 192-193
Agricultural Festival see Passover
Ahad Ha-Am, 163, 188
Ahasuerus, 71-76, 77, 81, 180
Airusin, 141
Akdamut, 111
Akiba, Rabbi, 101-103, 104, 105
Al Ha-Nissim, 57
Al Het, 33
Alenu, 18
Alexander the Great, 49-50
Aliyah, 19
Alkabets, Solomon, 14
Amalek, 23, 80
America, first Jewish community, 123
American Joint Distribution Committee, 147
American Nehemiah, 39
American Pilgrims, 39-40
American Reform Judaism, 127
American Thanksgiving, and Sukkot, 38-40
Amidah, 18
Amnon, Rabbi, 29
Amos, 173, 176
Amoz, 174
Amram, 87
Amsterdam Haggadah, 96
An Only Kid, 61, 99
Angel of the Sabbath, 12
Ani Ma'amin, 185
Antiochus Epiphanes, 50-54, 57, 59
Aramaic, 94, 134, 142, 160-161, 183
Arba Minim, 41-42
Arch of Titus, Rome, 60
Architecture, American synagogue, 129-131
Ark of the Covenant, 133-134
Aron Ha-Brit, 133
Aron Ha-Kodesh, 133-134
Art, and the Haggadah, 96-97
Artaxerxes, 181
Arur Haman, 81
Asarah Be-Tevet, 117
Ashi, 183
Ashre, 18
Atah Horayta, 45
Athletics, and the synagogue, 129
Atzey Hayyim, 133, 135
Av, 8, 31, 115, 117

B

Ba'al Ha-Bayit, 146
Baal Kore, 137
Baal Musaf, 137
Baal Shaharit, 137
Ba'al Tefilah, 137
Baal Tokea, 137
Ba'ale nefesh, 39
Babylonian calendar, 7
Babylonian Gemara, 183
Babylonian Talmud, 183, 184
Bar Kochba, 64, 101-105, 115
Bar Mitzvah, 19, 112, 140, 151-157
Bar Yohai, Simeon, 64, 104-105
Barley harvest, 108, 109
Barukh Dayan Emet, 148
Barukh Mordecai, 81
Bat Mitzvah, 112, 140
B.C., 6
B.C.E., 6
B'dikat Hametz, 91
Belshazzar, 180
Be-Midbar, 172
Besamim, 20, 162
Bet am, 120
Bet Ha-Knesset, 121, 127, 129, 130
Bet Ha-Midrash, 105, 121, 128, 129
Bet Ha-T'filah, 121, 129
Bet Hayyim, 149
Betar, 103, 115, 120
Bialik, Hayyim Nahman, 19, 163, 190-191, 193
Bialik Prize for Literature, 193
Bible, Books of, 171-182 see also particular book, e.g., Exodus; Isaiah; Psalms
   Prophets, 173-178
   Torah, 171-173
   Writings, 178-182
Bikkurim, 109
Bimah, 42, 125, 135
Birkhat Ha-Mazon, 17, 18, 57, 96
Birthday of the Flowers, 63
Bitter Herbs, 92, 93, 95, 163
Blintzes, 112
B'nai Jeshurun, New York City, 130
Boaz, 180
Bokser, 65, 104
Bonfire celebrations, Lag Be-Omer, 105
Book of the Kusari, 188
Book of Legends, Bialik, 190-191
Book of Life, 26, 27
Books, 163, 167-195 see also Bible; Siddur; Talmud
   illustrations, 170
   importance of, 167
   and invention of movable type, 168
   and invention of printing, 167-168, 170
   manuscript period, 168-170
   modern form, 169-170
   origin of, 167-168
   scrolls, 168-169
Booths, 37 see also Sukkot
Bows and arrows, Lag Be-Omer, 101, 104-105
Bradford, William, 39
B'rayshis, 171
The Bridal Canopy, 193
Bridegroom of Genesis, 46
Bridegroom of the Torah, 46
Brit Milah, 139
"Bull-roarer," 79-80

C

Calendar, Jewish, 3-9, 104, 183
Canaan, 89, 109, 110, 172
Candle lighting, 8, 13, 40-41, 56-57, 59, 92, 162
Cantillation, 152
Carob tree, 64, 65, 68-69, 104, 182
Caucasian Jews, Passover customs, 98
Cave of Machpelah, 148
C.E., 6
Cedar tree, 63, 64
Cereal harvest, 108, 109
Ceremonial objects, Jewish home, 157-164
Ceremonial objects, synagogues, 131-135
Charity see Tzedakah
Children, naming of, 139, 140
Chmielnicki pogroms, 123
Christianity, 61
Christians, calendar, 6
Chronicles, 182
Circumcision, 139-140
Citron, 41, 64
Commonwealth, Second Jewish, 119, 131
"Completion of the Sefer Torah," 132
Confession, prayer of, 33
Confirmation, 112
Congregation Shearith Israel, 123-124, 130
Congregational School, 128
Conservative synagogue, Shavuot Confirmation custom, 71
Crown of Solomon, 68
Crusades, 123
Cultural events, and the synagogue, 128-129
Cup of Elijah, 92
Curtain Purim, 83
Customs and ceremonies, Jewish home, 159-165
Cyclamen, legend of, 68
Cypress tree, 64
Cyrus, 59, 177

D

Dairy foods, and Shavuot, 112-113
Daled, 152, 161
Daniel, 178, 180-181
Darius, 49
Darmstadt Haggadah, 96-97
Date-palm, 110
David, 63, 64, 111, 173, 178, 180, 185
David and Goliath, 77
Day, Jewish reckoning of, 8, 12
Day of Atonement, 35, 40, 177 see also Yom Kippur
Day of Rest, 11, 17
"The Day of the Sounding of the Ram's Horn," 26
Dead Sea Scrolls, 169

196

Death, Jewish rites and traditions, 147-149
Debarim, 172-173
Deborah, 139
Der Kemfer, 192
Deuteronomy, 46, 171, 172-173
Dietary laws, 163-165
Drashah, 152, 154
Dream interpretation, 86-87, 180
Dreidel, 57-58
Dura-Europos synagogue, Syria, 120

E

Ecclesiastes, 43, 178, 180
Edomites, 176
Education, and the synagogue, 128
    see also Bet Ha-Midrash
Edward I, King of England, 115
"Eight Degrees of Charity," 186
Eighth Day of Solemn Assembly, 44
    see also Shemini Atzeret
Eighteen Blessings, 18, 57
    see also Shmoneh Esreh
Ekhah, 116
Eleazar, 54
Elijah, 92, 97, 140
Elijah's Chair, 140
Elijah's Cup, 92, 97
Elul, 8, 25, 28
Emek, 67
Emmaus, 55
Engagement, Jewish tradition, 141
England, expulsion of Jews from, 115
Ephraim, 31
"Epimanes," 50
Essen teg, 149
Esther, 71-82, 169, 178, 180
Eternal Jew, The, 192
Eternal light, 134
Ethics of the Fathers, 18, 153
Etrog, 41-42, 43, 44
Etz Hayyim, 132, 133, 169
Eve, 64
Exile, Babylonian, 7, 15, 16, 39, 119, 134, 169, 174, 175, 180, 182, 183
Exodus, 37, 89, 95, 115, 171-172
Ezekiel, 119, 175
Ezra, 16, 152, 169, 178, 181

F

Fast of Esther, 80, 116
Fast of Gedaliah, 30, 117
Fast of the Seventeenth of Tamuz, 117
Fasting, 30-31, 80, 116-117, 142
Fearful Days, 25 see also
    High Holy Days
Feast of Booths see Sukkot
Feast of Lots, 71, 77 see also Purim
Feast of Purim, 180 see also Purim
Feast of Tabernacles see Sukkot
Feast of water-drawing, 42
Ferdinand, King of Spain, 116
Festivals
    of Booths, 37 see also Sukkot
    of First Fruits, 109 see also Shavuot
    of Freedom, 85 see also Passover
    of the Harvest, 108 see also Shavuot
    of Ingathering, 37 see also Sukkot
    of Lights, 56 see also Hanukkah
    of Tabernacles, 37 see also Sukkot
    of Torah, 108 see also Shavuot

Fettmilch, Vincenz, 82
Fig trees, 64, 109-110
First Adar, 81
First Chronicles, 178
First fruits offering, 109-111
First Kings, 173-174
First Samuel, 173
First Temple, destruction of, 7, 15, 59, 115, 116, 117, 119, 141, 143, 180, 182
Five Books of Moses, 45, 46, 131, 132, 171-173, 188
Food, and dietary laws, 163-165
Forest of the Martyrs, 66
Four Cups of Wine, Seder celebration, 92, 95
"Four kinds," Sukkot, 41-42
Four Questions, Seder ceremony, 85, 94-95, 98
Four sons, Seder ceremony, 95
Fourth Commandment, 11
Frankfort ghetto, 82
Fruit harvest, 38, 109-111

G

Gabbai, 137
Gabbay Tzedakah, 145
Gamaliel, Rabbi, 90
Ganzfried, Rabbi Solomon, 187
Garden of Eden, 69, 167
Gate of Nicanor, 43
Gedaliah, 30, 117
Gemar, 183
Gemara, 183-184
Genesis, 171
Genizah, 194
Geshem, 44-45
Ghettos, Middle Ages, 121
Gift-giving, 71, 76, 80
Gimel, 58
Ginzberg, Asher, 188
Gopher trees, 64
Graetz, Heinrich, 191
Graggers, 79-80
Grain harvest, 85, 108, 109
Grape harvest, 109
Great Assembly, 177, 181
Great Sabbath, 22
Great Synagogue, Tel Aviv, 61
Greeting cards, New Year, 27
Gregorian calendar, 6
Gregory XIII, 6
Guide for the Perplexed, 187

H

Ha-Lahma Anya, 94
Habakkuk, 177
Had Gadya, 94, 99
Hadassah see Esther
Hadrian, 102
Haftarah, 19, 23, 80, 152, 155
Hag Ha-Asif, 37, 38
Hag Ha-Bikkurim, 109
Hag Ha-Katzir, 108
Hag Ha-Sukkot, 37
Haggadah, 22, 92, 94-99, 170
Haggai, 177
Haggeyd, 92
Hakafot, 46
Hakhamim, 154
Hakhnasat Orhim, 146
Halakhah, 184
Hale, Mrs. Sarah Josephs, 38-39

Haleff, 165
Halevi, Yehuda, 116
Hallah, 13, 16, 30, 40
Hallel, 43, 57, 94, 96, 185
Halutzim, 66, 67, 188
Haman, 19, 73-76, 79-82, 180
Hamantashen, 80
Hametz, 22, 91
Hamishah Asar Bi-Shevat, 63
Ha-Motzi, 30
Hannah, 51-53
Hanukat Ha-Bayit, 165
Hanukkah, 49-61, 162
Harbonah, 75
Haroset, 93, 95, 96, 163
Harrison, Peter, 125
Harvest festivals, 37-41, 89, 108-111
Hasidim, 105
Hasidim harishonim, 39
Hasmoneans, 54, 57
Hatach, 73
Hatan, 141
Hatan Berayshis, 46
Hatan Torah, 46
Havdalah, 18, 20, 35, 162
Hay, 58
Hazzan, 136
Hazon, 22
Heavenly Book of Life, 26, 27
Hebrew Union College-Jewish Institute of Religion, 127
Heder, 65, 122
Hegai, 72
Herzl, Theodor, 191-192
Heshvan, 8
High Court (Sanhedrin), 4
High Holy Days, 25-35
Hillel, 6, 96
Hillel the Second, 6
Hisda, Rab, 16
History of the Jews, Graetz, 191
Hol Ha-Mo'ed, 43, 92
Holy Ark, 31, 42, 46, 125, 133-135
Holy oil, 55, 59, 60, 64
Honi ha-Meaggel, 68-69, 182
Hopsch, Baron, 97
Hosea, 175-176
Hoshanah Rabba, 43-44
Hoshanot, 44
Hoshen, 133
House-warming ceremony, 165
Humash, 188
Huna, 183
Huppah, 142

I

Idol-worship, 50-52, 176
Illustrations, in books, 170
Immigration of Jews, 123-126
Inquisition, 32, 98, 115-116, 121, 123, 170, 187
Isaac, 28, 31, 140, 148
Isabella, Queen of Spain, 116
Isaiah, 173, 174, 175, 177
Israel, State of
    first Tu Bi-Shevat celebration, 66
    Hanukkah torch relay custom, 61
    Lag Be-Omer celebration, 105
    Menorah emblem, 60-61
    reclamation of land, 66-67
    Sabbath in, 19
Israel ben Meir, 97
Iyar, 8, 101

197

J

Jacob, 31, 85, 86, 148
Jeremiah, 116, 173, 174-175
Jesus, 6
Jethro, 88
Jewish Arbor Day, 63
Jewish Book Month, 128
Jewish Museum, London, 78
Jewish National Fund, 67, 111
Jewish State, The, 191
Jewish Theological Seminary of America, 127, 193
Jewish Theological Seminary, Breslau, 191
Job, 178, 179
Jocheved, 87
Joel, 173, 176
Johanan, 54
Johanan, Rabbi, 68
Jonah, 34, 176-177
Jonathan, 54
Joseph, 77, 85-86, 139
Joseph, Rab, 16
Joshua, 173
Josiah of Judah, 168
Judah, kingdom of, 174, 175, 176, 180, 182
Judah Maccabee, 54, 55, 58
Judah the Prince, Rabbi, 183
Judges, 173, 180
Judgment day, of trees, 64
Judith, 57
Julius Severus, 102-103
Justinian, 122

K

Kabbalat Shabbat, 13-14
Kabbalists, 14
Kaddish, 134, 149, 161
Karo, Joseph, 187-188
Karpas, 92-93, 163
Kashrut, 163-165
Kel Male Rahamim, 149
Keren Kayemet Le-Yisrael, 67
Keriah, 148
Keter Torah, 133
Ketubah, 142
Ketuvim, 82
Kiddush, 18, 121, 161
Kiddush L'vanah, 9
Kislev, 8, 55, 162
Kittel, 142
Kitzur Shulhan Arukh, 187
Knesset, 119
Koh Ribbon Olam, 17
Kohanim, 110, 119, 140
Kohelet, 43, 180
Kol Hanearim, 47
Kol Nidre, 31-33, 111
Kurdestan, Tu Bi-Shevat customs, 65

L

Lag Be-Omer, 101-105, 141
Lamentations, 116, 178, 180
Latkes, 57
Leah, 13, 148
Leap year, 5, 81
Lehem mishneh, 13
Lekha Dodi, 14
Levites, 43, 87, 140
Leviticus, 171, 172
L'Hayyim, 141
Libraries, 128, 163, 193

Lincoln, Abraham, 39
Lishkat Hashaim, 145
Lomed, 182
L'Shanah Tovah Tikatevu, 27
Luah, 8
Lulav, 41-42, 43, 44
Lunar year, 5-6 *see also* Calendar, Jewish
Luria, Rabbi Isaac, 14

M

Ma'amadot, 119-120
Maariv, 18
Maccabees, 54-56, 57, 59, 61, 163
Machatzit Hashekel, 82
Maftir, 152
Mahzor, 134, 161
Maimonides, 28, 164-165, 185-187
Malachi, 173, 178
Manna, 13
Manasseh, 31
Mantle of the Law, 133
Ma-ot Hittim, 90
Ma-ot Perot fund, 66
Ma-oz Tzur, 57
Mark Twain Society, 193
Maror, 92, 93, 96
Marranos, 32, 98, 123, 125
Marriage, and Jewish traditions, 140-144
Mashgiah, 165
Mather, Cotton, 39
Mattathias, 53-54
Matzah Shemurah, 90
Matzot, 89-90, 91, 93, 96, 163
Mazal tov, 27, 141
Mea Shearim, 19
Megillah of Esther, 71-83, 169, 178, 180
Megillot, 82, 169, 180
Meir, Rabbi, 183
Mekhirat hametz, 90-91
Memorial services, 34, 94, 148-149
Mendele Mokher Seforim, 188-189, 193
Menelaus, 51
Menorah, 55, 57, 58-61, 64, 110, 135, 162-163
Meron, Israel, 105
Messiah, 178
Mezuzah, 159-160, 165
Micah, 175, 177
Middle Ages, Jewish books, 169-170
Midian, 85, 87
Midrash, 82, 110
Migdal, 20
Mikdash M'aat, 120
Mill Street Synagogue, 124
Minhah, 18, 20, 116
Minor Prophets, 175
Minyan, 157
Miriam, 87
Mishloah Manot, 80
Mishnah, 94, 110, 136, 183, 184, 186
Mishnah Torah, 186
Mitzvot, 153
Mizrah, 160
Modi'in, 53, 61
Mohammedanism, 11, 61
Mohntashen, 80
Months, in Jewish calendar, 4-9
Moon, 3-6, 9, 23 *see also* Calendar, Jewish

Mordecai, 72-76, 77, 79, 81, 180
Morocco, Bar Mitzvah customs, 154-155
Moses, 11, 15, 19, 59, 64, 87-89, 108, 109, 111, 167, 171-173
Moses ben Jacob Ibn Ezra, 195
Mount Sinai, 11, 14, 28, 88, 89, 107, 108, 111, 112, 172, 182
Mourning, 148-149
Movable type, invention of, 168
Musaf, 18, 42
Myers, Myer, 125
Myrtle, 41, 43

N

Nahman, Rab, 16
Nahum, 177
Najara, Rabbi Israel, 17
Naming children, 139, 140
Naomi, 109, 180
Nazis, 99, 194
Nebuchadnezzar, 30, 72, 115, 117, 175, 180
Nehemiah, 39, 152, 178, 181-182
Nehemias Americanus, 39
Ne'ilah, 18, 35
Ner Tamid, 134
Nes Gadol Hayah Sham, 57, 58
New moon, 3-4, 5, 9, 23
New Year, 6-7, 25, 26, 27, 30
New Year of the Trees, 26, 63, 64
Newport, Rhode Island, and religious freedom, 124, 125
Nezer Shlomo, 68
Nile River, 87
Nineveh, 177
Ninth Day of Av, fast day, 31, 115
Nisan, 8, 26, 89
Noah, 64, 110
Noisemaking, Purim, 79-80
North African countries, Bar Mitzvah customs, 155-156
Numbers, 102, 140, 171, 172
Nun, 58

O

Obadiah, 176
Objects and observances, Jewish home, 159-165
Oifruf, 141
Olive trees, 64, 110
Omer, 104, 108
Oneg Shabbat, 19-20
Oral Law, 182-183 *see also* Talmud
Ozen Haman, 80

P

Palestinian Gemara, 183
Palestinian Talmud, 183
Palm, 41, 43, 64
Papyrus rolls, 168
Park Avenue Synagogue, New York City, 130
Parokhet, 133-134
Paschal lamb, 93, 94
Passover, 34, 85-99, 107, 141, 149, 172, 179
custom variations, 97-98
Haggadah, 22, 85, 92, 94-97, 98, 170

preparations for, 89, 90-91
Seder plate, 93, 163
Shabbat ha-Gadol, 22
and Song of Songs, 179-180
Patriarchs, 31
Pentecost, 68
Pepys, Samuel, 122
Peretz, Isaac Leib, 163, 189-190, 192
Pesah, 85-99 *see also* Passover
Pharaohs, 85, 86-89
Philistines, 59, 173
Philo, 120
Phylacteries *see* Tefillin
Pidyon Ha-Ben, 140
Pidyon Shevuim, 146
Pilgrim Festival, 85
Pilgrims, American, and Thanksgiving Day, 39-40
Pinski, David, 192
Pirke Avot, 18
Plagues, 88, 93
Plays and carnivals, Purim, 71, 77-78, 81
Plymouth, Massachusetts, 38-39
Pomegranates, 110
Pool of Siloam, 42
Poppy-seed cakes, 71, 80
Portugal, Passover customs, 98
Potato pancakes, 57
Printing, invention of, 167-168, 170
Procession of the Torahs, 45-46
Prophets, 171, 173-178
Proverbs, 179
Psalms, 28, 43, 57, 119, 178-179, 185
Pur, 76
Purim, 71-83, 169, 180
Purim of Bandits, 83
Purim of the Baker Woman, 82
Purim of the Bomb, 83
Purim Fettmilch, 82-83
Purim Katan, 81
Purim of the Poisoned Sword, 83
Purim of Shiraz, 83
Purim of Tiberias, 83
Purimshpiel, 77

R

Rabbi, 136
Rabinowitz, Sholom *see* Sholom Aleichem
Rachel, 101
Rain, prayers for, 44-45
Rambam *see* Maimonides
Ram's horn *see* Shofar
Rashi, 170, 187
Rebekah, 140, 148
Red Sea, 23, 89, 96, 132
Reform Jews
Passover observance, 89
Shavuot observance, 107
Sukkot observance, 37
Rehoboam, 174
Rejoicing in the Law, 45-47
Repentance, 34
Retzuah, 151, 161
Rimonim, 110
River Jordan, 89
Roasted egg, Seder celebration, 92, 93, 163
Rock of Ages, 57
Roman conquest of Palestine, 101-104
Romans, calendar, 6

Rosh Hashanah, 6, 25-30, 64
legends about, 26
morning service, 28
Shabbat Shuvah, 23, 31
Zodiac sign, 27
Rosh Hodesh, 9, 23
Rosh Hodesh Sivan, 141
Ruth, 109, 111, 178, 180

S

Sabbatai Zevi, 192
Sabbath, 11-23, 28, 37, 41, 43, 92
candle lighting, 13, 92, 161
Haftarah readings, 19
Havdalah, 18, 20-21, 162
in Israel, 19
legend of, 12, 14-16
meals, 15-16, 17
special, 22-23, 31
synagogue services, 17, 18-20
Torah readings, 18-19
welcoming of, 13-14
Sabbath of Blessing, 23
Sabbath of Comfort, 22-23
Sabbath Joy, 19-20
Sabbath of Penitence, 31
Sabbath Queen, 12, 14, 20-21
Sabbath Tefillin, 155
Sacrificial lamb, 94
Safed, Israel, Tu Bi-Shevat custom, 44
Saladin, Sultan, 185
Samaritans, 177
Samson, 109
Samuel, 23, 173, 183
Sanctuary of Shiloh, 59
Sanhedrin, 4
Sara, 148
Saul, 23, 80, 173
Scales, 27
Scholars' holiday, 101-105
"Scraper," 79-80
Scroll of Esther, 71-83, 169, 178, 180
Scrolls, 82, 168-169, 180
Second Adar, 5, 81
Second Chronicles, 178, 182
Second Commonwealth, 119, 181
Second Kings, 173-174
Second Samuel, 173
Second Temple, destruction of, 60, 115, 116, 117, 119, 121, 136, 180
Seder, 85, 90, 92-96, 97, 98-99, 163 *see also* Passover
Sefer Torah, 132
Sefirah, 104
Sefirat ha-Omer, 108
Seixas, Moses, 125
Selihot, 25, 27
Sephardic traditions, 65-66, 121, 156-157
Seudah, 83
Se'udah Shelishis, 20
"Seven kinds," 109-110
Seventeenth of Tamuz, fast day, 117
Shabbat ha-Gadol, 22
Shabbat Hazon, 19, 22
Shabbat Nahamu, 22-23, 116
Shabbat Shalom, 14
Shabbat Shirah, 23
Shabbat Shuvah, 23, 31
Shabbat Zakhor, 23, 80
Shaddai, 152, 160, 161
Shaharit, 18

Shalach Monos, 80
Shalosh Regalim, 38
Shammash, 17, 25, 56, 60, 136
Shanah, 183
Shankbone, Seder celebration, 93, 163
Shavuot, 34, 85, 107-113, 141, 149, 180
Shearith Israel, New York City, 123-124, 130
Shehitah, 164-165
Shekhinah, 120
Shel Rosh, 151, 161
Shel Yad, 151, 161
Shema, 18, 134, 161
Shema Yisrael, 185
Shemini Atzeret, 34, 44-45, 149
Shemitah, 144
Shemot, 172
Shemurah matzah, 90
Shevarim, 28
Shevat, 8, 26, 63
Shiloh, 58-59
Shin, 58, 151, 161
Shir Ha-Ma'alot, 43
Shivah, 149
Shlomo Molcho, 192
Shmoneh Esreh, 18, 57, 134, 161
Shneur, Zalman, 193
Shofar, 16-17, 26, 28, 35, 42, 137
Shohet, 126, 164-165
Sholom Aleichem, 163, 190
Shpieler, 77
Shulamit, 179
Shulhan Arukh, 164, 187-188
Shushan, 71, 72, 73-74, 76, 81
Shushan Purim, 81-82
Siddur, 134, 160-161, 185, 188
Sidra, 18, 46, 131, 137
Sidrah Be-shalah, 23
Signs of the Zodiac, 27
Simeon Bar Yohai, 64, 104-105
Simhat bet ha-sho-ayvah, 42
Simhat Torah, 45-46, 122
Simon, 54
Sivan, 8, 107, 109
Siyyum Ha-Sefer, 132
Slaughter of animals, Kashrut rules, 93-94
Sofer, 132
Solar year, 5-6
Solemn Days, 25 *see also* High Holy Days
Solomon, 59, 63, 68, 113, 141, 173, 179, 180
Song of Moses, 23
Song of the Red Sea, 132
Song of Songs, 113, 179-180
Songs of degrees, 43
Spanish Haggadot, 96
Spanish Inquisition, 32, 98, 121, 123, 170, 187
Spanish and Portuguese Synagogue, 124
Special Purims, 82-83
Special Sabbaths, 22-23, 31
"Stealing of the afikomen," 85
Stuyvesant, Peter, 123
Sukkah, 40-41, 47
Sukkot, 37-47, 64, 85
and American Thanksgiving, 38-40
and *Ecclesiastes*, 43, 180
morning service, 43
origin of, 37-38

199

Suleiman Pasha, 83
Sunset, 8-9, 12
Sun-year, 506
"Sweet Singer of Zion," 188
Synagogue
  ancient times, 119-121
  architecture, 129-131
  bodies, 131
  ceremonial objects, 131-135
  community program, 121-122, 126-129
  duties, 135-137
  and education, 122, 128
  first in North America, 124
  library, 128
  meaning of, 119
  Middle Ages, 121-122
  and new immigrants, 123-126
  offices of, 135-137
  Synagogue Council of America, 131
  three names for, 121, 129
  Touro Synagogue, Rhode Island, 124-126
  and Tzedakah, 145, 146

T

Ta'ame N'ginah, 152
Tabernacles, 37 see also Sukkot
Tablets of the Ten Commandments, 117, 133
Tallit, 134-135, 151, 152, 156, 161
Talmud, 134, 144, 164, 169, 170, 182-184
Talmud Bavli, 182-183
Talmud Torah, 128
Talmud Yerushalmi, 183
Tamar, 139
Tamuz, 7, 8, 117
Tashlich, 30
Tefillin, 151, 153, 155-156, 157, 161
Tekiah, 28
Temple
  desecration by Antiochus, 51-55
  destruction First Temple, 7, 15, 59, 116, 117, 119, 141, 142, 143, 180
  destruction of Second Temple, 59, 60, 115, 116, 117, 119, 121, 136, 180
  "feast of water-drawing," 42-43
  pilgrimages, 38, 85
  rebuilding of First Temple, 59, 177
  rededication of Second Temple, 55-56, 58
  Tishah Be-Av commemoration, 116
Temple Isaiah, Chicago, 129
Ten Commandments, 11, 15, 28, 89, 107-108, 117, 133, 134, 135, 172

Ten Days of Repentance, 23, 25, 26, 28, 31
"Ten lost tribes of Israel," 176
Ten plagues, 88, 93
Tenaim, 141
Teruah, 28
Tevet, 8, 117
Thanksgiving Day, American, and Sukkot, 38-40
Thanksgiving prayers, Rosh Hodesh, 9
Thermuthis, 87
"This Is Not the Way," 188
Tiberias, 83
Tishah Be-Av, 115-117, 141
  and *Book of Lamentations*, 180
  Shabbat Hazon, 22
  Shabbat Nahamu, 22-23
Tishri, 6, 7, 8, 26
Titus, 60, 101, 115, 119
"To the Bird," 190
Torah, 31, 43, 44, 45-46, 57, 63, 64, 80, 92, 103, 107-113, 131-135, 157, 169, 171-172, 180, 181
  festival commemorating, 107-113, 180
  Five Books of Moses, 45, 171-172
  holiday dedicated to, 45-46
  as Law, 131-182
  readings, 18-19, 152
  scrolls, 131-134, 169
  as "tree of life," 133
Torah she'be'al peh, 182
Torch relay, 61
Touro, Judah, 125
Touro, Reverend Isaac, 125
Touro Synagogue, 124-125
The Treasure, 192
"Tree of life," 132-133, 169
Trees, 63-69
Trey Asar, 175
Triumph of Freedom, 56
Trop, 152
Tu Bi-Shevat, 63-69, 182
Two Tablets, 135

Tzedakah, 31, 34, 90, 135, 144-147, 161, 186
Tzom Gedaliah, 30, 117

U

Unetaneh Tokef, 28-30
Union of American Hebrew Congregations (Reform), 131
Union of Orthodox Jewish Congregations, 131
United Jewish Appeal, 147
United Palestine Appeal, 147

United Synagogue of America (Conservative), 131
Unleavened bread see Matzot

V

Valley of Jezreel, 67
Vashti, 71-72
Va-Yikra, 172
Vincenz Purim, 82-83

W

Washington, George, 38, 124, 125
Weddings, and Jewish tradition, 140-144
Wesel, Moses, 96
Wheat harvest, 108, 109
Williams, Roger, 125
Willow trees, 41, 44, 63
Wine cup, holiday use of, 161
Winthrop, John, 39
Worms ghetto, 82
Writings, 171, 178-182

Y

Yad, 135
Yahrzeit, 148, 149
Year, in Jewish calendar, 5-10
Yehudah Halevi, 188
Yehudah ha-Nasi, 183
Yemen, Bar Mitzvah customs, 157
Yemenite Jews, Passover customs, 98
Yeshiva, 101, 122, 128, 146
Yeshiva University, 127
Yiddish literature, 188-195
Yiddish School, 128
Yigdal, 134, 161
Yizkor, 34, 94, 148
Yokhanan Ha-Sandlar, 183
Yom Kippur, 18, 23, 28, 31-35, 37, 111, 116, 149
Yud, 151, 161

Z

Zakhor, 80
Zechariah, 177-178
Zekher l'yitziat Mitzra-yim, 37
Zephaniah, 177
Zera, Rab, 16
Zeresh, 74
Zeroa, 93
Zionism, twentieth-century, 191-192
Zipporah, 88
Z'man Matan Toratenu, 108
Z'mirot, 17
Zodiac signs, 27